Managing Teams
FOR
DUMMIES®

Managing Teams

FOR

DUMMIES®

by Marty Brounstein

Wiley Publishing, Inc.

Managing Teams For Dummies®

Published by
Wiley Publishing, Inc.
909 Third Avenue
New York, NY 10022
www.wiley.com

Copyright © 2002 by Wiley Publishing, Inc., Indianapolis, Indiana

Published by Wiley Publishing, Inc., Indianapolis, Indiana

Published simultaneously in Canada

No part of this publication may be reproduced, stored in a retrieval system, or transmitted in any form or by any means, electronic, mechanical, photocopying, recording, scanning, or otherwise, except as permitted under Sections 107 or 108 of the 1976 United States Copyright Act, without either the prior written permission of the Publisher, or authorization through payment of the appropriate per-copy fee to the Copyright Clearance Center, 222 Rosewood Drive, Danvers, MA 01923, 978-750-8400, fax 978-750-4744. Requests to the Publisher for permission should be addressed to the Legal Department, Wiley Publishing, Inc., 10475 Crosspoint Blvd., Indianapolis, IN 46256, 317-572-3447, fax 317-572-4447, or e-mail permcoordinator@wiley.com

Trademarks: Wiley, the Wiley Publishing logo, For Dummies, the Dummies Man logo, A Reference for the Rest of Us!, The Dummies Way, Dummies Daily, The Fun and Easy Way, Dummies.com and related trade dress are trademarks or registered trademarks of Wiley Publishing, Inc., in the United States and other countries, and may not be used without written permission. All other trademarks are the property of their respective owners. Wiley Publishing, Inc., is not associated with any product or vendor mentioned in this book.

LIMIT OF LIABILITY/DISCLAIMER OF WARRANTY: WHILE THE PUBLISHER AND AUTHOR HAVE USED THEIR BEST EFFORTS IN PREPARING THIS BOOK, THEY MAKE NO REPRESENTATIONS OR WARRANTIES WITH RESPECT TO THE ACCURACY OR COMPLETENESS OF THE CONTENTS OF THIS BOOK AND SPECIFICALLY DISCLAIM ANY IMPLIED WARRANTIES OF MERCHANTABILITY OR FITNESS FOR A PARTICULAR PURPOSE. NO WARRANTY MAY BE CREATED OR EXTENDED BY SALES REPRESENTATIVES OR WRITTEN SALES MATERIALS. THE ADVICE AND STRATEGIES CONTAINED HEREIN MAY NOT BE SUITABLE FOR YOUR SITUATION. YOU SHOULD CONSULT WITH A PROFESSIONAL WHERE APPROPRIATE. NEITHER THE PUBLISHER NOR AUTHOR SHALL BE LIABLE FOR ANY LOSS OF PROFIT OR ANY OTHER COMMERCIAL DAMAGES, INCLUDING BUT NOT LIMITED TO SPECIAL, INCIDENTAL, CONSEQUENTIAL, OR OTHER DAMAGES.

For general information on our other products and services or to obtain technical support, please contact our Customer Care Department within the U.S. at 800-762-2974, outside the U.S. at 317-572-3993, or fax 317-572-4002.

Wiley also publishes its books in a variety of electronic formats. Some content that appears in print may not be available in electronic books.

Library of Congress Cataloging-in-Publication Data:

Library of Congress Control Number: 2002108098

ISBN: 0-7645-5408-5

Manufactured in the United States of America

10 9 8 7 6 5 4

®Wiley Publishing, Inc. is a trademark of Wiley Publishing, Inc.

Dedication

To the first team that I was a part of, from a very young age. Over the years we've grown busy with our lives and families and moved miles apart so that we seldom all get together. Sadly we've lost our wonderful team leaders, Goldie and Cyril, to whom I dedicated my previous two books For Dummies. But despite the years and distance, my original team remains intact and in touch — in fact, our chain letter has lived on for at least 25 years. I am eternally grateful to this original team — my siblings. So with much love, I dedicate this book to my brother Rick and my sisters Sheri and Julie.

Author's Acknowledgments

I want to pass on my thanks to a few people who helped make this book become a reality. First, I want to thank Norm Crampton, my project editor, who provided seamless guidance and support in the writing of this book. Despite changes at the publishing company through the year, Norm was the constant and someone easy to work with. I want to acknowledge as well Tere Drenth. She provided great assistance to me in my first two projects For Dummies and taught me the style that made this book go smoothly.

I also want to thank Holly McGuire, the editor who has gotten to know me and my work, for providing my third opportunity to be an author in the For Dummies series. She signed me up for this book. Holly has moved on from Wiley, but I know her talents and down-to-earth style and care are greatly missed.

My appreciation also goes out to Carl Welte, a fellow management consultant and colleague. Carl once again played the role of technical reviewer for my book. His experience and expertise in my business make his involvement in this project a must. Thanks again for all your help.

About the Author

Marty Brounstein is the Principal of the Practical Solutions Group, a training and consulting firm based in the San Francisco Bay area that specializes in management and organizational effectiveness. Marty's consulting work includes one-on-one coaching with managers and executives, assistance to groups working to become productive teams, and guidance and direction for organizations establishing practices for high performance and employee retention. His training programs target management as well as employee-development issues including leadership, team development, customer service, and effective communications.

As a consultant, speaker, and trainer since 1991, Marty has served a wide variety of organizations from high tech to government, for-profit to not-for-profit. He has a bachelor's degree in education and history and a master's degree in industrial relations. Prior to beginning his consulting career, he spent a couple of years as a human resources executive.

This is Marty's fifth book and third For Dummies book. He is the author of *Coaching and Mentoring For Dummies*; *Communicating Effectively For Dummies*; and *Handling the Difficult Employee: Solving Performance Problems*. He is the coauthor of *Effective Recruiting Strategies: A Marketing Approach*.

To contact Marty regarding consulting, speaking, or training services, call 650-341-8001 or e-mail him at mabruns@earthlink.net.

Publisher's Acknowledgments

We're proud of this book; please send us your comments through our Dummies online registration form located at www.dummies.com/register/.

Some of the people who helped bring this book to market include the following:

Acquisitions, Editorial, and Media Development

Project Editor: Norm Crampton

Acquisitions Editor: Pam Mourouzis

Copy Editor: Neil Johnson

Technical Editor: Carl Welte

Editorial Manager: Christine Beck

Editorial Assistant: Melissa Bennett

Cover Photos: © R. W. Jones/Corbis

Composition

Project Coordinator: Dale White

Layout and Graphics: Scott M. Bristol, Sean Decker, Kelly Hardesty, Joyce Haughey, Jackie Nicholas, Stephanie D. Jumper, Jacque Schneider

Proofreaders: TECHBOOKS Production Services, John Greenough, Andy Hollandbeck, Carl Pierce, Linda Quigley

Indexer: Aptara

Publishing and Editorial for Consumer Dummies

Diane Graves Steele, Vice President and Publisher, Consumer Dummies

Joyce Pepple, Acquisitions Director, Consumer Dummies

Kristin A. Cocks, Product Development Director, Consumer Dummies

Michael Spring, Vice President and Publisher, Travel

Publishing for Technology Dummies

Andy Cummings, Vice President and Publisher

Composition Services

Gerry Fahey, Vice President of Production Services

Debbie Stailey, Director of Composition Services

Contents at a Glance

Cartoons at a Glance

By Rich Tennant

page 7

page 299

page 37

page 139

page 239

page 73

Cartoon Information:
Fax: 978-546-7747
E-Mail: richtennant@the5thwave.com
World Wide Web: www.the5thwave.com

Table of Contents

Part IV: Developing Tools for Productive Team Players *139*

Introduction

In the ever-changing world of work, the idea of spending some or all your time working in teams is becoming more and more common. From solving problems, to tackling projects, to providing organizational leadership, the roles and importance of teams continue to grow.

Leading a team — a collection of individuals — is no easy job, however. Teams are a means for getting work done but they're not a guarantee of success. They produce far better results when team members work well together than when they don't. Getting your team members to work well together is no small feat.

But when teams gel, they can far outperform traditional work groups. Teams make it possible to bring together the variety of skills, perspectives, and talents that you need in the contemporary workplace. In fact, teams are becoming more and more vital for helping business organizations to achieve their objectives. Leading people to work together effectively in teams is the topic of this book.

About This Book

This book is written for you — managers at all levels who have some form of work group that you're trying to lead as a team. In many cases, this group o people reports directly to you. They may be nonmanagement employees, supervisors, or managers who report to you as part of your department, or executives who report to you as part of senior management for the whole organization. They're your staff and you're their boss. If you have the need and desire for them to work together as a team, *Managing Teams For Dummies* is your reference and guide.

This book also is written for anyone, manager or not, who is asked to take on the role of team leader. Your team members don't report to you — you're not their supervisor. But for some work reason, such as a project, you're spending time together and you are the person designated to make the team run and produce good results. So although you don't have direct supervisory authority over the team members, you still bear all management responsibility for the team.

Managing Teams For Dummies also applies to senior level management people who sponsor teams. Although you may not run a team directly yourself, you're spearheading the efforts of your managers who are leading teams, and you need to be able to coach and support them.

Even team members who don't have a leadership role can benefit from this book. Many of the strategies and skills you find here can help you to perform well as a team member and to support your manager. In short, this book is a practical guide for everyone with a role to play in making teams produce good results — your resource for meeting this major challenge.

Conventions Used in This Book

Throughout this book, the word *team* has a particular meaning. Though many people refer to their work groups as teams, I do not use *team* to denote just any kind of work group. In this book, team means a group organized to work together that shares an overall common purpose or role and shares responsibility for the outcomes of the whole group. A team is an interdependent, coordinated group of people. Unlike regular work groups in which people take responsibility primarily for their own area of work, *team* denotes people relying on one another for organizing and carrying out all the team's work and producing the outcomes expected by the whole group.

Team building as used in this book is different from the way that many people use the term. In the broad sense of this book, team building means the whole effort and campaign to lead a team to perform well together — an ongoing responsibility for the life of a team. In a more limited sense, team building is one strategy among a large package of team development efforts that enhance working relationships for strengthening team cohesiveness. But I do not use *team building* in this book to refer to those group activities of play and fun — often done off the work site — that are meant to transform everyone into one big happy unit. There's nothing wrong with big happy units, but they're not necessarily teams.

The terms *manager* and *team leader* are often used interchangeably in this book. They refer to the role of the person who's running and leading the team.

How This Book Is Organized

This book is organized into six main parts. Here's an overview of what you can find in each part:

Part 1: Getting Into Teams

Part I contains the first two chapters of the book — the conceptual foundation of the whole book. I talk about what teams are and the common types of teams that exist in business organizations, and I distinguish between ordinary work groups and genuine teams, pointing out the key differences. Part I also reminds you why teams flounder and why simply wishing a team into existence is not enough to help make it perform productively. No magic wands or special pills exist for turning a team into a productive unit. But your leadership in building a team structure on the three cornerstones — focus, cohesiveness, and accountability — can produce success, and I show you how.

Part II: Leadership for Team Success

This part defines your leadership role in running teams effectively. Chapter 3 introduces the concept of leading your teams as a coach, which is a critical theme for the whole book. I explain what leading as a coach means and how it's different from being the boss or supervisor who's a good worker or doer.

In Chapter 4, you gain tips and strategies for helping lead a team through its early stages of development. It's naïve to expect every transition into a team structure to go smoothly, and this part prepares you to handle the challenge. Chapter 4 contains coaching tips for dealing with the team member behavior and performance problems that sometimes arise as teams take shape.

Part III: Strategies for Building Productive Teams

This third part of the book takes the model of the three cornerstones for team success — focus, cohesiveness, and accountability — and develops them one chapter at a time. You gain a depth of practical knowledge and tools for applying the strategies associated with each cornerstone. You can pick and choose the tools you think best fit your teams, but the idea here is to build upon all three cornerstones. Teams that have a high level of focus, cohesiveness, and accountability work well together and produce strong results.

Part IV: Developing Tools for Productive Team Players

Teams need members who can work well together to accomplish the team's work — otherwise known as good team players. But the skills of a good team player are seldom taught to most people in grade school or high school. School kids are often well conditioned to work independently but aren't necessarily equipped to work collaboratively, the way they must work as team members.

Part IV focuses on giving you these essential team skills — effective interpersonal communication, planning, problem-solving, conflict resolution, shared decision making, and organizing and running meetings. The chapters are written like instructional guides. If you want to, you can discover the skills right along with your team members.

Part V: Managing Some Tougher Team Matters

Part V explores three of the more challenging team management situations: self-directed teams, project teams/task teams, and alternative team-compensation systems.

As the name implies, a self-directed team has no manager in charge. A project team or task team often is cross-functional and exists only until its project or task is complete. The compensation topic can be just as challenging as the other two, involving incentives, bonuses, and skill-based pay, not to mention rewarding good team performance through noncash means. Part V offers you many tips and strategies on all these topics.

Part VI: The Part of Tens

This last part of the book consists of three short chapters containing useful tips and insights on other team-related issues: leading a management team, getting a team back on track when its performance slips, and recognizing effective team members when you see them.

Icons Used in This Book

Throughout this book you may notice small graphics in the margins, called *icons*. These symbols are meant to grab your attention in particular ways, as I explain:

This icon signifies practical ideas and points that help you put into practice what you're reading.

This icon identifies a thought worth keeping in mind as you manage your teams.

A red flag about what not to do in running teams.

An "aha" idea or insight meant to stimulate your thoughts about managing teams.

A how-to skill that can help your team members on the job.

A teaching tip to help you translate team management theory into understandable information

Where to Go from Here

This book is written so that each chapter stands on its own. So if you like to skip around and explore team topics as they come to mind, you can easily do so without being out of place. Sometimes I refer to points, terms, and skills covered in other chapters, making it easy for you to fill in information when you need to. One suggestion: You may want to start by reading Chapters 1 and 2 because they lay the foundation for the rest of the book. Enjoy your journey!

Part I
Getting Into Teams

The 5th Wave   By Rich Tennant

"For a more aggressive approach, we have our
'Or Else' series of motivational posters."

In this part . . .

Part I shows you what a *real* team is and how it's different from a regular work group. This section also explores some of the factors that give teams trouble, and you see why simply wishing a team to succeed doesn't guarantee anything. I also introduce you to a model to guide you in building a strong team, and I explain the skills that you want your team members to learn so that they can work well together.

Chapter 1

Recognizing a Business Team When You See One

*E*veryone knows what a team is. You understood instantly as a school kid when you were chosen as captain and got to pick your team for the kickball game at recess. Maybe you also played soccer or were on the school basketball or baseball team.

Adults love teams, too. I'll bet you have a favorite team that you cheer for: win or lose (Go Cubs!). Yes, you know what teams are — they're the heart and soul of sports. For many people, the whole idea of *team* is based on the sports model.

More and more these days, you see another model of *team* that is associated with the way employees spend their time in the workplace. Many of us work in some kind of team from 9 to 5 — it's a growing trend in private- and public-sector organizations.

But when it comes to the workplace, you can throw away most of the sports analogies. For one thing, not everyone plays sports or is a fan. More to the point, asking people to work in teams isn't the same as choosing sides for kickball. The goals of work teams are usually more expansive than merely beating an opponent (though I have some things to say elsewhere about beating the competition).

The sports analogy, in fact, breaks down very early when you transport it to the business scene. Think about it: In professional sports like the NFL or NBA, potential team members must compete against one another to make the team or win a starting position. And though they wear the same jerseys and cooperate on plays, the pros have to show in every game that they're worthy to remain on the team. That's competition.

I'm not saying there's no competition among business employees — there's plenty! But asking people to compete against other members of the same team in the workplace destroys the team concept. For a business team to succeed, team members must cooperate, and that's no easy feat to achieve. If you're going to succeed as a manager of a team, you need to understand first what a business team is all about. That's what this chapter does — it lays the foundation, defining common types of teams in business organizations and explaining why businesses are using teams more and more to get work done.

Also in this chapter I show you how to tell the difference between everyday work groups and work groups that are teams. And I give you a checklist of factors to consider as you move into team management.

Giving "Team" a Business Meaning

The word *team* has a positive connotation and gets thrown around a lot in workplaces, usually with good intentions. But just because a group of people have a good time at lunch or get along well at work doesn't make them a team, not even if some manager or executive calls them one.

The way I use the word throughout this book, a team is *a group of people organized to work together to accomplish a common purpose for which they share accountability.*

As you can see in this definition, three essential factors define a team:

- ✔ **Putting people together to do work.** The left hand and right hand, as the expression goes, are meant to fit together. (For soccer fans, it can be the left foot and right foot — but enough sports references.)

- ✔ **Having an overall common purpose.** Team members all work to achieve the same end result.

- ✔ **Being mutually accountable.** That means that each team member is equally responsible with every other member for accomplishing the team's mission.

What distinguishes a team from another kind of work group is the way its members are organized to capitalize on the *interdependence* that exists among them when they're at work. In simple terms, they need to work together to get something done.

Sometimes you can see interdependence within a work group or even an entire department, yet the individual employees function in their specialized roles and focus on their own tasks and issues. Sorry, they aren't a team.

Telling the Difference between Work Groups and Teams

Teams definitely are forms of work groups, but not all work groups are necessarily teams. In fact, plain work groups are much more numerous than teams. Are you with me so far? To make sure, I'm going to talk about the differences between work groups that *are* teams and those that are not.

Imagine that you are a contestant on a TV game show and the emcee is about to ask you the question that makes you rich forever (or for a few months, anyway). You're in the spotlight and the audience is hushed. Here's the question:

"Teams are a form of work group, but not all work groups are teams. *What's the main difference between work groups that are teams and those that are not?*"

You think hard. You bite your lip, maybe. Your forehead glistens with sweat. Then you speak, slowly but with certainty: "Teams," you say, ". . . have an interdependence among members . . . whereas other forms of work groups do not."

"That's right!" the emcee practically shouts as the audience thunders applause. When the house quiets down and you are chitchatting about your keen insights into team structure, you casually remark that work groups function on three levels:

- ✔ **Dependent level**
- ✔ **Independent level**
- ✔ **Interdependent level**

The TV host finds this so fascinating he asks you to explain, and here's the gist of what you say.

Dependent-level work groups

Dependent-level work groups are the traditional work unit or department groups with a supervisor who plays a strong role as the boss. Almost everyone has had some experience with this work setup, especially in a first job.

Each person in a dependent-level work group has his or her own job and works under the close supervision of the boss. The boss is in charge and tells the employees the do's and don'ts in their jobs. Helping each other and covering for one another do not occur often and do so mostly under the direction of the supervisor. In fact, most problem-solving, work assignments, and other decisions affecting the group come from the supervisor.

A dependent-level work group can perform well in the short term. But for the long run, because group members operate separately and mostly at the direction of the supervisor, such work groups don't seem to go anywhere. Maintaining the status quo and keeping operations under control are what they do best. Creating improvements, increasing productivity, and leveraging resources to support one another are quite uncommon with dependent-level work groups.

Independent-level work groups

Independent-level work groups are the most common form of work groups on the business scene. Like a dependent-level work group, each person is responsible for his or her own main area. But unlike the dependent level, the supervisor or manager tends not to function like the controlling boss. Instead, staff members work on their own assignments with general direction and minimal supervision.

It's very common for sales representatives, research scientists, accountants, lawyers, police officers, librarians, and teachers to work like this, to name just a few examples. People in those occupations come together in one department because they serve a common overall function, but almost everyone in the group works fairly independently.

If members of an independent-level work group receive the managerial guidance and support they need on the job, such a work group can perform quite well.

Interdependent-level work groups

Members of an *interdependent-level* work group rely on each other to get the work done. Sometimes members have their own roles and at other times they share responsibilities. Yet, in either case, they coordinate with one another to produce an overall product or set of outcomes. When this interdependence exists, you have a team. And by *capitalizing* on interdependence, the team demonstrates the truth of the old saying: The whole is greater than the sum of its parts.

There's no "I" in T-E-A-M

Dave was asked to lead the adoption of a team-based structure in the operations department of his company. He accepted the assignment knowing he would have to confront years of tradition in the 50-member department.

Employees generally worked as specialists within their subunits and reported to a supervisor. Even though the overall work of the operations department reflected a genuine connection among employees, the traditional work group structure prevented employees from realizing the full benefits of interdependence. Each subunit did its own part in the process with little concern for what the other groups did. In fact, the groups often functioned as if walls were built between them.

Soon, those walls began tumbling down. Cross-functional teams that focused on developing the whole product process replaced subunits. As teams were implemented and became productive, Dave in his role as director often preached this simple message: "There's no 'I' in *team.*"

Beyond the obvious spelling part, Dave's message took awhile to sink in with some team members. But over time, their attention at work shifted from primarily their own welfare to how their team was doing and what it needed to accomplish. And at that point, members of the operations department were poised to make tremendous gains in productivity.

An *independent* work group can often be brought up to speed faster than an *interdependent* group. It simply takes more time to get a group of individuals to work as a team than to set a group of individuals off on their independent assignments. Yet when teams move into a high-functioning and high-producing state, where they capitalize on interdependence, they can outperform all other types of work groups. So, if you want a quick fix, don't look to teams: but if you want to see strong results for the long term, *do* look to teams.

To call a group a team does not make them a team: wishing for them to work as a team doesn't work either. For a snapshot of the main differences between work groups and teams, take a look at Figure 1-1. As you can see, work groups have a strong individual focus and teams have a strong collective focus. The individual is not lost on a team, but that person's work is coordinated to fit in with the greater good. Team concerns are much more focused on the outcomes of the overall unit rather than an individual's accomplishments.

Figure 1-1 also indicates that teams meet more often than traditional work groups. Work groups may meet periodically, based on the manager's style, primarily to hear and share information. Teams, by comparison, do much more than communicate when they meet. Team meetings are forums for planning work, solving work problems, making decisions about work, and reviewing progress. In short, meetings are vital to a team's existence. Chapter 12 gives you tips and tools to help get the most out of your team meetings.

Differences between Work Groups and Teams

Work Groups	Teams
• Individual accountability	• Individual and mutual accountability
• Come together to share information and perspectives	• Frequently come together for discussion, decision making, problem solving, planning
• Focus on individual goals	• Focus on team goals
• Produce individual work products	• Produce collective work products
• Define individual roles, responsibilities, tasks	• Define individual roles, responsibilities, tasks to help team do its work; often share and rotate them
• Concern with one's own outcomes and challenges	• Concern with outcomes of everyone and challenges the team faces
• Purpose, goals, approach to work shaped by manager	• Purpose, goals, approach to work shaped by team leader with team members

Figure 1-1:
Work
groups
versus
teams.

The last item in Figure 1-1 is crucial: Team leadership is participatory, in contrast to the primarily manager-driven nature of regular work groups. On a team, the manager or team leader frequently involves team members in helping shape the goals and plans for getting the group's work done — may as well get them involved, they've got to do the work! But in other kinds of work groups, managers more commonly work with staff individually to set goals and determine assignments. Of course, in many cases, managers just assign work with little discussion or collaboration with the staff members. And staff are then left to figure out what's expected and how best to get it done.

How Teams Help Managers to Manage

More than just a fad or a nice word to throw around, real functioning *teams* are becoming a common way to get work done. That hasn't happened by accident. The turn-of-the-century idea (I'm talking 1900, not 2000) that workers are little cogs inside big industrial wheels has been turned inside out — now you see the "cogs" repositioned in team arrangements that vastly increase their influence and speed of action. If there's a better way to respond to the sheer speed of business today, I haven't seen it.

The increasing use of teams in private- and public-sector organizations has been done to adapt to a number of specific changes in the business climate, mainly:

- ✔ **Dealing with competitive pressures.** Your company may produce the world's best mousetrap today. But tomorrow, your competitor may roll out an even better trap — along with an A-plus customer-service group. What's the team response when that happens? In a nutshell, it's the old proverb, updated: Two or more heads are better than one. When mousetrap makers need to think fast to answer a competitive threat, they understand that combining the talents of all their trap engineers just may get the job done faster than having members of your brain trust work separately, no matter how smart they are.

- ✔ **Responding to technological advances.** Advances in technology, especially in the use of computers, often change the way work gets done. Computer-driven manufacturing systems, for example, can reduce or totally eliminate the need for an individual to directly perform a piece of work. When that happens, the workplace needs more multi-specialists and fewer individual specialists. Teams are the natural gathering place of such multitalented generalists.

- ✔ **Meeting customer expectations.** Customers have high expectations and little tolerance for any delay. If your service is slow or sloppy, customers can take their business someplace else. So, if you say, "I'm sorry, the person who handles your problem is on vacation for two weeks," that's a loud *click* you hear on the other end of the line. Teamwork is the natural way for colleagues to share responsibility for accomplishing Job One: serving customer needs.

- ✔ **Doing more with less.** In some workplaces this phrase has been the battle cry of management for quite some time. "Got to hold the line on costs. Can't just hire willy-nilly whenever the volume of work spikes up. Times are tough, so do more with less!" To get more work done without increasing the payroll, companies are asking employees to share responsibilities — fewer Lone Rangers, more teams. The logic is neat: four people working together can provide more coverage and get more done than four people working independently.

✔ **Tackling complex problems.** Some of the thorniest problems are primarily internal, like improving the quality of an organization's products or services. *Multidisciplinary task teams* can do crucial work at times like these. I have seen it happen at some of my city government clients who created multidisciplinary teams to tackle community-service related problems. Instead of each department dealing with a community problem from its own perspective, you can find a total, integrated solution faster by bringing staff together from all the departments that are affected — from the police department to the library, if that what it takes. I have seen the same thing with some of my private-sector clients — multiple disciplines getting together to solve everything from order fulfillment bottlenecks to product development snafus. (Would you believe it — marketing and engineering working together on the same team!)

✔ **Matching the pace of change.** In some companies the *only* constant is change — if you don't keep up with it, you'd better get out of the way! When they need to spark creative ideas and move people together quickly to keep up with the changing needs, more and more companies look to their teams for answers.

✔ **Turnover-proofing the company.** With turnover much higher and more common in many places than ever before, even in some public-sector organizations, managers are chagrined when they flunk the *truck test:* "If one of your staff got hit by a truck tomorrow, can others in your group step in and do the job with minimal disruption in productivity?" But teams can fill the gaps because they are composed of people who — by team design — share responsibilities.

Reengineering customer service at city hall

Companies aren't the only organizations that are redesigning work processes to gain efficiency and serve customers better. So are municipal governments. One of the best examples on the city scene is the building and construction permits process. In the old days (I'm sorry to say that the old days still prevail in many city halls), developers had to run a treadmill of city departments, getting their tickets punched at the zoning, engineering, street, water, sewer, and other departments. It took time and an enormous amount of patience with the bureaucracy.

Many cities and towns have reengineered this process with a team approach. Instead of sending builders off on a furious chase after numerous departmental approvals, these municipalities have created "one-stop shopping" — a single customer-service counter that draws all the different departments together in the construction permit process. The result is faster and more convenient service to the customer — make that, to the *taxpayer*.

If you're like a lot of managers, when you hear that something works well for someone else, you want to try it yourself. Or if you have experienced success elsewhere, you may want to recreate it when you arrive someplace new. As teams grow in use, some will experience significant success — greater productivity than any other form of work group. And as word of this success spreads, so have managers' and executives' initiatives to give teams a try.

Introducing the Most Common Types of Teams

Practically all teams can be classified as one of five types, which I list below. Because of their objective, some teams work together indefinitely. Others have a short-term mission, and when their work is done the team disbands. It's common in many organizations for people to have regular job duties in a regular, old-fashioned work group that isn't a team, yet spend at least some time working in a genuine team setting to reach a short-term objective.

Here are the five most common types of teams that you can find in organizations:

- **Work-unit teams:** They are the most common and usually are ongoing. Work-unit teams are part of departments and have skills related to the department or work group's main function. Think of the *customer service* team, the *accounting* team, or the *technical support* team, for example. A work-unit team may not always have *team* in its name, but you can tell by the way team members work together and share accountability for an overall outcome that they are a classic team.

- **Project teams:** This second most common type of team often is cross-functional, meaning it brings together a few special talents — or quite a few, if necessary — to accomplish a project. Everyone has a role, and everyone needs to work with everyone else to reach the right outcome. Often time-limited, project teams can disband when they complete their assignment. But in some technical fields, like engineering, the nature of the work is one project after another and people spend whole careers in team assignments, moving to a new project when they finish the last.

- **Task teams:** Sometimes referred to as task forces (or even *committees*), task teams usually are time-limited and cross-functional. Team members have skills related to the task: they are brought together to study challenging issues or critical problems facing the organization or overall department and to recommend action — and they are growing in use in many organizations. Sometimes task teams also implement their recommendations. Sometimes they are kept on call to respond to whatever arises, kind of like a volunteer fire department! Some task teams operate over long periods with members rotating in and out. The membership changes but the work of the team lives on.

Speaking of teams. . . .

No absolute definitions apply to the following terms, but I want you to know how they are commonly used and the particular spin that I put on them in this book and when I work with clients.

Teamwork means the behavior of team members with one another. It describes the way team members get along and cooperate to succeed. You may see this sense of teamwork in work groups that are not teams, but you can't have effective teamwork without the formal deployment of teams. Teamwork, as I use the term, does *not* mean team development and management.

Team building in common use means some kind of social or recreational activity or special retreat designed to bond team members. But I use the term to describe something more rigorous — the ongoing hard work of creating and managing a team to function and perform at a high level of productivity. There's nothing wrong with the other sorts of team-building tactics, like ropes courses or mental gymnastics or bowling — teams need to have fun. I talk about team building in that context in Chapter 6. But the risk is assuming that that side of team building causes people to work better together at the office. One does not beget the other. Teams develop best when they work together on getting their work done.

Integration team unites various teams to ensure consistent policies and practices. For example, if the manufacturing department has a number of product teams performing similar functions, the integration team — usually made up of one member of each work-unit team — ensures that all teams are coordinated.

Steering team, usually composed of management staff and sometimes individual employees too, often oversees major organizational change or addresses department-level issues and can be the driving force for setting the direction that day-to-day work-unit teams follow.

Self-directed team, usually a work-unit team, operates with autonomy — all members share in managing the team's responsibilities. Although such a team usually reports to a manager, it generally does not operate with anyone in the role of day-to-day supervisor. Chapter 13 explores self-directed teams.

Team leader means different things in different situations. On some teams, especially work-unit teams, the manager is the team leader: in management teams, the top executive serves as the team leader. Both are roles that come with authority. But often with project teams and task teams, the team leader has no supervisory authority but serves as a facilitator and coordinator and is often the focal point for communications to and from the team. Sometimes the leader role is rotated among team members. Project teams may call this role *project manager* or *program manager.*

Sponsor, usually a member of senior management, is not a member of a team but the person who creates the team, provides overall direction and support, and expects to see results. The sponsor is not involved in the day-to-day workings of the team. In many team structures, no sponsors exist. But in the case of significant project and task teams, a sponsor at the executive level may be a critical component.

Team member is, of course, one of the group that gets the team's work done. Your job is to coordinate their work. Some members of the team may be with you only part time, especially if you're dealing with a task team, management team, or project team. Some team members may also be part of regular work groups, or managers of work groups, or members of other teams at the same time — all of which makes managing teams a challenging job.

Chapter 14 goes into greater detail on how to manage both project and task teams to achieve success.

✔ **Improvement teams:** As you can guess by the name, improvement teams work to make things better — usually work-related processes. In municipal government organizations, I've seen improvement teams streamline the registration processes for recreation programs and the application processes for obtaining building permits. *Quality circles* are a type of improvement team and became widely known as part of the total quality management movement in Japan and the United States. But you don't see them called by that name as much as you did a decade ago.

✔ **Management teams:** You can find so-called "management teams" all over the place. But seldom do you find one that functions like a real team. It's easy for a company to say it has a management "team," but aside from coming together periodically, the members may seldom do any collective work in running the enterprise. Each manager has his or her primary area of responsibility and does little beyond that for the greater good. Yet there are some authentic management teams — not many but at least some good examples — with leaders who involve the rest of the management group in working on issues and taking on responsibilities together for the greater organization. Chapter 16 offers some tips for helping management groups to really work as teams.

Looking Before You Leap: Factors to Consider in Adopting Teams

Teams are a way to organize people to get work done, but they are not a cure-all. Just because you create a team doesn't guarantee you're going to see any benefits from it. Another person's success with teams does not mean you'll have the same experience.

On the other hand, if you see opportunities to capitalize on the interdependence of employees, then creating teams may be just right for you. But before you announce, "Everyone, we're now a team!" take time to think and plan so that you can lead the transition into teams in an organized and purposeful fashion. (Don't worry, your employees will overcome the shock of seeing you look organized and leading with a purpose. Their shock may even turn into joy!)

This section provides you a list of factors to consider before moving into teams — factors to examine at the organizational level, the manager level, and the team member level. Generally, the higher you are in the organization, the more factors you need to consider and plan for to make the transition to teams successful.

Factors to consider at the organizational level

The first set of factors to consider are the so-called big picture items — organizational concerns that often reach beyond teams themselves, such as:

- The performance challenges your business faces

- The best structure for meeting those performance challenges, regular work groups or teams, and why

- If you go with teams, the types that are best

- Skill sets needed to perform the work, on both the team member and team leader level

- Other possible roles that may need to be filled, such as sponsor and management steering team, to help make teams happen and support their ongoing development

- The experience of teams elsewhere in the organization and the lessons you can learn from them

- Processes, practices, rewards, information systems, and related elements that need to be enhanced or put in place for teams to work

- The boundaries and level of authority that teams will have

- Resources that need to be invested, from people to money, to implement and develop teams

- The approach that will work best to start into teams — pilot program, transitional phase-in, or total immersion

The final item listed above focuses on how you begin. Sometimes, especially when fewer teams are involved, *total immersion* can work fine. This means that everyone who has anything to do with a team begins learning and working as a team right away — ready, set, go!

Sometimes you may want to take the *pilot program* approach — reconfigure one work group as a team and try them out for awhile. Once they get rolling, then you form other teams.

If your objective is to create a number of teams, a *transitional phased-in* approach may be best (see Chapter 4). This means you start with a few teams and give them some time and support to get working, then add a few more, and so on from there. It's the old row-row-row-your boat approach — move ahead in stages over time.

Factors to consider at the manager level

This next set of factors focuses on you as the manager responsible for leading one or more teams. You need to be concerned about:

- ✔ Understanding the purpose and overall goals of the team
- ✔ Providing guidance and direction as the team develops, and acquiring the skills you need to become effective as a coach and facilitator
- ✔ Acquiring the resources you need to train team members — and the tools they need to succeed
- ✔ Identifying the outside relationships your team needs to cultivate
- ✔ Identifying the obstacles your team must address
- ✔ Assessing your own willingness to share authority and decision making with the team

The last point above is one of the most crucial for a manager. If you are totally hands off in your leadership style, the team flounders. If you control everything, you stifle and demotivate the team. If you try to make every decision by consensus, it can lead to the analysis-by-paralysis syndrome, taking forever to decide anything.

Or you can adopt a more participatory approach. You can share some level of responsibility and get your team members involved in helping shape the direction and operation of the team. Chapter 3 provides guidance on leading teams so that members are involved and performing well. Chapter 11 gives you tools for managing the group decision making effort.

Factors to consider at the team member level

Team members are the lifeblood. Their performance and working relationships with one another make or break a team. So, from selecting the team members to developing them to work as a team, you want to consider these factors:

- ✔ The skills and talents, from technical to interpersonal, best needed to perform the team's assignment
- ✔ The mix of members who potentially can work well together

✔ The development each team member needs to perform and fit well on the team

✔ The level of motivation you have to work with — or the degree of resistance you need to work through — with various team members

✔ The key roles required by the team and the individuals who can play them best

You don't need to nail everything down before you launch a team. So don't let one or two free-floating concerns stop you in your tracks — some questions can be answered only as you move along. But do use the management factors above as your own personal team-management plan.

How many people does it take to make a team?

Okay, this is not the same as asking, for example, "How many dot-comers does it take to screw in a light bulb?" (I just made that up and don't know the answer — you're welcome to invent one.) But people often ask me the team-size question, and I don't really know. No set number or right answer exists. Technically, the smallest a team can be is two people. It's possible that two people can work together toward an end result that they are together responsible for making happen. This is different from the relationship between two people who need to cooperate and help each other now and then but focus primarily on their own areas of responsibility — they may call themselves a team but they are mostly independent operators.

I don't see many pairs or trios functioning as teams, although they can be structured to do so. More commonly, team size starts with four and runs into double figures. I have not seen too many teams work effectively once they got beyond a dozen members or so, but again no limit on size defines a team. Sometimes you can have subteams existing within one large team structure. But in this book, when I talk about teams I'm talking about units made up of four people to a baker's dozen (that's 13, if you haven't been to a bakery recently).

Chapter 2

Creating a Team Culture: Going Beyond the Magic Wand

*N*o magic wand or special pill exists that can instantly transform a work group into a highly productive team. Developing a team to achieve high levels of performance involves a lot of hard work — a continuous effort. So, when it comes to forming and leading teams, managers with a hands-off style or an impatient manner need not apply.

On the other hand, if you're willing to accept the discipline and do the work, welcome aboard! When I see managers who have an opportunity to create a *real* team — one with genuine interdependence, common purpose, and mutual accountability among its members — I urge them to go for it. My recommendation is based on a simple fact: Teams outperform any other type of work group. Teams work.

And yet some days, frankly, it doesn't look like teams work at all. Despite the positive connotation of the word *team,* the reality is that not everyone takes instantly and positively to genuinely working as a team. Teams can become rife with struggles and even self-destruct. In this chapter, I show you the symptoms of team trouble and explore the reasons some employees initially resist working in teams.

This chapter also lays the foundation for building a team and setting it on a path toward achieving high performance. I introduce you to a model for developing your team — the three cornerstones of *focus, cohesiveness,* and *accountability.* And I introduce you to the skills that team members need to perform well in team situations, because you can't just wave that magic wand and expect teamwork to happen.

I talk about discipline in this chapter and elsewhere in the book. Teams need discipline if they're going to gain benefits in performance. The way it's used here, *discipline* means an ongoing effort and hard work, initiating and following through on strategies and actions that drive teams toward achieving top performance. Of course, the lead driver for instilling discipline is the manager. That's you.

Understanding "The Terrible Twenty" — Why Teams Sometimes Struggle

Even when teams work hard, they sometimes flounder and fail. Why is that? Through the years I've asked that question of people attending my seminars, and here's what they tell me — I call them "The Terrible Twenty." You may recognize some of these problems.

- Team members shirking their responsibility, not pulling their weight
- Conflicts or personality clashes among team members
- Lack of cooperation among team members
- Cliques forming within a team
- Disruptive behavior by a team member that's left unaddressed
- Poor communication and withholding of information
- Disorganized team meetings that turn everybody off
- Little or no attention to the training and cross-training that a team needs to do its work
- Essential skills sets missing from a team
- Differing ideas among team members about what the team should focus on
- Apathy
- A dominating or controlling team leader
- A laissez faire or hands-off team leader
- Unclear team goals
- Unclear team purpose
- Constantly changing directions to the team from upper management
- Undefined roles of team members, sometimes leading to duplication of effort or tasks left undone
- Lack of resources — from tools to training

> ✔ Unrealistic expectations of the team by management outside the team
>
> ✔ Lack of cooperation or support from managers or others outside the team, throwing roadblocks in front of the team

As you look at this list of team problems remember that any one can pop up unexpectedly, especially if your style of team management is merely to wave the magic wand and wish the members well.

Sorting the problems by general type, you can see that they fit into three broad kinds of issues:

> ✔ **People issues,** brought about by things like poor interpersonal communication, poor leadership, and lack of cooperation
>
> ✔ **Structure issues,** stemming from missing skills or missing direction or poorly defined roles and goals
>
> ✔ **Support issues,** which can mean lack of training and essential team tools and lack of interest by management above the team — all factors that prevent teams from performing well

Concentrate on these three general issues as you develop and lead teams. This is the hard work of managing teams. Later in this chapter, I introduce you to three principles for building a high-performance team — strategies to help you avoid being plagued by issues concerning people, structure, and support.

Spotting Resistance

Don't be alarmed when you see some employees resisting your teams program — they're only being human! But they're also reflecting American culture, as I explain in the next four sections. I think you may be surprised how much resistance is simply bred into people by their experience. Take a look and you may even see yourself in some comfortable situation from the past, or *uncomfortable* team situation more recently.

Cultural orientation — the rugged individualist

If you've grown up in the United States or been reared on U.S. cultural exports, you may be well conditioned as an *individualist,* someone who can stand on your own without team support. American literature romanticizes the rugged individualist — the cowboy, the sheriff, the wildcatter. TV and movies glamorize the solitary hero. In school, you're rewarded for *individual* achievements. You compete to get into a prestigious college and work hard for good grades and a degree. And that's only the beginning! You compete against others for the job you want and for career-advancement opportunities.

So, from an early age and well into your working career, you're prepared and even rewarded for taking care of yourself and competing for what you want. And nothing is wrong with that! America is a great nation, in part, because of the wonderful achievements of many individuals. But you can see how this cultural orientation may make the transition into collective ventures — teams — hard for some people. Suddenly you have to change your focus. Rather than think only about your own needs, you need to think about the outcomes of an entire group of people, and working cooperatively becomes much more critical for success than functioning competitively.

Limited or poor experience with teams

For many, their first significant experience working in teams occurs on the job, sometimes after years of working in other group situations that may look like teams but actually aren't or as members of genuine teams that struggled for one reason or another. Or their prior experience may be limited to playing on a sports team, which is far different from a work team (see Chapter 1). Other people may remember their team experience in school. They worked on a project team in a class where they did most of the work and practically carried the team while others sat back and took equal credit! None of these experiences is motivating, especially when your livelihood is on the line.

Success as a solo

Some people are fiercely independent and enjoy working alone. That doesn't mean they don't like interacting with others. But what they like more is being responsible for their own work and seeing accomplishments from their own efforts. They like to do their own thing on the job and often are well trained to do so. They may work most of the time in independent work group situations, and when asked to double up by joining a task team or special project team, they may put less emphasis on the team. It isn't their main priority.

However, when the team becomes the biggest part of such individuals' job responsibilities, they may have the comfort level knocked right out from under them. The acts of coordinating work with others, problem-solving with others, and depending on others to do their parts of a job — all common features of team situations — render practically irrelevant the prized quality of working well on your own. No wonder some soloists have a hard time adjusting to teamwork!

The idea window is now open

John, a 15-year employee, is a member of a production team established at his plant a few months ago. Under a new manager and new team structure, employees are expected to work together on the whole production process and constantly are involved in planning the work and finding ways to make it more cost effective.

John had an idea for improving efficiency and presented it to his team. They approved the idea and implemented it. The cost to the company was about $50, but the savings turned out to be tens of thousands per year.

One day recently a top company executive came by to congratulate the team and in particular John for the magnificent cost savings that had been achieved. "When did you have this idea?" the executive asked John.

"Oh, about ten years ago," John said. "But when I came up with it back then, my supervisor told me my job was not to worry about those kinds of things, just do my work as I was told."

What a difference real teams can make.

Fear of change

Some people are happy with the status quo. They like their job situations and want nothing to change. For some, regardless of what the change is, fear and great discomfort set in as an initial reaction, affecting them for quite awhile before they work through it. Think about how you, as manager, are viewed: You come along and announce that you're organizing everyone to work in a team. Say hello to resistance from the defenders of status quo.

Other people may outwardly support the team concept, yet they hold unrealistic expectations about how quickly the team will gel and perform well. When they feel some bumps along the road to effective teamwork, they grow restless and disenchanted. "Maybe this change to teams wasn't such a good idea after all," they think. Patience isn't a characteristic of many employees, let alone their managers.

Winning Them Over

Don't be alarmed if some of your employees show signs of great discomfort and resistance as you move into teams. In fact, you may have more reason to worry if they all seem overjoyed at the prospect of teams and think everything's going to be wonderful. Teams can and do deliver wondrous results but rarely before hard work and some frustration. So just roll with the punches and help your people to get on board. Here are some tips for moving people along and getting them adjusted to a team situation.

✔ **Set a tone of patience and persistence.** Team members need to see you set the right example. When they see you're in control and not upset at every little ripple, they too calm down. When they see you stay the course and talk about where the team is going, they too look ahead and work through each day.

✔ **Listen a great deal.** Sometimes the best way to help people adjust into teams is to spend more time listening to them than talking to them. That means *active* listening, as I describe in Chapter 8. Seek your team members out. Hear what's going on with them individually as they work in the team, find out their concerns, and acknowledge their feelings. When you understand what's going on with your team members, they know that you care, and that knowledge can be a great boon in helping them adjust to the new team situation.

✔ **Provide ongoing communication.** Team members need updates from you, from one another, and from management above — news about the team's direction, progress, and performance, to name just a few of the issues for communication. Although e-mail is okay for passing on news, frequent, face-to-face communication in group and individual settings is far more effective. Make those sessions part of regular practice.

✔ **Get the team involved in planning its work.** Push as much as you have to on this one — otherwise, your *inaction* can spell disaster for the team. Get the members involved from the beginning in setting up the framework for performing their work. Meet with the team to develop goals and plans and to define roles and responsibilities. When you do all this, you relieve the team of waiting and wondering, the time when chaos and frustration can creep in and the resistance movement can declare victory. I talk more about strategies that provide team focus and direction in Chapter 5.

✔ **Help the team to overcome obstacles.** If the team needs resources, get them. If the team needs information, create access to it. You're the team's advocate to others in the organization, from peers to higher levels of management. So push, push, push! Don't let anything distract you from helping solve the team's functional problems. The best news is: The team often can figure out ways of solving problems as long as you're there to facilitate the effort.

✔ **Train them and cross-train them.** From team-oriented work skills to technical job skills, team members often need training and cross-training. You may need to tap other internal resources or even external resources to teach your people. Whatever it takes, get rolling with training so that team members can grow while they work as a team rather than suffer through trial and error. The key team skills you want your members to master are highlighted in this chapter at "Training Your Team in Six Critical Skills," and detailed throughout Part IV.

✔ **Deal at once with performance issues.** Whenever you see any performance problems — for example, team members slacking off or becoming disruptive — consider them signs of resistance that must be addressed right away. Do nothing and you may see these behaviors multiply, affect others, and drag down the entire team. In the early stages of a team's development, most members aren't ready or willing to address performance issues with other team members. That's where you as manager come in. Coach to correct first. That means taking individuals aside and giving them feedback based on your observations about their performance and then clarifying your expectations and asking what steps they'll take to meet those expectations. In most cases, a one-on-one like this refocuses people on the job and on conducting themselves professionally. Chapter 4 provides more specifics.

✔ **Focus on driving performance.** This tip sums up the previous seven tips. Performance is what teams are all about, and your main job is not to make everyone happy but to guide and lead the team to good performance, including everything from setting goals and assignments to monitoring progress and results. Chapter 3 gives you detailed advice on leading teams as a coach, employing the strategies that build discipline for higher performance.

Anyone seen a manager?

Company X decided to combine a couple of work units into one team. The groups previously had operated separately, handling various customer order processing and administrative functions that were closely related. The two unit managers got along well and supported the move — it made good business sense. "Let's give it a try," they resolved. Regrettably, that was about the extent of their commitment.

After a few months the managers discovered that their newly formed team was struggling, and they worried about the growing disenchantment of many team members. What to do? At the urging of upper management, the managers invited an outside consultant to interview team members and assess the situation.

The assessment was grim. Team members' roles were not well-defined — not even for the managers. Cross-training occurred only in bits and pieces with no one getting fully what they needed. Communication was sporadic. Database systems weren't fully upgraded and

adjusted. Team members who resisted the new work situation were mostly ignored. The human resources department did put on a workshop about adapting to change, but that was the extent of organized guidance and support. Through it all, team members tried to remain optimistic, but many became frustrated and let others know how they felt.

Follow-up on the consultant's report was sporadic, and eventually the two managers were assigned elsewhere in the company. If they were puzzled by the team's failure, they actually shouldn't have been. Merely supporting the team concept is not enough to help people overcome their discomfort and resistance when they begin to work as teams. You, as manager, have much influence on how well your team members make the adjustment. When you recognize that you, too, have to change and that the team needs you to positively and actively take charge, you are ready to become an effective team manager.

Introducing the Three Cornerstones: Focus, Cohesiveness, Accountability

If you want to show your team the road to success, pointing with your magic wand won't do any good. Neither will all your good wishes or days spent on retreat. What you must do is help the team set three main cornerstones in place as a solid foundation for all their teamwork (see Figure 2-1). The cornerstones are named:

- ✔ Focus
- ✔ Cohesiveness
- ✔ Accountability

In this section I show you how each cornerstone supports a number of specific team strategies and I introduce you to the other secret for achieving success with teams: training team members in the skills they need to work together effectively. Most of these team skills are not taught in school, and that's surprising when you think how critically important they are in moving people off a self-focused, I'll-do-it-myself orientation toward working well in collective efforts.

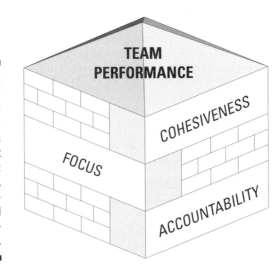

Figure 2-1: Three interlocking cornerstones support your team: Focus, Cohesiveness, and Accountability.

Managing teams that are going to work well together for awhile, from project teams to work-unit teams, is no easy feat. The key to success is heavily involving work groups in developing and utilizing strategies that build discipline for high productivity. Discipline is about continuous hard work and follow-through, not stop-and-start efforts.

What follows are definitions of each cornerstone and showcases of the strategies associated with the cornerstones that drive team performance.

Focus

The *focus* cornerstone supports the team's reason for being and helps define where it's going and what it needs to accomplish. Focus is about building the clarity and sense of direction that a team needs to perform well. Remember that strategies are developed with the team, not imposed on the team. More details about developing focus strategies are in Chapter 5. Some key strategies for developing a strong focus cornerstone are:

- ✓ **Establishing a team vision statement.** The vision statement describes the long-term outlook — where the team is going and what it will be like when it's performing at a high level.

- ✓ **Defining core values.** Core values are guiding principles. They're the handful of beliefs that inspire team practices and guide team members as they do their work.

- ✓ **Developing a team-purpose statement.** The purpose statement explains why a team exists and what it's expected to do, defines the team's overall role, and gives members a common agenda for doing their work.

- ✓ **Creating team guidelines.** Guidelines are the behavioral expectations that define how team members work with one another and provide a focus on professionalism and excellence.

- ✓ **Setting team performance goals.** Performance goals are the *big* end results that the team needs to reach within a set period of time. Goals are updated periodically to stay current with new challenges while continuing to serve as the driving force in focusing the team on what it needs to accomplish.

- ✓ **Planning projects and assignments.** That means figuring out the key steps for the team to follow in accomplishing its goals. The idea is, plan the work, and then work the plan.

- ✓ **Clarifying roles and responsibilities.** Figuring out who's going to do what is a strategy that often is devised at the same time the work is planned. Clarifying roles and responsibilities helps to avoid duplicating efforts and to prevent important obligations from slipping through any cracks — or any canyons — that may develop along the way.

- ✓ **Defining performance measurements.** With some teams, knowing what outcome areas to measure provides a strong focus. For example, when a team places a great emphasis on providing quality service to its customers, determining the areas of quality service to track or measure is important.

✔ **Setting team performance standards based on key factors.** If a team emphasizes customer service, for example, setting behavior or work standards based on good customer service practices gives the team a strong focus in that area.

Cohesiveness

The *cohesiveness* cornerstone helps the team to bond the various perspectives and talents of its members, creating a dynamic and positive work group. To repeat, these strategies are devised *with* the team, not imposed from its leader. Details about cohesiveness strategies are covered in Chapter 6. Some key strategies for preparing and setting the cohesiveness cornerstone are:

✔ **Developing backup coverage.** Backup means cross-training, preparing the team to pass the truck test, so that if someone is run over by a truck, someone else can step up and keep the team moving ahead.

✔ **Creating shared responsibilities or joint assignments.** Managers need to employ this strategy whenever they can — getting people used to working with one another and accomplishing important things. In earthy terms, this is like working side by side to dig a ditch, making joint decisions about how deep and how far and coordinating the entire effort. Shared responsibilities and joint assignments are great for *group* dynamics, ending I-do-everything-myself kind of thinking.

✔ **Problem-solving with operational issues.** Cohesiveness develops as teams solve problems together. So as problems arise, managers must pull their teams together to work on developing solutions. Show them the systematic ways that I cover in Chapter 9 to involve them in solving their own problems.

✔ **Employing team guidelines.** Post team guidelines on the wall, making them visible whenever the team meets, and periodically talk with the members about how they're following guidelines. Use the guidelines to direct discussion when the team is resolving problems and conflicts.

✔ **Addressing team functioning issues.** Sometimes conflicts come up, communication problems arise, or other group concerns become apparent. When such issues affect most team members, pull the team together to address these concerns and together find solutions. If the issues involve individuals, speaking with the individuals privately is okay. Chapter 10 provides tools for constructively resolving group functioning issues as a team.

✔ **Attending training sessions together.** From staging technical forums to receiving training on various team skills, having team members learn together — and from one another — is a great strategy for building a cohesive team.

✔ **Redesigning a work process.** Improving a work process to increase efficiency, or creating a new process, is a team activity that can pull team members together. By pooling ideas and playing off one another's insights, teams find better ways to get the work done.

✔ **Involving the team in interviewing and selecting new team members.** Especially useful with teams that are working together for long periods of time, current members can help you interview candidates for open slots on the team. Making members part of the process adds credibility to your decision to hire (or not) and enhances team support of new team members when they come on board.

✔ **Conducting activities to build relationships and promote understanding.** Stepping away from the work at times to strengthen working relationships often aids overall team performance. This strategy, sometimes referred as "the team-building stuff," may look like it's all about fun and games and getting to like your fellow team members. But it's really about enhancing group dynamics so that people pull together to get their work done. Some useful ideas about this strategy are covered in Chapter 6.

Accountability

The *accountability* cornerstone reinforces high standards and the sense of shared responsibility that a team needs to produce top results. It is about collectively extending concern for a team's performance and outcomes from the manager alone to the group. As with the other cornerstones, accountability strategies are carried out with the team, not laid on the team by its manager. Chapter 7 covers accountability strategies in detail. Some key strategies that surround the accountability cornerstone are:

✔ **Delivering team presentations to management.** When a team reports its results or recommendations to management, it puts its work on display. The formal presentation to which all team members contribute gives everyone an opportunity to shine and to show how the team has delivered well on its responsibilities.

✔ **Conducting periodic status review meetings.** Important with project teams and useful with any type of team, this strategy requires each member to report progress on their assignments. Status review sessions can build positive peer group pressure: Pete hears Mary deliver a strong progress report and thinks, "I can do that, too!"

✔ **Doing a team self-evaluation.** Best if done once a quarter or once every six months, a team self-evaluation poses questions like: How well has the team done in meeting its goals? How well have team members worked together? What kind of progress has the team made in working toward its goals? Manager and team members assess the answers and suggest and implement corrections and improvements where needed.

✔ **Conducting post-mortems.** Post-mortems are evaluation meetings at the end of a project or major event. They're conducted to review what happened, from what went well to what can be done better next time. The idea is to learn from the past so that successes — and not mistakes — are repeated.

✔ **Recognizing and celebrating accomplishments.** Pausing to recognize and celebrate team successes is important. Don't take the team for granted! From big parties to simple gatherings, how you celebrate with your team doesn't matter as long as what you do is viewed as positive by the team.

✔ **Assessing the effectiveness of team meetings.** Because teams spend much of their time in meetings, assessing how team members run their meetings helps keep them on a productive track. Jointly determining criteria for productive meetings and taking time when meetings end to ask "How did we do today?" reinforces the idea that meetings shouldn't waste time.

✔ **Carrying out peer feedback sessions.** One of the best strategies for promoting team accountability is using peer feedback sessions, so that team members exchange constructive feedback with one another about team member behavior and performance. Teams can use the guidelines they developed as a *focus* strategy to structure their feedback sessions. Such sessions challenge the maturity level of a team and its members and are useful for identifying problems as well as recognizing individuals making valuable contributions to the team. The feedback strategy can be introduced after a team has spent some time together and then used periodically, say once a quarter or every six months. See Chapter 7 for details on organizing and running a peer feedback session.

Make sure that you develop your team's skills by implementing strategies from all three cornerstones — focus, cohesiveness, and accountability. You need all three going strong together to maximize your team's performance.

Training Your Team in Six Critical Skills

Besides acquiring technical and job skills, teams need to discover the skills that are essential to working together — what I call the team skills or tools. Your job as manager is to find the resources that you need to impart these critical skills, devote time to this training, and make the training action oriented — what team members discover in the classroom they apply right away on the team.

Six critical tools that team members use when they work well together are:

✔ **Interpersonal communication.** Communicating with one another is so much a part of life in teams that it greatly shapes the general quality of a team's work. So, team members need to discover how to listen *actively* and to speak *assertively*. Chapter 8 goes into detail about these important communication tools.

✔ **Systematic problem-solving.** People are not born with problem-solving skills. Yet teams often deal with problems. Finding out how to attack *problems* instead of people and how to solve them instead of shooting from the hip is what systematic problem-solving is all about.

✔ **Planning and goal setting.** To get ahead, you must plan ahead and set goals. Individual team members, not just managers, must master these skills — planning the work, then working the plan. Chapter 9 gives you more insight.

✔ **Collaborative conflict resolution.** Conflicts are inevitable in team situations. Conflicts are rooted in differences — different opinions, different ideas. Working through these differences is key for teams to minimize interpersonal tension and perform productively. Chapter 10 shows you how teams can address and resolve conflicts.

✔ **Group decision making.** Teams share decisions much more than other kinds of management groups do. Chapter 11 shows you how to reach good decisions without long delays or chaos, and it provides tools that you need for building consensus as well as applying a consultative decision-making process with teams.

✔ **Meeting management.** People often dread going to meetings because of their many experiences in unfocused, chaotic, pointless meetings. But meetings are the backbone of a team's work, and discovering how to productively run your meetings is vital for team success. Chapter 12 provides you with tools for making meetings work, including how to effectively facilitate them.

Part II
Leadership for Team Success

The 5th Wave   By Rich Tennant

In the end, it was Edward Scissorhand's cousin, Jonathan Hammerhead, who brought the team to a consensus on their vision statement.

In this part . . .

This part is mainly about you, the team leader or manager. I offer you insights into behaviors that make the difference in your role as leader, plus practical suggestions for helping your teams work through their early stages of development. One entire chapter in this part shows you how to help teams deal with the ever-changing business environment.

Chapter 3

Leading Teams as a Coach

Coaching a team means working on two levels: the group level and one-on-one. That means shaping the talents of individual team members and then fitting them together in a powerful single unit — the team. It also means not sitting back and hoping that one wave of the magic wand brings everyone together in a team. That's a hazard I warn you about in Chapter 2.

Chapter 2 also talks about how transition can be tough on individuals — members of your new team — who've grown comfortable operating more or less independently. In the new team environment, where success depends heavily on *inter*dependence and mutual accountability, some free spirits may suddenly feel boxed in. Managers need to be patient, and in Chapter 4, I delve deeper into techniques that managers can use in helping team members adjust to their new environment.

But in this chapter, I concentrate entirely on you, the manager, and the best way for you to lead with teams — as a coach. Managing a team requires the application of a certain set of skills that you may not have needed much when you were in charge of a department of amiable and cooperative but basically independent workers. If you want to become an effective *team* leader, you have to make adjustments, too.

When managers move into team situations, they sometimes fall into what I call the *all-or-nothing trap:*

   ✔ **All** — you direct all activities of the team. You explain (to yourself) that they (your team's members) can't do anything yet for themselves. Although you're trying to be helpful, you actually come across as a dictator. In the process, you stifle team members' initiative, creativity, and quite possibly their entire motivation.

> ✔ **Nothing** — you stand back and let the team do everything for itself. You tell yourself, "I don't want to get in their way." In this hands-off style, you come across not only as uninvolved but also as uninterested, and you unknowingly plant the seeds for a bumper crop of chaos and frustration — not exactly the way to grow a team!

The key in managing teams so that they achieve high performance is finding that happy medium between the *all* approach and the *nothing* approach. This chapter shows you the way — how to be a coach but not a dictator. In this chapter, I talk about the way successful team managers behave in any situation, whether they supervise the team members or serve as a leader among peers. The pointers in this chapter even apply to coaches who at the moment have no supervisory authority at all, like when they're on temporary assignment in a cross-functional situation.

Working as a Coach, Not as a Doer or Boss

This first section defines what leading teams as a coach is all about. It distinguishes the role of *coach* from the way many managers commonly function, as a hands-off and distant observer or as a totally hands-on, dominating boss.

Coach versus doer

Managers in all types of organizations commonly function as *doers* rather than coaches. They put greater emphasis on doing work themselves and much less emphasis on developing and motivating staff members to do the job on their own initiative. With teams, managing as a doer can be problematic. The following story is a common one in many workplaces.

Joe M. was assigned to manage a cross-functional project team with a critical mission at a packaging industry plant in the Southeast. Initially, he met with the seven members of the team to scope the project and make individual assignments. Everyone nodded with understanding when Joe explained that the team's mission was crucial to landing a sizable, long-term contract. They took reams of notes as Joe spoke, and he felt pretty good as the meeting broke up. "They're ready to go," he thought. The project had a deadline of four months.

As the weeks rolled past, Joe was busy with his part of the project. He occasionally checked to see how individual team members were doing. But the entire team didn't get together on any regular basis.

At the beginning of Month Four, Joe became aware, almost by accident, of a big disconnect between the project's marketing and logistics functions. He heard a couple of team members griping about the problem. "We better meet quick," Joe thought. He pulled the team together in an emergency session. Working many extra hours during the next few weeks (Joe especially) with *only two* deadline slippages, Joe's team got the project done — in just under *six* months. Upper management was unhappy with the delay but kept the new customer on the line and finally reeled in the big new account.

Joe breathed a sigh of relief when the project ended, but he wasn't happy about the whole experience. Leading this project team was a difficult job. He encountered problems with team members sometimes getting off track from what they needed to focus on, occasionally duplicating efforts, leaving tasks undone, and clashing over what the project objectives were.

Characteristic of his own operating style, Joe often stepped in, picking up work that team members dropped and solving problems team members encountered. Sure, the team pulled together to get the project done, but Joe thought the overall quality of work wasn't as good as it should have been.

Why doers (like Joe) feel frustrated

I'm sure you can guess the main reasons Joe's team didn't produce as well as he expected:

- ✔ **Lack of planning:** The team didn't operate with any kind of documented project plan. Each team member had his or her own understanding of what should happen. Objectives and assignments weren't fully clarified. The results were conflict, duplication of effort, and work left undone.

- ✔ **Lack of regular progress review:** Joe met sporadically with individual team members. He didn't pull the team together unless a big problem surfaced. He didn't have any status review sessions so that team members could discuss overall progress and unsolved issues, no matter how trivial.

- ✔ **Joe acted as a doer, not a coach:** Joe was team leader more by title than by action. He did little actual coaching of team members as a whole or as individuals. He was the classic doer, rescuing the team by picking up any (and all) slack and confronting and solving most of the problems himself.

What coaches of teams do that doers usually don't do

Managers who are doers (like Joe M., earlier) often get stuck in day-to-day operations and tied up in their own work. For such managers, time is a constant squeeze; every day becomes a series of interruptions. Managers working as doers may be the top individual producers for the team, the ones who pull it through — just the way they did on projects back in school. Trouble is, they rarely have the organization and discipline necessary for leading a team and coaching its members.

Managers working as *coaches* are doers, too. They have tasks of one kind or another as they help the team achieve its goals, but, unlike doers, managers as coaches do work that's appropriate to their role. They function at a higher level, by leveraging their people resources — multiplying the effect of their team members by doing the following:

- **Meeting regularly.** Coaches pull their teams together, meeting on some kind of regular basis. At their meetings, they set plans, review the status of work, and address and solve problems. In doing so, they ensure that the team stays focused and on track. Coaches also meet with individual team members, keeping in touch and working with them so they perform well within the team structure. In contrast, managers as doers infrequently meet (if at all) with the entire team and thereby tend to leave issues to chance.

- **Managing by plan.** Managers as coaches want to clarify roles and responsibilities and define objectives and assignments with their team members so they can develop schedules and set action items when they meet together. In simple terms, everything the team does is part of a *plan,* and the coach manages the team *by that plan.* Although it may be adjusted over time, the plan serves as a guide for the team to follow. Coaches also ensure that all-important matters are documented, from big-level work plans to sublevel action items. Nothing critical is left to memory. Doers, meanwhile, tend to be more reactive, dealing with tasks and issues as they arise. They do much less in the way of planning for themselves, let alone their teams.

- **Giving lots of feedback.** Coaches regularly provide performance feedback about overall group effort to their teams and about individual matters one-on-one to their team members. Coaches cite examples of specific team behavior when letting people know what they're doing well and what they need to do better. The team and each of its members know how well they're performing when they work for a manager who functions as a coach. Doers give much less direct performance feedback. If big problems arise, they may say something. But they're often too busy with their own activities to stop and directly acknowledge the performance of their team and its members.

- **Helping resolve problems and conflicts.** When problems arise affecting how work gets done, coaches work with their teams to address and resolve the issues. Problems are a normal part of any work operation. Coaches work to solve problems, not to evade dealing with them or to assign blame. Doers, like in the story of our friend Joe, are diligent workers who look like they have all the answers. But coaches know that they don't have to shoulder that enormous burden all by themselves because they can involve others — team members closest to problems — to help work out solutions. When personal conflicts arise on a team, coaches get team members to work out their differences. Coaches know that conflicts left unaddressed fester and can disrupt a team. By comparison, doer types often steer clear of personal matters, hoping they will work themselves out — management by osmosis!

✔ **Pushing accountability.** Managers as coaches push team members to take responsibility and produce at high levels. The main techniques coaches use are regularly reviewing progress, addressing issues as they arise, and giving constant feedback — all in the name of high standards of performance. Hands-off doer managers certainly want their team members to achieve top results but seldom take any action to ensure that outcome, leaving much to chance. That laid-back approach ends in frustration when team members fail to perform as needed.

✔ **Putting an emphasis on mentoring.** A big part of coaching involves mentoring — challenging your people to do better and supporting their development. Such efforts can range from discussions about their career interests and mapping career paths to posing tough questions that help staff figure out solutions on their own. Mentoring emphasizes working with team members so that they can handle responsibility in a self-sufficient way.

Managers who lead their teams as coaches try to use the time they spend with their people wisely. Because they don't have much time to give, they emphasize *quality time*. A manager as a coach knows she doesn't have time to waste, so she makes every bit of it count. Doers don't seem to grasp that idea. They may not shirk hard work, but they just waste a lot of time and energy running from one activity to another.

Coach versus boss

Some managers with a broad doer streak in their makeup do, nevertheless, assert leadership. They're willing to step in and take charge of their work groups and often play the role of *boss* in doing so. As the boss, they call all the shots.

Meet Ann, a boss-manager

Ann was a take-charge type manager in the marketing department of a pharmaceutical company in the Midwest. She determined what each person in her group needed to work on and how that work should be done. When anyone complained, Ann pushed hard and those workers usually fell in line. At the same time, because all workers were somewhat interdependent, Ann wanted to see her group develop into a team, and she thought the opportunity was coming soon.

Ann's boss hinted that the rollout of a new over-the-counter product might be assigned to her. To get the work done and out the door, all five staff had to work closer together than they seldom had before. Ann coveted the assignment, but she said nothing to her staff members, reasoning that doing so might distract them from their current assignments. She'd clue them in if and when the project was assigned.

Then one day, 15 minutes before Ann was due at her boss's weekly staff meeting, he called telling her the important project was a go and that she needed to get it rolling ASAP. Ann sprang into action, running to each staff member's office delivering the good news and making assignments. "Drop what you're doing and make this your top priority," she declared, offering no assurances to their bewilderment. "Look — don't worry about what you're doing now," Ann said. "You know how to do what I've told you here. And make sure you work well as a team on this one!"

Ann felt relieved as she rushed off to her boss's staff meeting. Her project was launched, and she'd meet with her team next week for progress review and Q&A. What Ann didn't know was that her staff met informally as a team even before the scheduled team meeting to complain about their confusion and Ann's dictatorial style.

Why Ann's team struggled

A manager as boss takes charge and runs the group as she sees fit. However, she often leaves her staff in a dependent role, waiting to be told what to do and what's going to happen. This hit-and-run, tell-them-what-to-do style lets the team know who's boss, but it also leaves them in confusion. Without planning and two-way communication, people aren't prepared to work as a team. In fact, Ann, the heroine of the story, is causing a team to form. But her people are coming together for the worst possible reason: They have a common enemy — the boss!

Many managers like Ann try to be good bosses. They assert themselves and have good control over their groups. But their take-charge, do-as-I-say approach, although quick, usually doesn't lead to the development of a group as a finely tuned, functioning team. Table 3-1 shows five functions and compares the way a coach of a team handles them with the way a boss of a work group responds.

Table 3-1	Comparison of a Team Coach and a Work Group Boss	
Function	*Coach of Team*	*Boss of Work Group*
Communication flow with staff	Group level and one-on-one Two-way interactions	More often one-on-one More one-way interactions
Decision making, planning, problem solving	Involves team in issues affecting the group Consults to seeks consensus	Makes most decisions, plans Solves most problems affecting the group

Function	Coach of Team	Boss of Work Group
Control and responsibility of group	Plays leadership role and pushes accountability so that team members share in what affects the team as a whole	Nearly total control and responsibility for the group; the authority figure
Outcomes focused on	Performance results and development of team	Business, work getting done
Extent of guidance	Frequent. Teaches, supports, clarifies direction, gets resources, gives feedback, encourages, challenges	Rare. Guides more by telling people what to do

Teams need leadership to develop and perform, but managers who are absorbed in the work and control it with a heavy hand aren't providing the leadership that teams need. Their efforts lessen teamwork and heighten dependency — the opposites of what you want to achieve in managing a team.

Leading by Example

As a manager, you're in the spotlight — *all* the time. You're the most-watched person in the group and your behavior influences everyone else. I offer no guarantees, but when you set the right example you greatly increase the likelihood that you'll get the performance that you want from your team members. Set the wrong example and — do I need to explain the down side?

This section explores some key behaviors that you need to demonstrate to build credibility and respect for your leadership among team members.

Making your actions speak louder than your words

What you *do,* more than what you *say,* plays a big part in establishing your credibility as a team leader. Take the little test in Figure 3-1 to find out what your *actions* say about you. For each of the 10 leadership qualities, give yourself a frequency score.

Scoring Yourself on the Action Scale

Give yourself a frequency score on each of the 10 questions.

Frequency scale: 4 = quite often; 3 = some of the time; 2 = occasionally; 1 = seldom

_____ 1. I show up at meetings on time, my own and those called by others.

_____ 2. I do quality work in my technical area and meet deadlines with it.

_____ 3. I see plans and projects through from start to completion.

_____ 4. I stay calm under challenging and stressful situations.

_____ 5. I deal with problems in a responsive and solutions-oriented fashion.

_____ 6. I follow through and do what I said I would do.

_____ 7. I listen to and seek to understand viewpoints different from my own.

_____ 8. I openly communicate and keep others informed.

_____ 9. I take initiative to get work done or to tackle problems.

_____10. I function collaboratively with others in working through issues.

Figure 3-1:
Measuring
your
leadership
qualities.

Add up your score and see where you stand:

- ✔ If you score 33 and above, you lead by positive example.

- ✔ If you score 26 to 32, you show flashes of setting a positive leadership example but need to be more consistent.

- ✔ If you score below 26, you have a lot of work to do to become an effective team leader who functions as a coach.

All the behaviors listed on the leadership inventory are exactly what you'd expect from your team members:

- ✔ Producing good work

- ✔ Listening and communicating constructively

- ✔ Helping to solve problems

- ✔ Meeting commitments

As a manager, you can assert leadership influence through the authority of your position — known as positional influence — or through the character you show as demonstrated by your behaviors — known as personal influence. Employees, especially team members, tend to follow and want to work with managers they respect and care about most — those with a positive personal influence.

Your personal influence as a team leader and coach begins growing as you begin behaving the way you expect your team members to behave. The more consistently you demonstrate those behaviors, build relationships with each person on the team, and treat others with respect, the more your influence continues to grow. Add one more ingredient — a feeling of *involvement* on everyone's part — and you've formed a group of people who want to be part of the program with you. In short, you're leading as a coach.

Avoiding the credibility busters

You don't need to be perfect to function as an effective team manager. But you do need to avoid certain kinds of behavior that can damage your credibility — and disillusion your followers. Making apologies for your bad behavior won't make it go away, so here's my check-off list of credibility busters:

- ✔ **Starting, stopping, changing.** Team members need to see you stay the course and stick with the plan from beginning to end. Sure, good reasons exist for making mid-plan corrections. But if you change directions again and again because you haven't thought things through in advance — *with* the team, you leave the team confused and doubtful that any progress is going to be made under your leadership.

- ✔ **Shooting the messenger.** Managers often say to team members, "Tell me if you're having any problems — I want to know right away." And when a team member reports bad news, some managers explode in anger. That's called *shooting the messenger*. If your people don't feel safe bringing issues to you when they first arise, you may hear about them much later, when the molehills have turned into mountains.

- ✔ **Staying out of sight.** When managers of teams seldom are visible to team members, their leadership tends to have little positive effect. "Out of sight" definitely becomes "Out of mind" for most team members. They don't see you, so they don't know you; and as a result, you don't command much respect. You can give all the reasons you want for why you're wrapped up in other important matters, but excuses neither make up for your lack of visibility nor provide motivational leadership for the team.

✔ **Talking often, listening seldom.** One of the big credibility busters that I hear employees remark about is having a manager who talks too much but doesn't listen. When team members come to you discussing issues or sharing other news yet having to fight hard to get a word in, you prove that you're not a resource for them. Managers as coaches invite two-way conversations, and they can listen to understand.

✔ **Dominating more than facilitating.** Breaking this old habit is one of the biggest challenges many bosses face as they seek to become coaches and team leaders. The team needs you less to take charge and more to guide its discussions in planning and problem-solving — and in getting everyone involved. That's the essence of good facilitation, which I talk more about in Chapter 12.

✔ **Avoiding, avoiding, avoiding.** Problems are inevitable in every work situation. Some problems need direct involvement by the manager, especially when they involve sensitive issues like operations or person-nel that require negotiation with management upward and outward from the team. When the manager is one who never met problem he couldn't avoid, you have a team swamped in chaos and frustration.

✔ **Making commitments, failing to meet them.** Lack of follow-through is another deadly disease that kills manager credibility. This behavior is akin to a politician making promises on the campaign trail and forgetting them once elected. Politicians who don't follow through often get voted out at the next election. Team managers who make false promises lose their following even faster.

Looking Ahead While You Keep the Team Focused on the Here and Now

Leading teams as a coach goes beyond leading by example. It also requires communicating about the long term at the same time that you review progress on the current agenda — in other words, staying involved with the team on the day-to-day work while providing a sense of direction toward the future. This section explores the key behaviors you want to demonstrate in that dual role.

Looking forward to be forward looking

An important ingredient teams need from their leaders is a sense of direction. A sense of direction answers questions like: Where are we going? Why are we going there? And what are we going to accomplish in the end? To avoid becoming aimless, your team needs answers. This is what you can do to help give the team a clear sense of direction:

Stan's slippery slope

Stan inherited a team of four whose overall ability to deliver quality performance and work together effectively was less than he desired. He sometimes thought they were just plain dysfunctional. After a few months on the job, Stan persuaded management to let him bring in an outside consultant to coach him in developing his group as a more effective team.

The consultant conducted an assessment with Stan and the team members to identify the issues. He did a little work afterward with the team as a whole to help them run efficient team meetings. The consultant's primary role was to coach Stan to apply strategies for coaching and developing his staff to address the issues and become a highly productive team.

But Stan's management style was rather hands-off. As the consultant continued meeting with Stan, what Stan had to report regarding following through on his coaching efforts grew less and less. At the same time, the team members reported in follow-up assessments that Stan was less and less visible and didn't deliver on his commitments.

One positive result: Stan's four team members started pulling together rather than bickering. Now they complained in unison about Stan's lack of leadership. A team had formed over a common enemy! When management evaluated Stan's performance a short time later, the decision to say goodbye to Stan was easy. His credibility with the team had vanished during the course of six months.

After Stan left, the team was assigned to another manager. Within a month, she had implemented the coaching tips from the consultant and the team was moving forward positively in performance and teamwork.

✔ **Communicate a vision.** A vision is a picture of the future. It shows your team how it will function when it is thriving sometime in the future, and it serves as the guiding light for getting there. Good leaders provide a vision. Even if you lead a team with a fairly short time frame for its work, you want to communicate the overall good results that you expect to see in the end. A vision galvanizes people to move in a direction together, and that's what you want if you're seeking a high-performing team.

✔ **Talk up your vision and share other vital future information.** Communicating your vision is only the beginning of helping your team see the big picture. Make your vision a recurring theme. Bring it up in conversations with team members. Relate it to what's happening to team members in their work, to decisions the team is making, and to the evaluation of team progress. When you talk about the vision, formally and informally, to the whole group or individual members, it comes alive and, over time, grows stronger as the guiding light. And don't forget to share news about the organization's plans and progress. Let the team know where the business is going and how the team fits into the big picture. (You may need to take the initiative on this one, finding out from management above you. Again, no passive coaches need apply for team leadership roles!)

✔ **Set goals.** Working with the team, determine the important results the team needs to accomplish so its vision comes to fruition. Coaches focus people on producing results; doers tend to be task oriented — let's just get the work done. Without goals for results, people are busy but not necessarily productive.

✔ **Develop action plans.** Coaches manage by planning. Managers who function as coaches work with their teams to set plans that define how goals are to be achieved. The plans serve as the road maps, showing team members the key steps to be taken and the roles and assignments along the way. Plans may change as needs change, and that's okay. Plans minimize seat-of-the-pants operations and reduce team frustration.

Challenging and encouraging excellence

Managing as a coach means challenging and encouraging your team members to achieve high quality performance in their day-to-day work. Here are key things that you can do to encourage excellence:

✔ **Review progress regularly.** Coaches let their teams know how they're doing, individually and as a team. That way, everyone knows where he or she and they stand. (Progress reviews are covered in Chapter 7.)

✔ **Provide constructive feedback.** Constructive feedback means telling someone what you notice about that person's job performance. It acknowledges what was done well — called positive feedback — and what was done less well, where improvement is needed — called negative feedback. Although it can be written, professional-quality feedback is offered informally, often one-on-one in a conversation, and it meets these guidelines:

- The instance of performance that is being discussed is stated up front.

- For clarity, performance is described in specific terms, not generalities.

- Feedback is delivered directly and sincerely.

- Feedback states observations, not interpretations. You report what you've seen and not what you think about it.

When you're coaching and giving constructive feedback to acknowledge performance, look at this conversation as a two-step process. First, provide the observations-based feedback following the key guidelines of the tool. Second, if you're pointing out a problem, then have a discussion with the individual about how to correct it.

✔ **Support professional development.** A major part of encouraging excellence in performance is creating opportunities for team members to improve their job skills. Whether done through training classes, cross-training, new assignments, or all those ways, the method matters less than your support of continuous training as normal practice. In fact, sometimes you may even be the teacher, passing on your knowledge and experience in work areas and thus helping team members to improve their skills.

✔ **Address problems constructively and in a timely manner.** Achieving excellence means dealing with problems that can hinder top performance. It does not mean humiliating people who make mistakes or are performing at less than desired levels, nor does it mean sticking your head in the sand just to avoid hurting anyone's feelings. Managers who function as coaches handle performance issues by coaching to improve. They map out goals and plans with the team member, targeting improvement in performance, with a follow-up review of progress. Problems in getting the work done that affect the whole team are discussed with the whole team. Leading as a coach in these situations usually means acting as a facilitator who guides the team through problem-solving. It often means teaching the team to facilitate its own problem-resolution efforts without you being there — that's good coaching!

✔ **Recognize successes.** Taking people for granted is a *Demotivator with a capital D.* Good coaching, on the other hand, recognizes success and uses it to motivate more good outcomes in the future. How you recognize success, whether informally with positive feedback to individual team members or in a celebration for the entire group, is less important than making certain that you, in fact, *do* recognize success in some sincere fashion. Chapter 15 gives you specific ways.

Making Things Happen as a Catalyst and Advocate

Coaching the team as a catalyst or an advocate often is the most challenging behavior for a manager. As catalyst, you must make things happen *with* the team, not *for* the team, and, as an advocate, you must manage upward and outward, supporting your team elsewhere in the organization, as needed. Working as catalyst and advocate challenges you to be assertive, positive, action-oriented, persistent as needed, direct, and sincere. But you must guard against being passive — just sitting back or aggressive — coming on too strong and harsh.

Lights, camera, action

When you're a *catalyst,* you organize and cause action. Managers play an important role as catalysts, spurring action on big issues and thereby helping the team to move forward. In the following sections, I discuss a few critical action-oriented behaviors and skills for leading teams in the catalyst mode.

Facilitating the resolution of issues

To facilitate simply means to make easier. Sometimes managers need to intervene, making it easier to make a decision, address a problem, or resolve a conflict or other issues. Facilitating in these situations means bringing parties together, generating full participation in a discussion of the issue, and working toward closure and agreement on what needs to be done next. Your role as manager is to help this process work, but not to dictate it. (Chapter 12 provides you with tools to develop your facilitation skills.)

Your role as catalyst comes into play when the team needs training, especially in the skills that individuals need to work together as team members. Sometimes you can be the hands-on organizer of training; other times you may want to involve team members to assist you. However you manage the training program, you want to ensure that the training gets scheduled and is delivered. The same goes for your team's big performance events or change efforts. These are the kinds of things you want to be closely involved with, assisting team members so that everything happens according to plan — and following up to make sure that it does!

Feel free to join in the training sessions and participate with everyone else. Doing so helps you reinforce the training back on the job and shows you value the training — good leadership by example.

Bringing discussions to closure

People sometimes talk issues to death. The coach's job is to focus people on bringing discussions to closure and defining actions to be taken, which can be done by asking questions like:

- Specifically, what are you going to do to deal with that matter?
- What are your action items here?
- What are your ideas about solving that problem?
- When will you carry out that plan?

Keep the questions you-oriented so that responsibility rests with the team or team member. As you see in the examples, the questions are simple and don't lead a person to answer in any certain way. Give people space to think for themselves. Use what's called *open-ended* questions, like the first three examples, when you want to generate ideas or thoughts. *Close-ended* questions are those that can be responded to with a short definitive response, like *Yes* or *No* or a specific date, for example. Coaching managers use them when they want to get a commitment of action or agreement, like in the fourth example.

Serving as an advocate

An advocate is someone who defends or pleads a cause for someone else. Advocating is what your team needs from you, their leader, to help them perform successfully. Here are some of the ways you can be an advocate:

- ✔ **Get resources the team needs.** To perform well, your team may need materials, tools, time, staff, training, or all the above. Those resources are often beyond the team's reach — someone needs to go get them or budget for them. That's where you come in as manager. Don't wait until your team reaches a point of pain before you go after the resources they need. But use your head when dealing with the company bureaucracy, especially when you ask for more staff. Wait until the need is truly strong and you can make a solid case to win approval.

- ✔ **Broadcast team successes.** This isn't about tooting your horn so you look good. It's about making sure your team's successes don't remain secrets. When your group makes gains and delivers good results, let management know. People like to hear good news, so write up your team in a report and talk about them to other groups when you can. If battling for resources is the way it works in your organization, your record of success helps you win favor, especially from management above you. People support winners. And don't forget the other guys. Remember to support other teams when they need something from you or your team.

- ✔ **Make connections for your team.** A big part of your role is to know who does what around the organization so you can build working relationships that help get work done efficiently. Sometimes this means serving as the connection for team members who need support from other people.

  So make that phone call, do that introduction, write that notice of explanation, or join that sensitive meeting — whatever it takes to help your team members going forward and taking responsibility. Promoting self-sufficiency is a major aim of leading teams as a coach.

- ✔ **Help remove obstacles or barriers.** Because your team operates within a larger organization, it sometimes runs into organizational obstacles like policies or practices or an obstinate rule enforcer or two in the management bureaucracy. When these obstacles begin to rear their ugly heads, your team needs you as its leader to negotiate upward and outward to minimize, if not remove, these interferences or to navigate around them. But pick and choose your battles and methods carefully, and if you need to challenge someone else in management, do it privately not publicly. Remember, when you make success happen, people tend to listen to you. Your job as occasional barrier buster is a kind of advocacy your team really needs.

Drive performance, not happiness

Sometimes managers have what I call a misguided focus in leading their teams. They think that throwing a few team-building activities so that everyone can be happy and have a good time ought to do the trick. Right?

Gaining good results is not about how well your team members play with each other but how well they work with each other. Gaining results is not about how happy you make your team members feel. Happiness is an emotional state, and some people are happy only when they're miserable. My point is: You don't need to be a *cheerleader* to be a team leader or manager.

As the coach, your job is driving your team to *perform*. Being a mentor, an active listener, a planner and communicator of the future, an advocate, a catalyst, and at times a taskmaster demanding excellence are part of the key behaviors of the coach. These behaviors emphasize getting good results, which is what you're paying the team members to do. Coaching also emphasizes the development of the team and its individual members. When teams achieve success and team members grow in the process, one of the best byproducts you see is increased personal job satisfaction and morale. So, keep the focus on performance; that's the best way for everyone to win.

Chapter 4

Leading Teams through Change

Change: It's the one constant in today's business world. Many factors propel the constant change occurring in organizations — customer demands, the push for higher productivity, fluctuations in the economy, investor pressures, technological innovations, and expanding competition, to name a few.

Sometimes all it takes to push the change lever into high gear is new management at the top. Soon you're saying, "Hello, restructuring!" "Hello, downsizing!" "Hello, acquisitions!" And while you're at it, here's a new philosophy to incorporate into operations. (Oh no, it's another management flavor-of-the-month!)

As a result, trying to manage a group of people in today's ever-changing climate is quite a challenge — even more so when you're trying to develop a high-performing team. Just moving into the team mode is a major element of change. As I point out in Chapter 2, not everyone instantly embraces the idea, especially if it's different from previous work situations. Some people enjoy working on their own and being responsible for their own duties, but teams require coordinated group efforts and often the sharing of duties.

Managing teams is a lesson in change management.

This chapter prepares you as team leader to handle challenging situations of change that lie ahead, based on your role as coach, which I cover in Chapter 3. I provide you with strategies to follow as you manage the transition into teams and move forward. Strategies are far more effective than the *magic wand approach* where you just wave the wand and hope for the best. (I cover the nonsense of that idea in Chapter 2.)

This chapter also contains tips for dealing with challenges along the way — bumps in the road — especially the challenge of disruptive behavior and other forms of nonperformance by team members. So fasten your seat belt.

Instant Coffee, Instant Team? Managing the Transition

Add hot water and instantly you have a team! Not quite. Developing a team takes brewing time. It doesn't happen as quickly and easily as instant coffee. The hard work isn't merely forming into a team, it's moving forward and performing like a team. The amount of time it takes to reach good levels of performance varies, and you have no guarantees that you'll move forward at all. However, the one factor that can make a huge difference is your leadership.

This section shows you how to make a positive difference when taking on the role of managing a team. You get a plan of attack plus warnings about pitfalls to avoid, and you gain insight into how leadership by your example is crucial.

Looking out for the speed bumps

Teams go through a period of maturation as they form and develop. Some people like to quote psychologist B. W. Tuckman, who says a team goes through four stages of development, "forming, storming, norming, and performing." I've seen others call the stages testing, infighting, getting organized, and bonding. Whatever you call them, the ideas behind stages are

- ✔ When a team begins, its members go through a feeling-out process with one another.
- ✔ What follows is a stressful period of conflict as members get used to working with one another and adapt to the various styles people bring to the jobs.
- ✔ Then comes a period of acceptance and getting focused.
- ✔ At last, the team comes together and goes into high gear as a productive, supportive unit.

The reality of team development may not exactly follow these four stages, but the concept of stages is worth keeping in mind. Teams don't instantly come together and perform at high levels. They're likely to encounter some ups and downs before (and if) the ups finally outweigh the downs.

When managers don't lead their teams as coaches, they're likely to contribute more toward the downside than the upside. In the following sections, I discuss a few of the things managers do in early stages that hinder the development and maturation of teams. This is your list of pitfalls to avoid.

Letting confusion reign

Early on, team members often wonder, "What's my role? What's this team here to do? How do I fit in with the rest of the members? Where are we going with our work?" Managers commonly answer such questions with the tried-and-true method for heightening employee anxiety: "We'll cross that bridge when we come to it, so don't worry, be happy!"

When managers do little work to define their team's purpose, its goals, its future direction, and the roles and assignments of its members, anxiety usually increases while team-member performance usually declines. This continuing confusion often breeds chaos and conflict among team members — not exactly the track to follow to gain high performance.

Instilling no discipline on the team

Sometimes managers take the stance that work has to be done, so everyone should get to work and get it done! They ignore practices that build the discipline to guide team performance. For example, team meetings occur irregularly and usually are unproductive, work plans aren't defined (if plans are set at all), and progress review is overlooked. Problem-solving as a regular practice often is replaced by lingering problems or a lot of finger-pointing. Managers wish for everything to turn out well, but they often find that wishing isn't enough to help.

Becoming absorbed in their own work

Some managers seem to be controlled by their *doer* sides. If that's where you are, your own to-do list takes precedence over what you need to do to lead your team. The pressure of getting your own work done clouds the vision that your most important role is guiding your team to good performance.

When you take on more than you reasonably can handle, you find yourself in a reactive mode. Every problem becomes a crisis, and your team members sound like they whine over every little thing that goes wrong. For managers, stress builds when delegation fails and, as a result, team development becomes a bumpy ride with no clear destination in sight.

Sitting back and complaining about the change into teams

Managers sit back and complain about changing into a team's environment more often when they haven't directly created the teams they're assigned to lead — a kind of juvenile response, I think. When a need for teams exists and a manager is asked to lead the effort, well, that's all part of the job of being a manager.

You may feel much of the same stress and confusion that your team members feel during the transition period into teams, but that's no excuse for adding to the distress with your own bad behavior. When you complain about management above you or grumble over confusion with your own role and when you do little to get the resources your team needs and let everyone know that moving to teams is not a good idea, you demotivate team-member performance and destroy your credibility as a leader.

Getting your team focused early on

You know what *not* to do in the early stages of team development. Okay, what, then, *do* you do? The answer: As coach you get the team involved in shaping its foundation, direction, and continuing education. In the following sections, I share some strategies that greatly help. (Many of the how-tos for executing these strategies are described in Chapter 5.)

Setting the team's purpose

The team's purpose answers why the team exists and what its overall role is supposed to be. Sorting this out and developing a purpose statement with team members in the beginning days of the team's formation is critical for getting everyone on the team moving in the same direction. Setting the purpose reduces the so-called *hidden-agendas problem* that can plague teams — everyone with his or her own, usually unspoken, opinion of what the team's purpose is.

Before working with your team on its purpose, you may first need to manage upward, finding out from your team sponsor or management above you what they have in mind as your team's role. This intelligence is valuable input for your team members to have as they define the team's purpose statement.

Developing team guidelines

Team guidelines are expectations. They answer the question: What do we expect from one another as a part of this team? The guidelines are a handful of key behaviors (developed by team members with the coach as facilitator) that clarify performance expectations inside and outside of team meetings.

When team members define their own guidelines, they, of course, buy in to the expectations.

Planning the work

As you work with your team, set goals, define the milestones along the way, and decide who's doing what. That way, instead of diving into the work in any old sort of haphazard fashion (a common work method, I'm sorry to say) your team members have clarity about what they are to do. Goodbye, confusion!

Creating work plans as a team also helps identify what resources and training team members have. At the same time, you communicate your vision of where you see the team going and what you expect it to accomplish, providing a strong sense of direction to the team members. Thus you're building an organized and focused team — by George, you're "norming" already (to quote one of psychologist B.W. Tuckman's stages from earlier in this chapter).

Getting the resources and the training they need

Getting your team what it needs is where much of your hands-on work comes into play. You are the team's *gofer* when it comes to equipment, tools, and anything else that your people need to work effectively. And when team members see you playing this active role, they find focusing on work much easier.

At the same time, lining up the essential training resources is essential. What cross-training do people need? Figure out a schedule and implement it. What team skills do *you* want to discover with your team? Start early and continue over time. Because you want to establish regular team meetings from the beginning, finding out how to run a productive meeting is a good training class to start with.

Give your team members the tools they need to function as a team and virtually nothing can stop them.

Smile and "absorb"

Team members need to see you showing a positive demeanor day-in and day-out. They need to see that you believe in teams and want to make them work, and that you're focused on leading *this* team. At the same time, they need to see that you're patient, calm under stress, and can listen openly to their concerns. Listening, truly active listening, as I touch upon in Chapter 8, enables people to be heard and, when they have concerns, provides them with a safe way to get those concerns off their chests. You then can refocus them and send them back to work in a better frame of mind, instead of hearing them vent their concerns openly among other team members.

Listening like this is part of the "absorbing" function that managers need to perform in the early stages of a team's formation. It's normal for team members to have concerns, and sometimes the best medicine for them is having someone with whom they can safely discuss them. Channeling their concerns and helping them act on matters that truly need attention is your role. But as manager, you stay in control, taking care not to vent your own concerns or frustrations. If you do anything with your own concerns and worries, take them upward.

Tom Hanks on leadership

Every now and then the movies provide a good lesson in leadership. The acclaimed movie *Saving Private Ryan* offers an example of the "absorbing" function of leadership. As you probably recall, the story concerns a World War II army unit of eight soldiers whose mission is to do anything it can — even venturing behind enemy lines if necessary — to find and safely return a certain Private Ryan, the only survivor among five brothers engaged in the war, to his home and his family.

Soon after the mission begins, the soldiers complain openly about their disdain for the assignment — because it's like trying to find "a needle in a stack of needles." One soldier asks the unit's leader, played by the actor Tom Hanks, "Captain, how come you're not complaining about this job?"

The captain responds, "I don't gripe to you because I'm a captain. Griping goes one way, up, only up, never down. You gripe to me, I gripe to my superior officers. Up, get it?"

Persist and follow through

Stick-to-itiveness is a managerial behavior that definitely sets a good example in the early stages of a team's development. When team members see you persist and keep moving forward despite the bumps and bruises along the way, they're more likely to join you by pitching in. If you're not abandoning ship or barfing overboard when rough waters hit, they too recognize that a team's development is hard work and not always smooth sailing.

In addition, when you do what you say you will do, when you meet your commitments, and when you deliver on time with your assignments, no one can argue with your word, your actions, or your performance. Follow-through is a major credibility builder and a behavior that helps you to set the tone of excellence that you want to see in your team's performance.

Reinforcing early and often

Good old-fashioned positive reinforcement starts a team in the right direction and maintains a good course. That means you need to recognize when the team and its members produce good results in their work and show good examples of cooperation and assistance that enhance teamwork. Don't take progress for granted! Give positive feedback when you see good actions and outcomes.

In coaching teams you want to work on two levels — group and individual. Acknowledge good behavior and performance that individuals do individually. Acknowledge good behavior and performance that the team does collectively. Celebrate team successes together.

Being open and action-oriented

Another lead-by-example difference is behavior that shows you're willing to listen to team members' input and ideas and, in fact, getting the entire team involved in planning and acting on those plans. As a result, plans are set, decisions are made, and problems are addressed. The team sees you consulting them, sometimes seeking their consensus, and then moving discussions forward into plans of action. As a catalyst for making things happen, you set the tone, projecting to team members that taking responsibility and acting upon it are to be expected.

Mentoring with messages

On the mentoring side of coaching, an important action you must take with staff members is providing them with messages that guide their thinking and understanding. Messages are best when they're positive and relatively brief. They're the nuggets of wisdom or points of importance from your experience that show people the bigger picture, from development of the team to their personal development.

Communicating these messages is meant to be an informal process, sometimes one-on-one and sometimes in group settings. Explaining your overall vision to people and informing them that the ride is likely to be bumpy — and that you're not expecting perfection — reinforces the goals and guidelines the team has set and helps everyone maintain focus. All that remains is for you to lead the way, practicing what you preach.

Plugging in the channels of communication

Managing change, especially the work that needs to be accomplished in teams, means that you must provide more communication (formally and informally) than typically occurs with the status quo in a regular work group. And this enhanced communication works best when it's live and in person.

Group level communications

Teams need to meet to function, so you must establish the practice of meeting from the team's inception and maintain it as you move forward. Depending on what team members need, you may have to meet once a week or even once a day initially. Having purposeful meetings is key, and I talk about that in detail in Chapter 12.

Teams have many good reasons to meet. Making decisions, setting plans, and conducting progress reviews are a few. More important, teams need to meet so they can address and resolve problems that inevitably pop up along the way. In the early stages of team development, the issues sometimes concern tuning in to individuals' needs while meshing them together with the team's needs.

Sharing news and information is helpful at meetings, but teams must do so much more than that. You may find that sending out e-mail updates on what's happening is more useful than pulling people into a meeting solely for an update. When team meetings go beyond passing along information, becoming forums for addressing issues and getting work done, communication is enhanced and, most important, productivity goes up.

Individual level communications

Meetings are the formal means of promoting communication within the team. At the same time, you want to supplement this effort with more informal means so that you stay connected at the individual team-member level. Walking around periodically in the work area for brief chats with team members, having lunch out with individuals, and holding ad hoc, one-on-one discussions away from the work area are useful ways of getting you plugged in to what's happening with your team members.

These informal means of communication give you a chance to spot problems early, channel people to deal with concerns constructively, and discover issues the team can address at its meetings. Of course, you often have to listen more than you talk during these informal check ins and visits, but, more important, these strategies make you visible and approachable — two key ingredients for effective team leadership.

Hanging on When Business Changes Set Teams Spinning

It's enough to make you dizzy — managing all the major business changes that can come your way, that is. Sometimes you feel like they're pouring down on you, enough to knock your team back into chaos and conflict. But, of course, you're expected to easily incorporate them and make everything run smoothly — the magic wand approach to change management. This section arms you with strategies — precise steps — for becoming an effective *change manager* for your team, beginning by explaining to your team why change is occurring, where it's likely to take you, and how you'll get there.

When e-mail doesn't connect

E-mail is useful for passing on messages and information. It's handy for making simple announcements that require no explanation or providing news and updates on what's happening in an organization.

However, where e-mail runs into trouble is when it's used for discussing issues or problems or when it becomes the primary means of keeping in touch with people. Lacking the richness and complexity present in live, personal communications at team meetings and in one-on-one discussions, an e-mail message can easily be interpreted the wrong way by the receiver. E-mail doesn't replace a live two-way conversation.

For more about the uses, misuses, and abuses of e-mail, check out Chapter 13 in my book *Communicating Effectively For Dummies* (Wiley Publishing).

Step 1: Explaining the need for a change

Managing change effectively with your team begins with their understanding the need for change and the thinking that's driving the change process. The list below explains what you need to cover when you talk with your team. Again, if you're not sure of the answers, ask management above you.

- ✔ Why we're changing
- ✔ What's driving the change — competitive realities, market factors, the economy, or other reasons
- ✔ Why change is urgent

Even when employees don't agree with a particular change that management has requested, if they understand the thinking behind it, accepting the change becomes much easier. But when people can't explain (to themselves, to their significant others) why a big change is rolling down the pike, they often resist helping to make it work.

So as you communicate the need for the change remember to:

- ✔ **Put the best light on the topic.** If you have any personal reservations about the change, set them aside and just stick to the facts. Be *positively* honest, not negatively honest.

- ✔ **Come across as clear and confident.** If you sound unsure, you'll only stoke everyone's anxiety.

- ✔ **Be sincere and straightforward.**

- ✔ **Convey a sense of importance about the reasons for the change.**

Step 2: Communicating a picture of the future

After your team members understand the reasons for the change initiative, they need to view a picture of the future so that they have a sense of direction and an understanding of what will be accomplished by the change. They want to know about:

- ✔ The opportunities or gains that lie ahead
- ✔ The outcomes desired
- ✔ What the change will mean for the organization and its business
- ✔ What the change will mean for the team
- ✔ How the team can help make the change work for the organization

Address these issues clearly and positively. When you show team members the big picture and the forecast, you prepare them to make change happen.

Step 3: Developing the transition plan

Work with your team to figure out how you're going to move from where you are today to where you need to be tomorrow when the change initiative is in full force and running successfully. Your transition plan needs to extend ahead at least three months. Six to nine months is even better so that you have a strong focus on the future environment under the change. Some key elements to address in the transition plan are

- ✔ Performance goals the team needs to reach
- ✔ Key steps or milestones along the way
- ✔ Roles and responsibilities of every team member
- ✔ Processes, systems, or other work practices that may need to be created or modified
- ✔ Resources the team needs need to support the work
- ✔ Training the team needs and when it is needed
- ✔ Other issues that must be addressed to help the team manage the transition

Step 4: Implementing the transition plan

In this step you take action, executing the plan. A good transition plan addresses key elements identified in Step 3 and maps out a schedule for completing them. From this point on, you manage by your team's plan, which keeps everyone focused on what everyone needs to accomplish to make major change work within the team.

Transitional or interim work practices sometimes are set up to manage early stages of a change initiative. This may mean establishing a small unit within the team that oversees certain temporary functions or responsibilities, a trial run for a new practice or method, or temporary policies to guide the initial implementation.

A few other steps that you can take to get the transition plan off to a good start are

✔ Clarifying the goals and keeping your people focused on them.

✔ Obtaining the resources that your team needs as fast as possible.

✔ Initiating training.

✔ Celebrating endings.

Celebrating endings means saying goodbye to the past as you move in new directions. Sometimes major changes in organizations require a team to end certain practices — practices that people may have liked and found effective. When that happens, having some kind of celebration to recognize the good of the past helps people gain a sense of closure and develop a frame of mind for tackling the future. No harm in having fun every now and then at work!

Keeping your team flexible and focused: Building the rubber band team

The first four steps for leading your team through significant organizational or business changes prepare them to understand why the change is happening, where to go with it, how to get there, and how to implement it. Step 5, on the other hand, provides you with strategies for dealing with some of the challenges that can derail a team as it tries to make change efforts work. I call this "building the rubber band team."

A good rubber band is loose and elastic yet can withstand stress. It bends but does not break. That's what you want your team to be like as it moves forward, dealing with a major change initiative and the nuances of smaller changes that may also come into play.

This last step in this five-step approach for effective change management is really difficult work once implementation of the change has begun. Yet it's the key to maintaining your team's flexible and readiness to deal with whatever challenges may arise.

Step 5: Monitoring progress and adjusting plans

People work so hard initiating an important change that they sometimes forget to monitor progress and adjust plans as needed. The idea in this most important last step of the change management process is having your team live by its plans.

Conduct regular status review

Meet with the team regularly, such as once a week to once every two weeks, and have each member report progress on his or her assignments. A good status review meeting (which I describe in more detail in Chapter 7) helps team members with planning and staying on track. On the planning side, team members define what they're going to get done — with your assistance as needed — over the next week or two. As for staying on track, they must be prepared at the next meeting to report progress on what they said they'd do. That's how you promote accountability and keep team members focused on delivering results as they work through a change.

Maintain face-to-face communication

Whenever a major change comes along, a top priority for managers is maintaining frequent communication with their people. Regular working meetings are important, of course. In addition, continuing your informal one-on-one interactions is important.

When you're in the office, touch base with your people a few minutes each day to see how they're doing. This communication strategy, called *MBWA — management by walking around,* is helpful. MBWA simply means connecting with your team members individually through a few minutes of small talk, usually on nonwork-related topics for starters. Upon that base, you build rapport and become more approachable to your staff.

Periodically, maybe once every couple of months, you can do a *pulse check* with your team members. By that, I mean assessing their progress and finding out what concerns they have as they work through a change. A pulse check is best conducted in a one-on-one conversation in which you ask open-ended questions — questions that get your team members talking about what's working well and what isn't working so well for them.

Recognize good performance

As team members work through a change and make progress, keep the positive feedback flowing to deserving individuals and to the team collectively for its overall good work. Encourage team members to pass along the positive feedback, especially when people assist and support one another.

In addition, periodically discuss with the team where it stands today compared with where it was when the change initiative began. Sometimes the best way to recognize performance is stopping to reflect on how far you've all come together. People often are so consumed by hard work in their jobs that they lose sight of the progress they've made. And when the team scores a success, don't forget to celebrate!

Positive reinforcement is one of your most important tools for building high levels of performance in teams.

Keep on training and tracking what you're discovering

People can embrace change when they have the tools and skills that they need to do the work. From cross-training to training on team skills or other technical skills, encourage those learning experiences, include them as part of the job, and adjust the schedule or curriculum as needed. In addition, as part of status review, occasionally ask team members to report what they've done to apply their training on the job. Doing so reinforces the importance of training and promotes accountability as well. If you're spending time and money on team-member development, especially to implement a major change, measuring the return on your investment always is a good idea.

Evaluate progress and update the plan at least quarterly

When rapid change hits your team, stop at least quarterly to evaluate overall progress by asking

- ✔ How far have we come?
- ✔ Where are we falling short?
- ✔ What issues are affecting us?

Use these questions to conduct the assessment. Then, with the team:

- ✔ Update the transition plan. Incorporate new facets that may have come up regarding the change initiative.
- ✔ Note any issues that need to be worked out as you move forward.

Such efforts amplify the transition plan as the team's living document, its guiding light where work is concerned and a key to the ongoing management of changes effected through and by the team.

Dave, the prototype manager as coach

I once worked during a three-year period with a client who made a major transformation into a team structure and later had to cope with major business change. Dave, the manager who emerged as the prototype manager/coach, did much to build and keep his teams flexible and focused in their changing world.

In the early going, Dave implemented training in team skills and cross-training on job skills as normal practices. He communicated frequently with his teams in group and individual settings. His teams had their own regular meetings where they found out how to set plans, review progress, and reset plans as necessary.

Because of all these efforts, Dave's teams of nearly 50 people not only made tremendous productivity and morale gains but also became quite adaptable to change. In fact, when they first moved into the team structure, many of the people were some of the most rigid that I'd ever seen. Three years later, those same people had become the most flexible and adaptable set of employees that I've seen in an organization.

When people have major change initiatives thrust upon them, most need at least some time to adapt to their new situations. So be patient. Don't expect instant ready-to-roll team members who efficiently handle new challenges. By employing strategies that keep your team moving forward, as outlined in this chapter, along with a patient tone in your leadership, your people can get over the humps and bumps that often come with change.

Pushing Roadblocks Out of the Way

Leading a team across an everyday business landscape is tough enough. Nobody needs the added hassle of unexpected obstacles that get tossed in your way. But, it happens all the time. Sometimes a team member (of all people) lays down the speed bumps! Sometimes they come from elsewhere in the organization. In any case, you're the team's point guard and they're counting on you. In this section, I talk about three common impediments and what you can do about them.

New directives from on high

By new directives from on high, I'm talking about your boss or the executives above your boss. Bosses usually mean no harm and simply want to help you work through the change process. But they often just don't see what havoc their brainstorms create and how much unnecessary work they may be drumming up for your team.

To overcome this obstacle, plan on some face-to-face, one-on-one conversations — yes, with the boss. Remember the rule when you challenge upward: Do it privately, not publicly. Here are some tips:

✔ **Assume management means well.** This is the safest assumption, and it helps you focus on people's actions, not their intentions, and it helps *you* to stay positive and maintain your self-control. (But don't fall for the myth that the change drivers in top management know something about change management.)

✔ **Ask for the "gold."** That means, dig out the nugget of great worth that's driving this request you have received from above. Ask:

  • What's the rationale for what you want my team to do?

  • What do you want to accomplish?

Those questions prompt your key decision makers to think through what they're asking and the outcomes they're seeking, because they may not have fully figured those things out. By capturing this "gold," you sometimes get a chance to change the request for action before you must act upon it. Sometimes you can show upper management that no action is necessary at all. Other times, when you gain a better understanding of management's need, you can address it in ways that don't require extra or unnecessary work. You can head toward those happy endings by saying something like, "If this is what you'd like to accomplish, here's how my team can help get that done," or "Let me tell you how that issue is already being handled."

✔ **Talk about priorities.** Major change initiatives seldom succeed when they come cascading down like an avalanche. Changes work better when they come in small bites, more like adjustments than totally new courses of action. (Again, don't assume that top management has figured this out.) So when it looks like another flurry of snowball changes are coming your way and management makes them all sound crucial for your team to adopt, talk with management about priorities. Stay positive yet firm and informative, but don't go overboard with details. Don't whine! Offer recommendations that get them thinking, like: "Based on the resources we have and where we've made progress so far, my recommendation is. . . ." The idea is to invite management to problem solve with you. Help management get a better picture of what's possible by first understanding how your team resources are deployed on current assignments.

✔ **Document agreements and plans.** When you and representatives of upper management seem to agree on plans and priorities, recap your understanding of the agreement verbally and get their confirmation. Then close the meeting by saying you'll write it up and copy them on it. A written record is a much better future reference than memory. In fact, you can't count on impulsive bosses to remember what they wanted from you and your team even yesterday, let alone last week.

Cold shoulder from other groups

Sometimes the biggest obstacles to making change efforts work within your team come from other groups in the organization. Your team may depend on their support in the form of providing essential information, responding to your inquiries or requests, or applying their special expertise to help you solve problems. These are legitimate interdepartmental requests, yet for one reason or another the other guys aren't responding. Here's a process to help you tackle this impediment:

1. **Assume they mean well.**

   When you're dealing with problems, your approach plays a major part in how well others receive you. If you think the other group is plotting a conspiracy against your team, your suspicions will show all over your face. But if you assume that they mean well — the safest assumption — you're much more able to focus on issues and be in control of yourself.

2. **Go in to solve problems.**

   Let the others know you have a problem and are there to solve it with them.

3. **State your team's problem objectively.**

   Describe what has happened, perhaps as a sequence of events. But resist the temptation to interpret what you have observed. Provide no negative opinions — "Just the facts, ma'am." Tell what your people have experienced but don't comment on their experience.

4. **Listen to their side of the story.**

   You may often gain some information that adds perspective to the situation. Listen and learn; don't argue or debate.

5. **Solve the problem together.**

   Discuss possible alternative solutions, and don't hesitate to ask for what you need when you need it. Gain closure.

Working your way up the ladder, if necessary

If the person placing obstacles in your team's path is below the manager level, quite often you can coach your team members to talk to that person on a peer-to-peer level and solve the problem without further recourse. If the peer approach goes nowhere, it's your turn at bat. And if you find that you're mostly dodging wild pitches to the plate, it's time to move up the ladder and speak to the manager.

When you're getting no response to what you need, the question is — Why? Sometimes the answer reveals a concern that you can address at once. Sometimes the reply is less direct and you need to persist, emphasizing how the support of management is essential for good results throughout the organization. Helping people to see the greater good may nudge them off pure self-interest. If, in the end, you're still stuck, then go to the next person up the hierarchy, taking care to let that person know you have made good faith efforts to resolve the matter at a lower level.

When you need to go over someone's head, it's also a good idea to let that person know what you're going to do. Say it in a straightforward and matter-of-fact manner, summarizing your efforts so far, such as:

> *"I've come to you to address a concern regarding the support my team needs from you. Thus far in our discussion, you've not been able to offer any assistance to help alleviate this concern. If you can, I'd like to work that out with you now. If it's best that I seek this help from your manager, then I will proceed that way. You tell me."*

Saying it that way informs the other person that you intend to resolve the issue and removes any element of surprise if and when you speak to that person's boss. In essence, you're saying that going up the chain of command is a last resort and you'll do it only if the other person chooses that option for you.

Monitoring progress

Your direct and assertive intervention often removes any obstacles and gains the support that your team needs from others in the organization. You may need to set a time to meet with the other parties again and review progress. Doing so promotes follow-through and accountability. At the least, find out from your team how the support is coming along. And, if all is going well, pass along your appreciation to the former obstacles (don't call them that!), who, no doubt, have become your team's good helpers.

A counterproductive team member

Sometimes the biggest obstacle a team faces in its development or its effort to implement a significant change comes from the inside — from the actions of a team member. You may observe disruptive outbursts, chronic complaining, low quality or sloppy work, or very little work, period. They all equal unsatisfactory performance. If it only amounts to an incident here or there, you can pull the person aside for counsel and correction. But if the problems persist and shift into patterns, the effect on a team's morale and productivity can be devastating when the situation is left unaddressed. Aim your initial efforts at coaching to improve the performance of the person involved by:

✔ **Stating your concerns.** In a private conversation with the team member, begin by talking about the behavior or work that's below par.

Cite specific instances, not generalities, and talk about what you've observed, not your interpretation. Here's the difference between an observation and an interpretation:

- *Observation:* "I've noticed that when team members or I ask for your assistance on assignments, you react by turning and looking away or you say that someone else should do the work, not you."

- *Interpretation:* "You're very snarly and resistant when team members or I ask for your assistance."

✔ **Exploring reasons for the problem.** Let the employee respond to the concerns that you've raised. Don't debate the issues, just hear the person out. Then, try to uncover the reasons for the problem so that you can also pinpoint a solution.

✔ **Finding a solution and forming an action plan together.** As you move toward the solution stage, clarify your expectations by describing the kind of performance you want to see. Then brainstorm together about the steps the employee can take to meet your expectations. Ask questions instead of dictating action. (Instead of saying, "Step One should be . . ." ask "What do you think Step One should be?") That's one way to keep the team member actively involved in solving his or her problem. Then ask what support you can provide to help make the solution work. As you talk together, have the team member write the agreed-upon ideas into an action plan so that the two of you have a guide for going forward. Don't leave it to memory — people forget!

✔ **Following up periodically.** End the private conference by setting a time to meet again in the near future to review progress. And plan on periodic follow-ups after that to keep the improvement rolling.

In most cases, intervening like this to *coach for improvement* gets what you want from the team member. But if you don't see any improvement, termination may be your only recourse. Actually, that may not be necessary. Quite often, when people know that below standard performance isn't going to be tolerated, they quit.

Don't tolerate actions by certain team members that poison the overall team's chemistry and performance. But remember to intervene early and coach for improvement first. Quite simply, the earlier you act to address an unsatisfactory pattern of performance, the more likely you are to gain improvement in the team member's performance and the team's morale in general.

Part III
Strategies for Building Productive Teams

The 5th Wave   By Rich Tennant

POSSE MANAGEMENT SEMINAR

Sheriff

"... and remember-a posse ain't a posse until it's good and riled up. Which is why I've brought one of the country's foremost rilers to speak with you today."

In this part . . .

Part III explores in depth the discipline that teams need for peak performance. Here, you gain strategies for building productive teams atop the three cornerstones of *focus*, *cohesiveness*, and *accountability*.

Chapter 5

The Focus Cornerstone: Seeing Where the Team Is Going, and How

In This Chapter

▶ Implementing the strategies that set a foundation for a team

▶ Defining the work to be done and who does what in the process

▶ Exploring other focus cornerstone strategies that strengthen a team

*T*he time for getting to work and making your team go is upon you.

You need to plug in the strategies that are necessary for building discipline in your team. *Discipline,* remember, means driving performance to achieve top levels of output and quality.

The discipline-building effort begins in this chapter, providing you with the hands-on feel of the *focus cornerstone,* which is one of the three key cornerstones (along with cohesiveness and accountability) that are needed for building high-performing teams. Imagine, if you will, holding a camera. When you put it into focus, you get quality pictures as long as you keep your hand away from the lens. Teams also need focus so they get quality performance. The focus cornerstone defines why a team exists, where it's going, and how it plans to get there.

In this chapter, I outline two critical foundation-setting focus strategies that you want to use in almost every team situation. In addition, I define two other strategies that you can use in most situations to help guide the team in its work. Toward the end of the chapter, I provide you with an overview of other focus strategies and tell you how they can help your teams. So get ready to work. It's time for focusing and saying goodbye to the three Cs that spell team disaster — chaos, confusion, and calamity.

Not every strategy applies to every team situation, but employing more focus strategies tends to be better than using fewer of them, because a team with a strong focus knows what it needs to accomplish. A strong focus is much better than being led by chaos, confusion, and calamity.

Laying a Solid Foundation Before Building the Whole House

Every kind of team that plans to be around for awhile needs to put together two critical pieces of its foundation — a team-purpose statement and team guidelines.

Even when the team has existed for a long time without these two elements, they're worth putting in place because they can sharpen a team's focus so that it's ready and continues to perform well.

Writing a team-purpose statement

A *team-purpose statement*, as the name implies, defines the purpose of a team and why it exists. I'm not talking about a lofty mission statement that you sometimes see for entire organizations. A team-purpose statement is simple and focuses on the team itself.

A team-purpose statement is best when it's boiled down to one sentence. Otherwise, nobody remembers it. The idea is to simplify the statement so that every member of the team can recite from memory why the team exists.

Steps for creating a team-purpose statement

When creating a team-purpose statement, do so *with* your team not *for* your team.

As is true of all the strategies in this book, your team members must be a part of the process. People support most that which they help create. Before you and your team start to work, briefly explain what a purpose statement is: "A one-sentence statement that defines why the team exists or what the purpose of the team is." Getting into more details, you then can explain that a clearly articulated team-purpose statement answers these questions:

✔ **What's the team's role?**

✔ **What does the team do, or what's its overall function?**

✔ **How does the team want others outside of it to view the team?**

When writing the purpose statement, your team needs to follow these steps:

1. **Using the three team-purpose-defining questions as a guide, have each individual member of the team write a one-sentence purpose statement.**

   You want everyone to write only one sentence that responds to all three questions, not one sentence for each of the questions.

2. **Ask team members to write their finished sentences on something large enough to post them on the wall for everyone to read.**

   Something like a piece of flip-chart paper will do

3. **Begin a discussion by asking team members to point out the common themes or ideas they see in the various sentences.**

   List those themes as they're called out.

4. **Ask team members to suggest new sentences that incorporate those common themes.**

   Write the new sentences on a flip chart for all to see and lead the discussion with your team toward deciding which statement does the best job of

   - Capturing the common themes

   - Answering the three defining questions (listed earlier)

   - Expressing the ideas clearly and meaningfully

5. **Keep the discussion going preferably until you've boiled your statement down to one (but not more than two) sentence(s) that everyone can support.** Getting everyone to buy in to the final statement is *consensus,* which you want to have for implementing strategies like this one. (Chapter 11 provides insights into making consensus decisions with your team.)

For example, take a look at these sample team-purpose statements. They're based on real ones:

✔ Our marketing team is committed to functioning as a cohesive unit by developing and executing strategies and services that position, promote, and achieve high visibility, customer satisfaction, and profitability for our company's software products in the marketplace.

✔ Our administrative team is dedicated to providing our customers, the employees of this company, with top quality facilities, purchasing, and office services in a courteous, responsive, accurate, and efficient manner.

✔ Fulfilling customer orders completely and accurately and shipping them on time is what our operations team makes happen.

✓ The policy task team's purpose is to create and implement key personnel and operational policies that provide the company and its employees with guidelines that are as useful and helpful in operating the business as they are in making it a great place to work.

The value of a team-purpose statement

After you finish crafting the team-purpose statement, make sure that every member of the team receives a copy of it. You also want to post the statement in a highly visible area so that it remains a part of everyone's consciousness. Getting fancy with huge posters or banners isn't necessary, unless, of course, your team likes that style.

Talk about the team's purpose from time to time, such as when you and the team plan and schedule your work or when you evaluate progress. A clearly articulated team-purpose statement provides a sense of direction and alignment for the members.

Alignment means that everyone on the team is pointed in the same direction. Sometimes when teams form and get into their work, members develop differing ideas about the team's overall purpose. When these differences aren't discussed and sorted out, they create obstacles for team members who are trying to move in the same direction. People with hidden agendas may seize an opportunity to stir up dissension. Creating the team-purpose statement early in the process helps your team members sort out possible differences and serves as the guiding light as the team moves forward.

Creating team guidelines

The second foundation-building focus strategy, which also is good to execute early in the process, is establishing team guidelines. Similar to the team-purpose statement, team guidelines are best established by creating them together *with* the members of your team, not merely *for* your team. That's how you can garner everyone's support.

Team guidelines spell out expectations. They are like codes of conduct or commitments, and they define the important behaviors expected of team members as they work together in and outside of team meetings.

Steps for creating team guidelines

As team members gather for one of your team's early meetings, you can explain what team guidelines are and how to write them. Tell your team that a good set of team guidelines spells out what each member can expect from other members while building and sustaining a cohesive and productive team. Try not to exceed ten guidelines: You want to create a working tool, not a rulebook.

Each written guideline should be

✔ Stated as one clear sentence.

✔ Stated in a positive way — telling what *to do* versus what *not to do*. For example, say, "Treat each other with courtesy and respect," rather than, "Don't be inconsiderate, malicious, and rude."

✔ Defined as an observable behavior — something another person can see.

Guidelines describe how people act, not necessarily how they think. Observable behavior is key.

Sometimes people come up with a guideline like, "Display a positive attitude." Nothing is wrong with a positive attitude, but attitude is more about what goes on inside someone's head than how that person is acting. Behavior is a better way to describe someone's actions. You can observe people's actions or behaviors, but you can only make assumptions about their attitudes or dispositions. Whenever you try to get inside people's heads and tell them how to think or feel, watch out — you're stepping into a minefield and it will blow up on you. (Don't even try it at home.)

Follow these steps to create guidelines with your team:

1. **Ask each of your team's members to write three or four guideline sentences, using the three-guideline criterion that I listed earlier in this section.**

2. **Have them write their guideline sentences on flip-chart paper and post them on a wall for all to see.**

3. **Together with your team, identify common themes or ideas that emerge from the various examples.**

   Look for similarities. List common themes that you see.

4. **Collectively craft each common theme into its own guideline sentence.**

   Sometimes someone may have stated the guideline well from the individual inputs that were posted. If it works in capturing the point, use it.

5. **After you identify and apply all the common points, if any potential guideline statements remain that team members believe are important, discuss them and, as long as team members agree, add them to the list.**

   But remember, limit the list to ten or fewer items.

6. **Check for consensus to ensure that everyone on the team supports all the guidelines.**

For example, the following sections represent a few samples of team guidelines based on what real teams have done:

The Public Relations Management Team Guidelines

The management team members will

1. Communicate openly, honestly, and directly with each other.
2. Actively listen to show understanding and respect to what other members have to say.
3. Support one another and the decisions made by the team.
4. Challenge the status quo and show openness to new ideas.
5. Provide and be receptive to constructive feedback.
6. Focus on generating and implementing solutions.
7. Demonstrate that managing and developing people is a priority.

The Team Guidelines of the Policy Task Team

The policy task team members will

1. Come to all team meetings on time and prepared.
2. Follow through and meet commitments with assignments.
3. Actively and constructively participate at team meetings to help the task team get its work done.
4. Support all decisions made by the team.
5. Listen to each other with attentiveness and openness.
6. Maintain and respect confidentiality.

The Patrol Team A-Shift Team Expectations

To be a strong and positive team, we will

1. Communicate with one another in a direct and constructive manner.
2. Take all concerns directly to the source and work to resolve them constructively.
3. Show respect to everyone with whom we have contact.
4. Follow through on all assignments and perform all tasks at a high quality level.
5. Give and receive criticism constructively.
6. Offer help and give help so we can rely on one another.
7. Share information timely and openly.
8. Keep the patrol cars clean and neat.
9. Focus on results and allow for different ways to get a job done.

Communications Dispatch Team Guidelines

The communications dispatch team will follow these guidelines:

1. **RESPECT. Accept team members for who they are as well as what role they have, and treat one another in a courteous, considerate, and understanding manner.**

2. **SUPPORT. Actively reinforce individuals' ideas and the decisions the team makes.**

3. **PATIENCE. Exercise self-control over your actions and realize some things take time.**

4. **TEAMWORK. Demonstrate collective effort, cooperation, and active involvement to help the team reach its common goals.**

5. **JOB FOCUS. Provide high quality to all internal and external customers.**

6. **ACCOUNTABILITY. Take responsibility for your actions and meet your commitments.**

As you can see in the various examples of team guidelines, styles vary. One example repeats the phrase "Team members will . . .", while another leads with an action verb, and a third gives you a key word and then defines what it means to the team. The common thread running through these examples is that each is stated in a positive way, is describing an observable behavior that's important for team members' to follow, is action-oriented, and is written in one concise sentence. That's what makes the team guidelines concrete and meaningful.

Go with whatever style you want, but decide up front and be consistent.

The value of setting team guidelines

Print copies of the team guidelines for all members of the team. Keep copies handy for awhile at team meetings, so that everyone becomes aware of the guidelines.

The truth about any of the strategies in this book that drive team performance is that some people may have reservations about what you want them to do. But, if you think implementing the strategy is useful, such as strengthening the team's focus by developing guidelines, be persistent. Team members adapt quite well when they discover how a strategy is being used to help the team perform well — all the more so when they're involved in applying the strategy.

After you explain a particular strategy that is new to the team, ask your team members what value the strategy has so that they clearly understand before you put it into practice.

For example, team guidelines add value by

- ✔ Creating a common set of performance expectations and understandings
- ✔ Encouraging desirable behavior for good teamwork and performance
- ✔ Enhancing team member self-management
- ✔ Helping orient new members into the team
- ✔ Serving as a way of evaluating member and team performance

Processing the process

At this juncture, a little reflection and analysis can help you become a better manager. If you really want that deer-in-the-headlights look from your team members when you're talking about a new and unfamiliar topic, simply tell them, "Just do it!" That approach, of course, doesn't work. In getting work done and implementing strategies, you need some kind of process.

A process simply is a way of getting something done — and, you hope, done well. Certainly you don't want a process just for the sake of having one, but rather for helping you achieve good outcomes. For example, when facilitating meetings, which I discuss in Chapter 12, you want to use processes that help you deal with issues — that's part of the million-dollar secret for making meetings really work.

In establishing the team-purpose statement and guidelines, the process that I recommend is a good one to employ when you're working in other areas with your team. Figure 5-1 shows you how the process flows.

The acts of writing team-purpose statements and developing team guidelines follow the same process, and you can use that process in many other situations, the same way a baseball manager uses a utility infielder. Using Figure 5-1 as a reference, you can develop a team's work product by following the guidelines in the next two sections.

Individual inputs

You explain the strategy, and then you enable each team member to provide input on the issue at hand. In developing a purpose statement and team guidelines, for example, team members individually write their ideas and post them for all to read and review. Discussion doesn't begin until the input of the individuals has been gathered.

Collective work

Now the team pulls together and works from the individual inputs. Here are some good steps to follow for this next phase:

1. **Begin discussion by identifying the common themes among individual ideas listed.**

   Whenever an idea is mentioned in similar fashion two or more times, it's considered a common theme.

2. **Discuss and together craft the end product around the common themes.**

   In this case, you're talking about a purpose statement or a set of guidelines.

3. **Discuss and determine if any of the remaining ideas are important enough to add to the work-product.**

4. **Close the discussion by checking for consensus and thus ensuring that you have everyone's support for the outcome.**

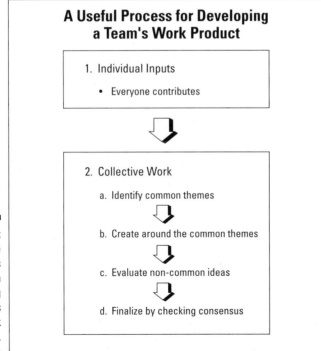

Figure 5-1:
How the process flows in developing a team's work product.

A simple, well-organized process helps you lead your team from discussion through finished work, supported by consensus. Such a process works because it

- ✔ **Equalizes participation.** At the individual input stage, one person's ideas are no better than anyone else's. As a team you're discussing and evaluating people's input, not people.

- ✔ **Increases team-member involvement.** In group situations, some people are more vocal while others are quieter. By starting with the input of individuals, everyone is contributing and yet no one is dominating. With more ideas presented for collective discussions, more people have a tendency to speak up and help the team create its end product.

- ✔ **Enhances efficient use of time.** Seeking common themes first is key to efficiency, simply because doing so is much easier than sorting out differences. Agreement builds momentum in finishing the task.

Remember the process. Many kinds of teamwork issues can be plugged into it to yield worthwhile results.

Goals and Roles, Like Bread and Butter

Goals are targets to achieve or results to produce.

Roles are the parts that people play.

In Chapter 2, I point out that when goals are lacking or unclear, and when key roles are left undefined, teams often struggle. Goals and roles go together like bread and butter, or peanut butter and jelly.

This section provides you with a road map for setting team goals and determining the corresponding plans and roles. Start with the goals and then work out your plans. Remember that you do this *with* the team, not *for* the team. Once everything is set, you have a team that's ready to kick butt.

Setting goals, not activities

Goals define what a team needs to achieve. Their focus is on results, not on activities. Knowing the difference between goals and activities is important.

People are often activity-focused in their jobs. Ask them what they do and they can tell you all the things they're working on right now. When they're organized, they can show you a long to-do list. But when you ask them about the important results they need to accomplish with all that activity, you're likely to come face to face with the trout-look — that mouth open, glazed expression. They simply don't know how to respond. "Just get stuff done" is a common reply.

Ask people, including team members, to state their goals and they'll write

> **Complete Project X by July 1, 2003.**

That isn't a goal; it's an activity. A goal defines a result to be accomplished, like this:

> **Complete Project X, resulting in a 10 percent reduction in material waste from current levels, by July 1, 2003.**

A goal defines a meaningful outcome. It answers the important so-what question — so why is the team working on this effort or assignment?

 You want to establish just a handful of goals that all members share in and contribute to in one way or another. Otherwise, establishing more than a handful of goals will probably result in a laundry list of activities, or more work than you can reasonably accomplish. The goals that you develop also must cover a set period of time, such as the next six months and certainly not longer than a year.

Making sure that your team's goals are results-focused means applying the *S M A R T* criteria, as follows:

- ✔ *S* **is for Specific and clear.** A good goal statement is one sentence. It's so clear and specific that even people outside your team can read and understand it.

- ✔ *M* **is for Measurable.** The goal that you establish can be measured in one or more ways by quantifiable means (numbers) or by qualitative means such as surveys to gather feedback, testing, or documentation, or simply by inspecting the finished product. You may have to create the measuring instrument whenever nothing suitable exists.

- ✔ *A* **is for Action-oriented.** Goal statements begin with action verbs. Among words that work well are *create, design, develop, implement, produce,* and *achieve.*

- ✔ *R* **is for Results-focused.** The goal statement answers the question, "What is the important result that needs to be accomplished?" It doesn't explain *how* but rather *what,* which gives meaningful purpose to the goal.

- ✔ *T* **is for Time-framed.** The goal has a target date, a time of completion. It's an estimate — no one's going to be shot if the date is not reached. But without a target date, work may never end. Target dates help teams focus on accomplishing results.

Four parts = one goal

An easy way to write an effective, one-sentence goal statement is writing it with these four parts, in sequence:

Action verb + Topic of goal + Result to be achieved + Target date

Here are a few examples that follow this useful structure of establishing team goals.

- Achieve through all spring and summer recreation programs and events an average customer satisfaction rating of 90 percent through the current cycle of March 1 through September 1, 2002.

- Implement communication, training, and other problem-solving strategies that result in a turnover rate in the department of less than 15 percent by the end of the year, December 31, 2002.

- Develop and implement a project-management process for the capital-improvement program that results in the completion of the 25 outstanding projects within 12 months, according to defined budgets, quality standards, and set schedules by December 31, 2003.

- Create and implement marketing strategies that result in a monthly hit rate on the company Web site of 250 and a revenue stream of $1,000 per month by October 1, 2003.

Making Plans, Assigning Roles

After the team knows the important results that it needs to accomplish — its goals, you can help team members establish the work plan for getting that job done. You want to determine two things:

- **How goals will be achieved?**
- **Who will do what?**

Planning how to achieve goals

By determining with your team how goals will be achieved, you're defining the main steps (not all the little tasks) that need to be completed along the way. In the next two sections I describe two useful planning strategies.

Going-forward approach

When planning your strategy, start with today and outline each major step needed to reach the goal. You arrange these steps in sequential order, each with a target date that takes you from today until the date by which the overall goal is to be achieved. This approach helps you and your team set reasonable target dates for its goals, because everyone sees what's involved from start to finish. Even when the target date is prescribed, using this approach helps you figure out what efforts are needed to meet that deadline.

Backward-planning approach

Using this approach, you start with the end date by which your goal is to be accomplished and work backward to the present day. Working in reverse, you outline each main step that you need to take all the way back to the present day.

The going-forward approach is the more common of the two planning strategies. When faced with a hard deadline, a team sometimes finds that working backward in planning what must be done is easier. For example, if the show is set for April 1, the team needs to have all:

- ✔ Programs ready by March 24
- ✔ Stage sets completed by March 21
- ✔ Ushers lined up by March 17
- ✔ Flyers and promotional materials sent out by February 15 and so on

Go with the approach that works best for the work at hand and with what your team finds most useful for the situation.

Be sure to document the agreed upon work plans and make copies available for each team member as a reference and reminder. People who are more visually inclined may like seeing the plans outlined in the form of flowcharts or graphs. Figure 5-2 shows you an example.

Defining who does what

As your team creates the work plan for reaching its goals, a picture emerges of what needs to be done. So, making assignments for who is going to do what becomes a natural progression.

Setting the Work Plan

TEAM GOAL: Achieve with all spring and summer reaction programs and events offered an average customer satisfaction rating of 90% through the current cycle of March 1 - September 1, 2002.

<u>Step 1</u>

Analyze data on customer feedback from last year's programs by Jan. 1.

<u>Step 2</u>

Define changes to make to the appropriate programs to increase customer satisfaction by Feb. 1.

<u>Step 3</u>

Lesson plans finalized, incorporating changes by March 1.

<u>Step 4</u>

Administer customer survey at the conclusion of each program and event starting April 1. Progress monitored along the way, too.

<u>Step 5</u>

All survey results from the spring and summer offering are tallied by Sept. 1, and the report evaluating results is completed by Oct. 1.

Figure 5-2:
A step-by-step flow-chart clearly presents the work plan.

Don't assume that your team members automatically know what part they play in the process just because they've had a look at the work plan. Even when certain assignments seem an obvious fit with the skill sets of only one or two team members, don't assume that everyone understands and will act accordingly. When you don't define roles, you can expect to see some tasks unnecessarily duplicated and others falling through the cracks. And when those things happen, say hello to the notorious three Cs — *Chaos, Confusion,* and *Calamity.*

Quite simply, talk with the members of your team so that their roles are clearly defined. In many cases, assignments may involve two or more team members working together. Talking about specific roles for each goal also helps you sort out and balance workload issues. Don't forget that documenting these assignments lets everyone know who's doing what in each work plan.

Overall team goals sometimes are purposely broad because everyone plays some part in helping accomplish them. You'll sometimes want to set goals at the individual level to connect or align team members with team goals. These goals are more specific to individuals and are subsets of the team goals. Aligning individuals with team goals is best accomplished by using what I call a *Performance Planning Worksheet.* Figure 5-3 is an example.

In Figure 5-3, *Goal* is what an individual team member must accomplish to help the team achieve its goal. You want to make sure this language is S M A R T (which I define in "Setting goals, not activities" earlier in this chapter) so that it focuses on results. An individual's goal usually is a subset of the team's goal.

Action Plans are key steps that an individual takes to achieve a goal. Each step is written as a complete sentence with a target date, and steps are listed in order. If these action steps have any requirements, such as "work with so-and-so to do such-and-such," they need to be indicated.

Measurement describes the quantifiable and qualitative evidence that tracks and shows achieved results.

Ties To Team Goal in the far right column of Figure 5-3 creates the alignment. That's where you indicate the corresponding team goal, referring to it by its number.

Not every team member aligns with every team goal. Because of varying responsibilities, some people may align with only three of the five team goals. But that's fine. Not everyone has to do the same things for a team. However, making sure that every team goal has one or more team members assigned to make it happen is important.

Aligning Individuals with Team Goals

Performance Planning Worksheet The period from _____ to _____

	Ties To Team Goal
Goal:	
Action Plans:	
Measurement:	
Goal:	
Action Plans:	
Measurement:	

Figure 5-3:
A worksheet relating individual team members' goals with overall team goals.

A good process for aligning individual member goals with their team's goals is

1. **Making certain that everyone involved attends the meeting at which team goals are set.**

2. **Asking each team member to write his or her performance plans on a worksheet like the one in Figure 5-3. As team manager, you work with them individually, as needed, clarifying their goals and roles in helping the team to achieve its goals.**

3. **Assembling everyone again to present individual plans to the group, which helps you and everyone on the team to**

   - See and understand how others are helping the team achieve its goals.

   - Sort out any differences or problems related to roles and responsibilities.

   - Ensure that every important aspect of the work is covered.

4. **Asking team members to finalize and send copies of their personal performance plans to everyone on the team.**

You may want to establish certain administrative roles that simply help your team manage its business better. Here are a few to consider:

- ✔ **Organizer:** Ensures that arrangements are made for every team meeting or special event, from advance agendas to materials distributed at the meeting.

- ✔ **Recordkeeper:** Keeps the official files and records of important work and information that the team produces, including meeting agendas and minutes, status reports, purpose statements, guidelines, and team work products.

- ✔ **Communications liaison:** Ensures that important news and information about the team's work is passed along to the right sources inside and outside the team.

- ✔ **Librarian:** Maintains important research materials and educational resources that team members need from time to time. The librarian may also be someone who retrieves those resources for the team.

You can give these roles any name that you like, and you can certainly add others as needed. You can assign one person permanently or the job can rotate. The key, however, is discussing these needs upfront with the team and settling on who will handle them.

Avoid making yourself the one who does all the administrative stuff — it's good to delegate!

Double Dosing the V's: Vision and Values

Now you need to consider two more strategies that help strengthen the focus cornerstone. They include developing a team vision statement and defining the team's core values. I introduce this idea in Chapter 2, but this section gets down to the details. I help you envision visions and value values — puns intended.

Establishing a team vision statement

A team vision statement is like drawing a picture of a team when it's successful in the future, describing its long-term outlook — what the team will look like when it's at a high level of performance. Vision statements generally are broad and meant to last a long time, so they're best used with ongoing teams A vision statement doesn't have to be unique or special, just a clear and meaningful description of the team in a positive future state.

Follow these steps when preparing a vision statement with your team:

1. **Define what a team vision statement is and why the team needs one.**

   Stuck getting started? Reread the last full paragraph.

2. **Describe your view of the future.**

   You are the team's leader, so don't hesitate to share your picture of where you want the team to go. Just remember to keep your ideas at the big picture level — skip the detail for now. You want people to grasp the overall concept first and then fill in the specifics.

3. **Follow the process that I describe in Figure 5-1, moving from individual drafts to common themes.**

Write an *umbrella statement* first and then add the key features. The umbrella statement serves as an introductory sentence or two that sketches the broad vision. The key features are items that you list that support the umbrella statement, which often guide the development of team goals and strategies.

Here is an adaptation of an actual team vision statement created by a management team:

> This team seeks to become a financially self-sustaining city department, one that doesn't rely on general funds, intent on delivering recreational programs and services that meet the needs of its customers. To do so, the team will be characterized by
>
> • Managers who are key drivers who develop staff and execute business strategies that achieve self-sustaining results.

- High customer satisfaction with all the programs and services supported by the team.

- Teamwork at all levels of the department.

- Staff who continuously look for ways of improving operations and services and take responsibility for delivering results.

- A work environment that promotes and supports learning and professional development.

The opening sentence of this example is an umbrella statement that defines the broader view. Beneath are five supporting key features that provide a more vivid description of how this future state will appear and how it will be accomplished.

Measuring the value of a team vision statement

Teams that are expected to be together for awhile benefit the most from developing vision statements. A vision statement contributes value to your teams and

✔ **Provides a sense of direction.** People at work want to know where they're going and what the future holds, especially members of teams. A vision statement gives them this sense of direction. Its positive outlook helps rally people together, especially when they've helped to write it.

✔ **Helps you set goals and plans.** A vision statement provides a first glimpse of work that lies ahead. In this way, defining the big picture prepares the team to establish its goals and plans for fulfilling the vision.

✔ **Serves as a reference for evaluating progress.** Reaching the objective described in a team vision statement may always be a work in progress; nevertheless, the statement is a useful reference for gauging how the team's doing.

✔ **Helps you lead the team.** A critical part of leading your teams as a coach, especially in times of change (see Chapters 3 and 4), means providing them with a picture of the future. It is part of good leadership because it gives you and your members a look at where you're going together. Regardless of whether you go through the formal development process of a vision statement, good leadership still needs to give people a picture of the future. Having an actual defined vision statement that others help create makes this important leadership strategy easier to apply. From there, live by it in your ongoing conversations with team members, so that when they operate in the day-to-day, they're focused on moving ahead toward a positive future.

A good team vision statement lasts a long time. When it must be changed every six months or a year, it's probably too narrow. The vision statement must be broad enough to be able to answer "Yes" to the question: "Even if the nature of some or much of the work changes and new demands are made on the team, will the vision statement still be relevant?" You may want to apply that test question when you and the team think you have a vision statement nailed down.

Defining core values

Core values are guiding principles that govern behavior and reinforce the organizational culture or climate that you want to maintain within a group. Core values are not wishes but rather are shared beliefs or behaviors that people truly and strongly hold. Core values answer the question: "What do we stand for as a team?" Because they're *core* values, they are few in number, and yet they characterize what your team is all about.

Some organizations determine core values at the executive level as a means of guiding the entire enterprise. Although core values are seen in practice less often at the team level, they can be useful at that level in pulling a team together and enhancing its sense of purpose and organization

The strategy of defining core values, as is true of the strategy of writing a vision statement, applies more often to a team that's going to be around for awhile. You apply the strategy *with* your team, not *for* its members. (I hope you're catching on to this *with-them-not-for-them* dance step. It's one of the million-dollar secrets that can lead your team to a higher level of performance.)

Remind team members that core values define how your team functions, not what you want to become one day. Therefore, you must be honest: They aren't values when you're not living by them. For that reason, it's best to employ this strategy after a team has been together for awhile and has had a chance to develop some character or identity in how it operates. By defining the values at that point, you not only reinforce them, but you also make them serve as a focus for the team in

- ✔ **Setting goals and work plans.** Ask if those goals and plans coincide with the team's core values?

- ✔ **Recruiting, hiring, and orienting new team members.** Will new members fit in with the team's values and therefore be positive assets to the team?

- ✔ **Evaluating team performance.** As the team produces results, has it kept its values alive and well so the team maintains its positive character?

Figure 5-1 provides you with an effective process for setting core values.

A good question that can stimulate people's thinking about core values is:

> ***What beliefs, practices, and principles do we share and consider important on this team?***

Following the step-by-step process outlined in Figure 5-1, and working off the common themes or ideas generated by individual team members, you can shape the final list of core values by paring it down to five at most. You want a list of core items rather than mere laundry or wish lists. Then, of course, distribute the list of core values for everyone to live by.

Ask your team members to identify core values in a single word or a brief phrase. Then have them build a sentence explaining what that word or phrase means to everyone on the team. Here are a few examples:

- ✓ **High Standards.** The continuous drive toward improving and delivering top results.
- ✓ **Openness.** The willingness to listen, share ideas, and consider diverse points of view.
- ✓ **Commitment.** Continuous support for the team and its members in their group and individual endeavors.

Because you're probing for the team's core values, the statements that you settle on need to stand up to this test question: "If the nature of some of our work or much of our work changes, or if new demands are made upon us, will these values continue to apply to us as guiding principles?"

Some S & M action — standards and measurements

Here are two more strategies supporting the focus cornerstone that you can use to drive team performance. These strategies of establishing standards and measurements tell you, among other things, what to track and focus upon as the team seeks top performance results.

Setting team performance standards

As I define it, a *performance standard* is a level of performance or a work practice to maintain to produce consistent, high-level results. Standards can be set at the policy or guideline level and at the operating-procedure level.

Avoid using the term *minimum standard*. That's an oxymoron. When a standard isn't meant to guide achievement at *high* levels of performance, it isn't a useful standard. Setting a minimum standard is like establishing an Olympic qualifying time so slow that even the slowest of runners can join in the action. So, stick to high standards in what you establish with your team.

Standards established at the policy or guideline level usually address important areas of performance that many, if not all, of the team members share, such as customer service, quality, documentation, and even teamwork. When you draft these kinds of standards with your team, follow the short-and-sweet approach. Make them as clear and concise as possible. For example:

- ✔ Maintain a turnaround time of 30 days or less for processing all vendor invoices.

- ✔ Maintain past-due collections of more than 60 days to 5 percent or less of your total accounts.

- ✔ Maintain an accuracy rate of 95 percent on all coding work.

- ✔ Maintain all project documentation so that it is complete, organized, and 100 percent accurate by the end of each project assignment.

I recall members of one work group who shared responsibility for serving their company's internal customers. They began pulling together as a team and drafted the following customer service standards for this important function.

On a consistent basis, the team will

- ✔ Follow up to ensure customer needs are fully met.

- ✔ Deliver customer service in a manner that is courteous, understanding, and helpful.

- ✔ Provide time frames for completion-of-service requests and advise in advance if a change in status is needed.

- ✔ Provide thorough and accurate solutions and service, doing the job right the first time.

- ✔ Show proactive efforts in anticipating and responding to customer needs.

- ✔ Take responsibility for providing information, assistance, and service that the customer requests.

Performance standards are good for teams because they help them gain

- ✔ Targets to shoot for in their performance — much like goals

- ✔ Sharper focus on excellence in performance

- ✔ A more accurate measuring stick for tracking results

You can read my mind about how to develop performance standards by, again, checking out Figure 5-1 and applying what I cover in "Processing the process" section earlier in this chapter.

Developing SOPs — standard operating procedures

Sometimes teams need to establish *standard operating procedures* or *SOPs*. That kind of performance standard often applies to teams that deal with business operations, such as processing, order fulfillment, financial management, and production.

SOPs define how certain functions are performed, often outlining a step-by-step routine or establishing consistent practices that ensure accuracy, thoroughness, and high quality. In other words, SOPs are supposed to prevent sloppiness.

When you want to develop SOPs with your team, I recommend this process:

1. **Collectively (that means everyone!) determining what areas of your work can benefit from having written procedures.**

2. **Asking team members to select the SOPs that they want to write. They can work individually or in pairs (what used to be called onesies and twosies).**

3. **At a follow-up meeting with the entire team, reviewing drafts for clarity and completeness.**

Because SOPs guide the performance of key tasks, they contain some detail. But no one's going to read them when they're multiple pages long. So make them as short and sweet as possible — logical and concise, with minimal jargon.

Avoid letting your SOPs turn into staunch rules. That can happen when team members forget that procedures *guide* performance toward good results. Results are paramount; arguments about methods for method's sake usually are a waste of time.

People carry out tasks in different but equally valid ways, so enable your team members to work in their own styles while following SOPs. Keep the focus on consistent results, because whenever a team member comes up with a better way of carrying out a function, by all means have that member share the new insights and then update SOPs as needed. And certainly, as work progresses, whenever anyone spots a function that can benefit the team by becoming an SOP, let the good times roll — create that new SOP *on the fly*.

Deciding what to measure and how to measure it

Another focus cornerstone strategy that you may want to use with your team involves defining *performance measurements*. Sometimes referred to as performance indicators, this strategy determines what to measure and how to measure it — what progress in a team's performance is important to track. The idea with this strategy is a familiar one: If you can't measure something important, you can't achieve it. Or, put another way, for a team to focus on and achieve good results, it needs to measure key factors of performance that are important for achieving good results. As you may have guessed, this strategy supports the focus strategies of establishing team goals and team-performance standards.

By looking at what you do for your customers and then deciding what things you can measure, you can establish performance measurements. Don't forget that every team's list of customers includes the obvious outsiders who buy things from you and your inside customers — other work groups and individuals elsewhere in the organization you support.

For instance, assume that you run a fulfillment team with overall responsibility for packaging and shipping every order that your business receives from its external customers. With your team, you may decide that the following performance indicators are important to measure:

✔ Daily volume of orders shipped by type of order

✔ Number of orders returned for correction

✔ Number of orders shipped on time and to the right location

✔ Number and type of customer complaints

✔ Number and type of customer compliments

When you figure out what's important to measure, determine with your team how to measure it. The most common and useful ways of measuring performance factors are

✔ Documenting, on an activity log, the volume and kind of transactions that occur

✔ Utilizing surveys to gather customer feedback

Computers usually enter the picture as an easier and faster way of compiling and analyzing data. So you may also need software, but whatever it takes, performance measurements help a team:

✔ Show what's most important to concentrate on for delivering good results

✔ Provide timely information on performance

✔ Spotlight problems while they're still easy to correct

Chapter 6

Everyone Working Together: The Cohesiveness Cornerstone

In This Chapter

▶ Exploring strategies that encourage people to work together and communicate

▶ Utilizing strategies so that team members learn from one another

▶ Employing the so-called team-building activities

*T*he English language has a great expression, "You can lead a horse to water but you can't make it drink." Teams sometimes are like horses. You can organize people to capitalize on the interdependence of their work, but that doesn't guarantee they work well together.

This chapter contains strategies for building discipline so that people *do* work well together — even if they *don't* personally like one another. You can think of all the strategies in this chapter as part of the *cohesiveness cornerstone* that I talk about in Chapter 2.

The strategies I present in this chapter help you lead members of your teams, showing them how to interact, handle problems, and learn together. I also include a section about what sometimes is called *team building,* by which I mean building working relationships and promoting understanding among people — not loving one another or even climbing rocks together.

Cohesiveness is not about making people happy with themselves or with one another on the team. Happiness is an emotional state. You may know from your personal life that trying to influence the happiness of those near and dear to you is tough enough without trying to make people happy at work. My advice is don't even try it in your professional life. The truth is, some people are happy only when they're miserable.

An example of my point about happiness and teams is evident in what happened with the Oakland Athletics baseball team in the early 1970s, when they won the World Series three years in a row. You may recall that the Athletics' dislike for their manager and sometimes each other was well known, leading, on occasion, to brawls in their own clubhouse. That aside, when they came out on the field, the Oakland team had the discipline to pull together and perform superbly. They were cohesive.

Teams are a means of performing work. People don't have to like one another any time at work. However, they do need to put aside their differences and concerns long enough to do the job. "United we stand, divided we fall."

Divisiveness is the opposite of cohesiveness. Whenever your team splits apart instead of pulling together, it's headed nowhere but down. Managers who utilize the *magic-wand approach* to leading their teams sometimes watch as this happens before their eyes. They simply throw people together, tell them to go work and play well, and then (waving the magic wand) hope the rest takes care of itself. Guess what! That often is the formula for breeding divisiveness.

In this section I talk about strategies that emphasize pulling — if not pushing — team members together to drive performance. Goodbye, divisiveness!

Hipbone's Connected to the . . . Building Connections

In building the strength of cohesiveness necessary for a team to perform productively, you must have strategies that connect people. Even when team members usually work on their own, something that connects, or binds, each individual member to the rest of the team is needed. The following sections present a few important strategies for building these vital connections.

Meeting regularly

Teams need to meet on some kind of regular basis to build strong connections among all members of the team. For some teams, regular may mean a few minutes every day, an hour once a week, or a couple of hours every few weeks. The idea is communicating and working together but not meeting simply for the sake of meeting — and for goodness' sake, not just because it's that time of the week. Chapter 12 provides you with tools for organizing and conducting meetings that accomplish results.

The forum that meetings offer enables team members to

- Communicate important news
- Set plans and coordinate schedules

 ✔ Solve problems

 ✔ Make decisions on issues affecting their work.

Leaving the meeting schedule to a kind of we'll-call-one-when-we-need-one basis often creates fragmented communication between members of a team. Ad hoc (or special case) communication alone won't enable people to think and coordinate as a team. But, on the flip side, meetings that never address issues, doing no more than merely passing information around, aren't of much value either.

Sharing responsibilities

Another useful strategy for pulling team members together involves how assignments are made. As much as you can, make assignments in a manner that enables people to work with one another to get the job done — joint efforts. When working on projects, making these assignments often means mixing different disciplines so that each person's expertise is brought into play.

Joint assignments are great for breaking down tensions and I-work-solo styles. Remember, people neither have to like each other nor have the same work styles just to work together. But when they depend on one another for achieving a shared outcome, they often find a way of putting aside or resolving their differences so they can get the job done well.

Finding a good meeting plan

I remember one operations team that had its ups and downs trying to find an effective meeting routine. Over time, they settled on a two-part approach that worked well.

First, they met every day to start each workday. Team members grabbed their coffee and gathered in the meeting area, covering a few essentials with their team leader, such as any important news or results from the previous day's work, decisions about who's going to do what today, any scheduling issues, or other important announcements. This meeting ran 15 to 20 minutes and helped everyone become focused. A few members referred to it as their *Hill Street Blues* meeting, naming it after the television show that usually began with a meeting of all police officers before they went out on patrol.

Second, the operations team met every week or two for an hour to an hour-and-a-half to work on issues. The team leader prepared an agenda for this meeting, which often focused on planning and problem-solving.

For a team that began by hating meetings because they seemed like a waste of time, the operations team found ways to make meetings a normal part of their operations and a key part of building a strong level of cohesiveness.

When you see an opportunity for using the joint efforts of a team to get work done, use these tactics to create good combinations among members of the team:

✔ Explain what work needs to be done and how many people are needed to do it to members of your team.

✔ When asking who wants to do what, suggest (but don't direct) that certain individuals take on certain assignments. "John and Sue, how about you two handling the market research aspects of this project?"

✔ Recruit people individually by talking with them privately before the team meeting, designating with whom you want them to work on a given job. In addition, when you know that certain people have a hard time working with certain other people, a joint assignment can be a useful way to get them to move beyond their hang-ups.

✔ Coach team members individually by preparing them for the upcoming work needed. But first, solicit any concerns or reservations they may have. Then you can focus on helping them move forward.

✔ Positively reinforce the individuals who perform well with shared responsibilities.

Developing backup coverage

Any work team that has a lone specialist for a member may be in a vulnerable position if anything were to happen to that person. You want to be able to pass what I call the *truck test,* meaning if anyone on the team ever happened to be run over by a truck (which you never wish on anyone), your team still can function. And, don't forget, people like to take vacations, too.

Executing a backup strategy usually involves cross-training. To make sure that cross-training occurs and backup coverage is in place:

✔ Ask the skilled team member — who, by the way, will train the backup person or persons — to create an outline of key tasks and functions that need to be performed and therefore taught to backup personnel. When you're fortunate enough to have detailed procedures manuals, that's great. However, when such documentation isn't in place, you don't want to create a cumbersome assignment for the trainer. Nevertheless, you want the cross-training to begin as soon as possible.

✔ Ask the parties involved in the cross-training — the skilled team member or trainer and the trainee — to establish and document a schedule that indicates when training will take place, how long each session will be, and for what period sessions need to continue until the backup person is properly prepared to perform with relative independence.

> ✔ When training is complete, ask the trainee to perform the essential functions of the job under supervision of the more experienced team member.
>
> ✔ When the backup person can perform independently, end the supervision and enable the backup person to work on the new tasks periodically. Ask the experienced person to evaluate and provide feedback on the now well-trained trainee's work.

Sometimes the *buddy system* can create the backup that you need. Using the buddy system means that every team member has a fellow member or two who can support and cover for him. The system is set up so that everyone has an assigned buddy. Some cross-training may be involved. Sometimes the system may require that you direct and encourage the team members to share information, keep each other in the loop, and reach out and ask for assistance from their newfound buddies.

When team members have a good understanding of what their teammates' work involves and can cover for each other, pitching in to help one another becomes much easier — and is easier to encourage. Asking for help becomes accepted practice; working as a lone ranger does not. In short, when you have a team pulling together, you have a team that's ready to produce.

Take a look at the way your workspace is laid out. Do the team members sit near one another or far apart? Are cubicle walls so high that people can't see each other when they need to? Get everyone as close together as possible. Especially with work-unit teams, proximity helps people to informally support one another.

Putting Team Guidelines into Action

In Chapter 5, I show you how setting guidelines or expectations actually sharpens a team's focus. (That's the *focus cornerstone.*) In this section, I present three strategies for using team guidelines to influence a strong sense of cohesiveness. (That's right — the *cohesiveness cornerstone.*)

Publishing and talking about guidelines

Team guidelines have to be visible if you want them to influence how people work with one another in getting the job done. So, as you establish the guidelines with your team members, be sure to talk about ideas for making them visible. Three common ways are the following:

✔ Creating a poster for the team's common work area.

✔ Giving all team members a copy of the guidelines to keep at their workstations.

✔ Making sure a copy of the guidelines is available at every team meeting.

Periodically, you can also end a meeting by having team members evaluate how they applied the guidelines during the meeting. The same tactic works well even when only a few individual members meet to work on an issue or to address a problem

Encourage team members to speak up when they witness another person carrying out the team's guidelines. Positive reinforcement enhances team cohesiveness.

Guidelines aren't excuses for publicly scolding members of your team. So you should avoid encouraging team members to use the guidelines as "gotchas" on each other. Sure, when someone isn't living up to the team's expectations, you want to address the issue.

Solving an operational issue

Operational issues are any matters that have to do with getting work done. These issues pop up all the time in every kind of work situation. When team members solve operational issues together they're applying basic team guidelines and shoring up the cohesiveness cornerstone. Chapter 9 covers problem-solving models in detail, but the basic steps are

1. **Defining the problem.**

   After defining the problem, if you also need to analyze it to better understand the circumstances and causes behind the problem, then do that, too. (See Chapter 9.)

2. **Getting some proposed solutions out on the floor.**

3. **Evaluating the ideas.**

4. **Deciding what will work best, and implementing it.**

Take care that everyone understands the problem before you go looking for solutions — no need to have solutions flying around in search of problems!

Remember at each step to ask individual team members for their input first so that everyone has a chance to contribute. When you begin general discussion, look for common themes before sorting out any differences.

Problem-solving as a team sends the message that it's not *your* job to smooth over every little bump the team encounters. Your role is to facilitate. That means ensuring that problems are addressed, and if necessary, following through to make sure things happen the way they should. What a relief — you don't have to do everything yourself!

The process of solving operational issues as a team also encourages individual team members to raise issues about what they're encountering in their work. In effect, the process says to everyone that finding solutions is a jim-dandy thing to do, while blaming others and complaining about problems isn't. (Hello, team guidelines!)

Addressing a team-function issue

Sometimes teams just don't work right because of a problem with, for example:

- ✔ Information sharing
- ✔ Coordination of tasks
- ✔ Interpersonal clashes and tensions

Group functioning issues like these, if left unaddressed, can become big impediments to team performance and can lead to the formation of factions and plenty of griping in the hallways. Believe me, you don't need any of that.

Addressing these issues tests a team's mettle. If you shy away from these kinds of issues, a team never matures and comes together. Accept the fact that some team members may feel uncomfortable at first in addressing these group dynamics issues. Don't let the comfort level, yours or theirs, guide your judgment. If the issue is affecting the way the team functions, it's important to address. You can follow a simple guideline that I learned about as a kid: When you're getting into a swimming pool with really cold water, just dive in. (Through the years I've found a better strategy: Pick a well-heated pool or just stick to the Jacuzzi.)

When a matter involves only certain individuals on a team, address it only with those individuals. When the matter concerns all team members, address it with them collectively. Your role is to facilitate or support the conflict resolution meeting.

In addressing a team-function issue:

- ✔ Prepare for your role by having a conflict resolution *model* in mind. You can find one of these tools in Chapter 10.
- ✔ Make sure team guidelines are visible and identified as the ground rules for the discussion.

✔ Start the discussion by inviting individual expressions — everyone contributes — without comment or judgment by others.

✔ Steer the discussion toward resolutions that will make the situation better.

✔ Close by recapping what action will be taken and by whom. Set a follow-up time for meeting again and reviewing progress. (That's the *accountability cornerstone* coming into play.)

Teams that can resolve their concerns and conflicts together are teams that can perform at a high level of professionalism.

Adding Adhesive to the Cohesive: Learning and Building Together

In this section I talk about three team management steps that can help you to further strengthen the cohesiveness cornerstone:

✔ Selecting new team members

✔ Developing your skills together

✔ Redesigning the work process to make it better

You can't pick your family, but you can pick new team members

Teams that function over long periods of time often see members come and go. And, of course, the dynamic of a team is greatly affected by its members. You have an opportunity to add to your team's sense of team unity by involving existing members in the process of interviewing and selecting new team members.

Defining the role and job requirements

The first step in selecting someone new for the team is agreeing on the duties and functions of the new team member. Sometimes they're the same as any other team member or, in other cases, the same as those of the departing member. In any case, hiring someone new also can enable you to redefine the work that your team needs to do better.

So, you need to ask yourself and your team members what job-related skills and experiences the team needs in a new team member? Determine these qualifications, along with the personal qualities and behaviors needed, so there's a high probability that whoever is selected to fill the vacant position will work effectively with the team.

Be specific. For instance, don't be content to say that "flexibility" and "initiative" are important qualities and let it go at that. Define specifically what you mean, like this:

- ✔ **Flexibility:** Team needs someone who is comfortable with changing conditions, able to adapt to them, and able to take on different assignments as necessary.

- ✔ **Initiative:** Team needs a self-starter, someone who does his own work and helps others without being told.

Determining the roles you want people to play in the interview process

Team members play various roles in the interview process; they don't all do the same thing. You may want one or two members handling the upfront screening of candidates, others focusing on certain aspects of the job during the interview with applicants, and still others focusing on aspects of the team during the interview. Whatever the case, work this out with team members in advance so that your people can prepare.

Don't have every team member interview every candidate during the preliminary round. That isn't a good use of time — for team members or the candidates. Instead, do upfront interview screening yourself or by designated team members. Later, all team members can interview the top few candidates.

In the early rounds of interviews, screen more candidates with fewer people. In the later rounds, screen fewer candidates with more people.

Avoid *panel interviews* — three or more people interviewing a candidate at one time. Panel interviews uncover only a limited amount of information about a candidate. In the group situation, building rapport with the candidate is as difficult as asking follow-up questions that reveal a person's background in depth. A good interview is a fact-finding mission. Five people separately interviewing one person one at a time will gather more information than five people interviewing one person as a group.

Coaching your team members to conduct effective interviews

Just because the opportunity to help in the hiring process excites many of your team members doesn't mean that they'll know what to do when it's time to conduct an interview. So, teach them yourself or have someone else do it. After you do, they'll be ready for future hiring situations. The following sections offer a few good pointers for conducting an effective interview.

Discussing what you can and what you can't ask in an interview

In brief, people do fine when they limit questions to job-related issues. But they may create potential problems when their questions focus on personal matters. Questions — even if implied and spoken out of innocence — that focus on race, ethnicity, religion, age, gender, or factors of personal background or affairs (from lifestyle to leisure time) are the ones to keep off limits.

Showing team members how to shape questions for good fact-finding

Most questions in an interview need to be *open-ended* rather than *close-ended*. Close-ended questions usually can be answered in only a word or two, such as the following:

- Did you work in a team situation in doing that project?
- When did you work at that company?
- How many people did you have on that team?

Open-ended questions seek an explanation or an expression of thoughts, feelings, and ideas. They can't be answered in only a word or two. Here are examples of open-ended questions:

- Describe your greatest challenge in that job and how you dealt with it.
- Tell me the main responsibilities you had in that role.
- What did you most like, and least like, about your last job?

Showing team members how to phrase questions that reveal how a candidate matches up with job requirements

Some useful ways of gathering job-qualification information are

- **Asking informational questions.** Gather information about a candidate's work experience and background.
  - Tell me what duties you performed in that position.
  - Describe what kinds of work teams with which you had involvement.
  - What contributions did you make in that role?
- **Asking behavioral questions.** Invite a candidate to tell a story about some past work experience that demonstrates how he or she applied a kind of behavior.
  - Give me an example of a difficult customer situation you were faced with and how you dealt with it.
  - Describe a situation from your work experience that demonstrates you're an effective team player.

- Tell me about a time when you were part of a team faced with a tight deadline and what happened in that situation.

✔ **Asking introspective questions.** Ask an applicant to assess himself and his preferences in a work situation.

- From pluses to minuses, assess how you function in team situations.

- How would co-workers from your last job describe you as someone to work with and why?

- Describe the kind of work situation in which you thrive the most.

Assigning team members to prepare questions in advance of their interviews

Have them try out new-member interview questions on one another so they can polish the queries and enter the interviews focused and ready to go.

Making the decision

When the interviews are completed, gather all the team members for an evaluation discussion. The objective of such a meeting is to make a hiring decision. Follow these steps for a fruitful meeting:

✔ Ask team members to come to the meeting with written evaluations of the finalists they interviewed. The evaluations must focus on matching the candidate with job requirements — evidence gained versus selection criteria. This is a much more objective technique than just opening the floor for discussions about general impressions or people's likes and dislikes about the candidates.

✔ Ask each member to report individually. Record their main points on a flip chart as you facilitate the session. Hold off on any discussion until everyone has spoken.

✔ Let fly with a give-and-take discussion between you and the team members, focusing on the pros and cons of each candidate as compared with the job requirements. As you join in the discussion, use your questions to probe for the full content of what you hear team members saying — and to float any trial balloons that may seem useful.

✔ When the discussion runs its course, announce your decision as the hiring manager and explain it.

The name for this process of facilitating a group feedback session is *consultative decision-making*. It's different from making decisions *by consensus*. (I talk about both forms of group decision-making in Chapter 11.) Briefly, in the consultative approach, a primary decision-maker uses the group's input to reach a decision. In consensus approach, the group reaches a decision when all agree to support a final outcome. The consultative approach usually works best in a hiring decision because not everyone may agree on the best candidate but involving everyone in the decision helps build understanding and support for it. Of course, if you're a team leader but not a hiring manager, the consensus process may be your operating method — unless the team is willing to hand you the final decision.

When your team isn't hiring a new employee but rather is taking on a new member from elsewhere within the organization, you can assign team members to find and screen possible recruits and thus help determine who will work best for the team. Again, as team manager, use the consultative approach for making your decision.

Training and Learning Together

Skill development is one key aspect of increased performance that often is overlooked. When you show people more about how to do their jobs and how to work effectively with one another, you increase the likelihood that they'll perform better. When team members go through training efforts together and, through that process, can learn from one another, you add to the cohesiveness of your team. To enhance this process of development and cohesiveness, I suggest conducting

✔ **Technical forums:** Gatherings at which team members explore and discover more about the technical issues related to performing their jobs. Sometimes such a forum may mean bringing in an outside speaker or a speaker from elsewhere in the organization. Often, a team member or two make presentations about areas of expertise.

✔ **Team skills workshops:** Scheduled times when team members learn about working together. You can see Chapter 2 and Part IV of this book for more detail, but briefly those skills are

- Interpersonal communications

- Systematic problem-solving

- Conducting productive meetings

- Planning and goal setting

- Conflict resolution

- Group decision-making

Who leads a workshop is less important than the fact that you're periodically spending time learning skills as a team. And, don't forget, this book is a great resource in any situation.

✔ **Customer service sessions:** For teams with work that has a strong service emphasis, a workshop may be devoted to reviewing articles or books about customer service. It may also involve analyzing how customer problems were handled in the past, drawing lessons from those situations — examples of good service and bad.

✔ **Cross-training:** A useful strategy for building connections among team members for assuring coverage of important functions of a team's work, the idea of cross-training is that people who know particular job functions show others who don't know those jobs so that the learners can help perform those functions. I provide details of cross-training in the section on "Developing backup coverage" earlier in this chapter.

✔ **Sharing from outside education** — Team members are selected to attend outside training activities and then share what they learned when they return so that the whole team benefits. This is routine in many organizations because of travel and budget limitations. It means that the week that one team member spends in Hawaii for that special conference is something the whole team can benefit from (well, maybe not from the sand and surf).

Training and learning together as a team must become commonplace if you intend to gain the most cohesive effect. Remember the benefits of involving team members in scheduling, organizing, and delivering these learning events on a regular basis. Ensuring that they happen is your role as manager.

Taking time for periodic professional development sends a message that learning technical and team skills is important and creates the kind of team where people want to stay.

Working the Process So You Can Process the Work

Work process is the way that tasks or job functions are done. The *re-engineering movement* was all about work process and had a pretty good head of steam going for awhile in the 1990s, but at times, efforts became cumbersome and complicated, which is the opposite of the way they're suppose to be. The main idea, however, is using people who do the work to create better and more efficient ways of doing it. And, that makes sense.

Redesigning the work process also enhances a team's cohesiveness. The strategy applies best to work-unit teams that share an overall job function. Sometimes, task or improvement teams are formed to redesign work processes, such as order fulfillment or manufacturing, that routinely cut across various departments. You may want to apply a work process strategy when

✔ You see a need for greater efficiency in how a team does its work.

✔ A team has a hard time keeping up with the demands of its internal or external customers.

> ✔ You anticipate future demands that will make today's processes obsolete.
>
> ✔ Current processes limit cooperation and mutual help — too many single task specialists and not enough multitask specialists.

To keep your team's redesign or process-improvement efforts simple and productive, I suggest that you

> ✔ **Outline what happens today.** Account for every step of a work process from start to finish. Put it on paper for all to see. Everyone must understand what you're doing today before you can take steps to improve the process.
>
> ✔ **Identify bottlenecks, confusing factors, and problems.** Analyze them from the perspectives of your internal and external customers. When something comes between your customers and your team's good products or services, that's usually an area that needs improvement.
>
> ✔ **Explore ideas for process improvements.** You may have many choices. Sometimes, only small adjustments or additional cross-training do the job. Other times, however, you may need to forget old ways and start over from scratch, making even wholesale changes. Encourage team members to be creative and think outside the box. (That's one cliché that actually seems appropriate. And, by the way, where exactly is that box that confines everyone's thinking so much of the time?)
>
> ✔ **Evaluate ideas for implementation by set criteria.** The criteria may be
>
>   • Helping to serve customers
>
>   • Creating better coverage and teamwork
>
>   • Saving time
>
>   • Reducing redundancy
>
>   • Simplifying
>
>   • Accomplishing some or all the above

Following this routine helps the team not only to devise better work-process ideas but also to implement them, and that's the whole idea behind the cohesiveness strategy. Even when some improvements involve technology or computer-system enhancements, go after them.

You may want to test an idea for improvement before officially implementing it. Conducting a trial run for a set period of time sometimes is safer than full-scale immersion, especially with a major change. Similarly, when a transition from old to new ways is necessary, plan it out with your team and determine whether you need to bring anyone outside the team into the loop.

Debriefing at the firehouse

Some of the best efforts in learning together that I've ever seen occur in the public sector. For example, I've known fire captains who routinely conduct debriefing sessions with their crews after returning from service calls. The firefighters discuss how the call was handled, emphasizing the services delivered. People aspects and technical and safety matters are discussed.

Debriefings of that nature are prime examples of team members learning together. These informal but routine sessions highlight what was done well and reveal how to make little improvements the next time out. In the firefighting business, the next time can be right around the corner, and those little improvements may actually save a life.

 With your team, periodically review the work-process changes that you make to ensure those changes are in place and that projected efficiency gains are occurring. Make adjustments as needed.

Getting Into Team Building

Teams are a means for achieving performance. When teams are instilled with discipline — focus, cohesiveness, and accountability, they can achieve a high level of performance.

But there's more. As team members work together, relationships develop. Teams are made of people, not fiber or bricks. So periodically working on these relationships is useful for promoting understanding and acceptance and thus, ultimately, greater cohesiveness. That's what I mean by team building and what I explore in this section.

 Some managers think team building means going off on some one-day outing, having fun playing games or climbing rocks, and then the whole team bonds and lives happily ever after. As I note in Chapter 3, how well a team plays together may have no bearing on how well it works together. Your job as manager is not ensuring everyone's happiness — that's a no-win situation — but rather leading the team to higher levels of productivity.

Occasionally focusing on working relationships is useful when the overall aim is improving the way team members work together toward an ultimate goal of stronger performance.

By all means, have fun with your team, but remember that team building is an ongoing effort, not just a one- to two-day event. The purpose of team building isn't fun for fun's sake. The purpose can be expressed in this simple formula:

> *Building understanding and acceptance*
> + *Increasing familiarity*
> = *(or leads to)*
>
> *Enhanced cohesiveness and performance*

You can find ideas for useful team-building activities and events from many sources — certainly many more than I have time to talk about in this book. So, in the following sections, I discuss a handful of good ones, classified in two categories — social activities and team-related exercises. Any of them can be done as a stand-alone event or part of a working meeting.

Social time

Social events can be highly organized or highly informal. Not every style fits every team, so go with what your team likes.

✔ **Coffee chats.** Usually good with bagels first thing in the morning as a breakfast deal, the coffee chat is a time when the entire team just sits around and chats for maybe half an hour or so every week or two. It's actually a team meeting with a simple and friendly agenda. Therefore, one simple rule applies to coffee chats: No talking about work! It's a time for team members to relax together before taking on the work that awaits them.

✔ **Lunch outings.** Every team I've ever seen likes to eat — a common theme among many of the social examples here. Going out for lunch together, as a team, is another way for team members to relax together and build familiarity with one another. Lunch outings are different from a few team members going out to lunch on their own. It's the entire team together. A lunch outing usually needs to be scheduled so that everyone can get together. Put it in your team budget — you can pick up the tab for these occasional outings. Sometimes a lunch fits in well after a working meeting. Lunches don't require an agenda, but you can plan to discuss a topic or two, or ask that certain people sit by certain others to mix everyone up. Vary what you do. Just make sure that you have a good time and go to a decent restaurant. Stay away from the fast-food havens.

✔ **Barbecues and potlucks.** These are eating-in events, not going-out-to-eat activities. Done on an occasional basis, with a team that likes to cook, a barbecue can be a great time for a team to work together (that's the cooking and cleanup stuff) and relax together (that's the eating stuff). Barbecues can also be good events to include guests from outside the team as a means of building goodwill. If you don't have a grill or don't want to cook, there's always the potluck luncheon. Team members sign up to bring a dish or the dishes (I was good at bringing paper plates and napkins), and then they gather around to enjoy each other's contributions. Although no one to my knowledge has ever correlated calories-in to performance-out, I know that sharing a meal can help reduce the stress a team often feels in getting its work done.

✔ **Special occasions.** These are team get-togethers celebrating birthdays, recognizing length of service on the job, acknowledging personal anniversaries, or appreciating other special occasions in a team member's personal or professional life. Sometimes the gathering includes a meal. Other times, it's a half-hour cake-and-ice-cream social with some off-key singing. One team that I've worked with schedules a special-occasion celebration once a month. They have birthday people each telling something about themselves that others may not know. This usually produces some good laughs.

✔ **Bringing dinner in.** Sometimes teams go through crunch periods of heavy work volume or they face deadline pressures that keep everyone working late. One of the more appreciated social gestures at such times is bringing dinner in.

✔ **Reward outings.** Maybe a reward outing includes dinner on the town, a movie, a ballgame, or a theater show together. The idea of this team-building event is that it's done as a reward for the team achieving an outstanding level of performance. It's an outing the team has chosen as its reward. You've budgeted for it, so you can take care of most, if not all, of the cost. Sometimes including spouses and significant others also enhances these events.

✔ **Recreational activities.** As a reward, or just for fun, this is a sports-type activity that the whole team can enjoy — perhaps a softball game, a kickball game, a volleyball game, or even touch football. It may be part of a team picnic. Choose an activity with which everyone is comfortable — nobody has to be a superstar.

Some people don't like physical activities. So don't push sports when you don't have a group of sports-minded, active people. Trekking in the wilderness or climbing tough terrain may be depicted as wonderful bonding experiences but may not be suitable for many teams. The idea is to have some fun together. Avoid turning a social gathering into a highly competitive event that can be a big turnoff. By the way, schedule events at the end of the day so that people don't have to go back to work — if you catch my drift.

Exercising without Breaking into a Sweat

This section provides you with another handful of activities that promote stronger working relationships among team members. These activities involve more talking and working than socializing, eating, or getting physical — but having fun is highly recommended just the same. These exercises work best when they are special meetings or special features within regular team meetings.

Icebreakers

Use these short activities at the beginning of a team meeting or special event. They're usually only a few minutes long, and they work best when you

- ✓ Explain how the activity works.
- ✓ Get them going.
- ✓ Debrief everyone afterward, sharing observations about how the team worked on the activity and what lessons people learned from it.

A-to-Z task

If the team is small enough, everyone can work together. Otherwise, you may want to organize into subgroups of four or five people. Provide a sheet of flip-chart paper with the letters A through M written down the left side and the letters N through Z written down the center. The team's mission is to find objects in their possession or within the meeting room that start with each letter of the alphabet and then place those actual objects on the sheet (just one object per letter), trying to fill all 26 letters. Set a time limit of three to four minutes. This icebreaker helps team members see how they organize themselves and execute efforts in their work. Often you witness a mad scramble of people working individually at first, and then pulling together only when time is running down. You may also witness plenty of creativity and positive energy.

Keep the balls in the air

With team members standing in a circle, this activity begins when one person tosses a kickball to someone else who isn't standing next to him, and each of the recipients does the same until everyone touches the ball once before it returns to the person who started the game. Whatever order the team follows in this first toss-around becomes the order that they must follow for the rest of the activity. Have team members practice a few times, so they become familiar with the order. Keeping the ball moving without hitting the ground for as long as possible is the objective. When the ball hits the ground, play continues from the point where it left off, but the timer goes back to zero.

As the activity gets rolling, the facilitator introduces an additional ball to the program once every minute by handing it to the person who started the game. That person works the additional ball into the routine. After a few minutes, the team — if it can get to that point — will have balls in motion equal to the number of people in the circle. Time how long they can keep all the balls in the air without hitting the ground.

In the debriefing, talk about how the team worked to keep the balls moving as more and more came into the mix. Relate this experience to the way a team works together when more demands and changing priorities are thrust upon it. Good lessons can be drawn from this activity.

Quiz game review

You may have to divide a larger team into subgroups of four to five people for this game. A quiz game is good way of reviewing and reinforcing recent team training. Remember, a little friendly competition can be fun. Obviously, the quiz questions are based on recent training

As you ask questions, team members huddle for a couple of minutes to come up with answers. Each team member then writes the answers in his or her own notes for a facilitator to check. (This prevents one dominant person from carrying the whole team.) The facilitator selects any team member's answer to a given question, and, if it's correct, the team scores a point or more, depending on the value the question was given.

In debriefing, discuss what team members did in helping one another to find the answers. This icebreaker reinforces important work lessons and good teamwork.

Working activities

The activities that I list here are much more involved than icebreakers and take much more time. Working activities involve all team members contributing to a final outcome, and you usually want to allow an hour or more. Here is a good general process to follow:

- ✔ State the objective of the exercise; that is, the final outcome, and then give instructions.
- ✔ The team members perform the activity. Make sure they have all the materials they need.

✔ When the work is done, the teams or subgroup teams present their results to the entire group.

✔ In a debriefing discussion, share observations about how team members worked with one another and about the lessons learned.

Solve the murder mystery

Each team member is given one or more clues about a murder mystery. Working together only through conversation, and without showing the clues to one another, the team solves the murder by telling who the murderer is, what the motive was, when the murder took place, where it happened, and what weapon was used.

Design the promotional plan for a fictitious product

Team members are given a fictitious product, such as a banana peeler, orange peeler, or vacuum cleaner, to promote. Their job is to write a description of what the product does and develop a visual presentation for advertising the product. This work activity not only promotes team dynamics but also stimulates creativity. Materials like construction paper, flip-chart sheets, crayons, markers, and scissors usually are good to have on hand.

Put together the puzzle

Team members are shown the final, assembled look of a complex puzzle, one with many pieces. Each member then is given an equal number of pieces of the puzzle. The team's objective is to build the puzzle together. How they organize their work and help each other is up to them.

Create the team story for publication

Usually working in subgroups of four or five, team members create a single story that involves each person and helps others discover something about them. They create an illustrated book that tells the story and then present it to the entire group. Have magazines, construction paper, crayons, markers, regular paper, scissors, and tape on hand for this activity.

Build the greatest mousetrap

Building the greatest mousetrap is another exercise that's best for a subgroup of four or five people. Team members are given materials like Popsicle sticks, toothpicks, and glue and then instructed to build the world's greatest mousetrap — or gadget, object, ship model, or replica of some great product. In a debriefing, they must tell the story of their products, how they work, and how they benefit humankind.

Describe personal styles

Each team member fills out a questionnaire that is aimed at defining his or her likes and dislikes in various work situations — an inventory of the person's "style." The Myers-Briggs product is the best known of a wide variety of personal-style inventories that you can purchase. Scoring and interpretation are provided. The value of defining personal styles is that they help people gain an insight into their and their workmates' personalities and work styles. This exercise works best when team members share their results with one another.

Personal-style inventories lose value when they are used to categorize people and create expectations about the way they will act, which is known as stereotyping, or when they suggest a formulaic method of working with another team member who has a different style. But when the instrument is used to promote understanding, it leads to some lively and beneficial discussions. The key is for team members to accept one another's styles, not expect everyone to be the same every day, and to employ respectful and effective interpersonal communication tools — tools I talk about in Chapter 8.

Stimulate conversation

People take turns sharing their experiences and perspectives related to a thought-provoking topic. The discussions can range from exploring work-related matters to personal ones. It's often best to allow the participants to take the topic in any direction they want. The exercise usually is done in pairs or small groups of up to four people.

The objective of a conversation-type activity is building understanding and familiarity among team members. Whenever anyone thinks this kind of stuff can become too touchy-feely, remind the participants of the objective. In fact, as people gain insight into and understanding of one another, they often become more accepting of team members' idiosyncrasies and different work styles — the root cause of many interpersonal problems that affect team performance.

If you decide to try the activity, follow this process:

- ✔ Designate conversation groups, from pairs to quartets.
- ✔ Explain what is to happen: a conversation in which everyone participates.
- ✔ Set a time limit for the entire exercise — usually three to four minutes per person.
- ✔ Provide a conversation-starting topic and let the discussions commence.

Sometimes you may want the discussion to continue for more than one round, rotating pairs so that participants have a chance to mix with others.

Debrief when the conversation is over. Have team members share observations of what the experience was like talking with and listening to their various partners. Aside from personal information, ask what they learned from the experience? If you want to promote more openness and think that members are willing, ask each one to share some highlights about what they discovered about their partners.

Toss out stimulator topics like these to get the conversation rolling:

- ✔ A turning point in my life (professional or personal)
- ✔ A significant change I've experienced in my life (professional or personal)
- ✔ What I want to be appreciated for in my work
- ✔ Something important to me
- ✔ A strong interest of mine
- ✔ A change that I think can enhance our team
- ✔ An interesting difference or two between you and me

Whenever you select the last topic on the list, first have team members identify their differences and then let them explore the differences in conversation. It's a great exercise for building awareness, understanding, and respect among team members.

When your goals are strengthening working relationships and enhancing performance, team-building activities can help, but it takes more than a one-day stand. So, remember to work these activities into the program on a regular basis, as special events or as part of regular team meetings.

Chapter 7

Taking Responsibility: The Accountability Cornerstone

In This Chapter

 Exploring strategies for evaluating team performance

 Using peer feedback for building team-member accountability

 Carrying out strategies that reinforce responsibility

*G*imme an F! Gimme a C! Gimme an A!

What does it spell? Nothing!

What do those letters stand for? Plenty! Namely, they stand for the three cornerstones for building team performance:

  ✔ Focus (Chapter 5 tells you all about focus).

  ✔ Cohesiveness (Chapter 6 tells you all about cohesiveness).

  ✔ Accountability. That's the topic of this chapter, including strategies for building your team on the accountability cornerstone.

You'll find in this chapter that the *accountability cornerstone* is a foundation for your team members to begin sharing in the team's overall results while remaining responsible as individuals. Distributing the burdens and successes of the team's work to everyone who is part of the team is your obligation as team manager. In nautical terms, although you may be the captain of the ship, every member of the crew shares responsibility for bringing the ship to its destination — and popping the cork to celebrate a successful voyage.

Evaluating the Team's Progress and Results

Teams don't perform as well as they can when most of the responsibility for the outcome of their work rests on your shoulders as manager. So, as manager, you need to instill a shared sense of accountability by including the team when assessing its progress and evaluating its results. This section explores the following three strategies for doing so:

- ✔ Holding status review meetings on a regular basis
- ✔ Reporting team results outward and upward in the organization
- ✔ Evaluating the team's overall performance

Each strategy can help your team focus on how it's performing while work is in progress and assess how it has performed once the work is done.

Conducting status review meetings

The name says it all: At a status review meeting, the team reviews the status of its work. You see how each team member is doing by checking off action items on the list of assignments given to him or her. Another key objective of the meeting is planning ahead for the next set of work assignments.

You may have participated in a good old-fashioned staff meeting typical of so many regular work groups, where all the members take turns talking for a few minutes about what they're doing. Because most of what's said doesn't pertain to others in the group, heads drop from drowsiness as people drone on. Occasional sparks may fly when someone tells about something that actually affects someone else, but those are rare occurrences. In regular work groups, people tend to do their own things in their jobs, so less of what concerns them pertains to the other members.

By comparison, when working in teams, each team member's part of the work affects the greater good of the team, so hearing what others have achieved is relevant to everyone else on the team. In addition, a good status review meeting focuses on what people are *getting done*, not merely what they're working on. The spotlight is on results, not activities.

For status review meetings to be useful, they need to happen on a regular basis . . . say once every week or two, depending on what the work dictates and on what team members need. The following three sections describe a good process to follow when you facilitate a status review meeting.

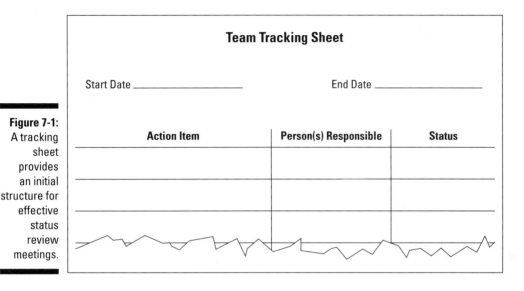

Figure 7-1:
A tracking
sheet
provides
an initial
structure for
effective
status
review
meetings.

People report progress first

The team tracking sheet shown in Figure 7-1 provides you with a structure for the first part of an effective status review meeting, which is like the team's show-and-tell time. Each team member reports what he or she has done, or not done, on the assignment for the team. A summary of this account then is written into the status column. Once the status column is completed for all team members, you have the minutes for this segment of the meeting ready to be published.

Make sure that you assign the task of filling in the status column and publishing the minutes to a *recorder* (sometimes called the *scribe*). You're facilitating the meeting, and you don't need to be doing two things at once. Share responsibilities with others on the team. Chapter 12 talks more about running a productive team meeting.

Next come the issues

Issues rise to the surface during individual team member reports and often can be discussed right away. Sometimes, no issues arise, so everything hums along. But at other times, issues or problems can be so big that separate meetings are needed to really tackle them.

Issues often center on team members not getting their work done. When that happens you merely need to ask questions like:

- ✔ What are you going to do to complete that assignment?
- ✔ What help do you need from other members of the team to get that work done?

✔ What steps need to be taken to overcome the obstacle that you've identified?

As your team's coach, do more asking than telling when you want to address issues. You don't need to have all the answers yourself. But you do need to ensure that issues that require answers get those answers. Involving the team members in the process by asking more than telling helps address the issues and reinforces accountability at the same time.

Finally, set action items for the next period

The meeting closes by pulling out a new team tracking sheet (Figure 7-1) and setting action items for the next period. Begin by determining when the next status review meeting will take place. Then ask each team member to name the action items they plan to accomplish by the next status review. In this planning phase of the meeting, you can help team members focus on the right assignments and remain realistic about what they can get done.

The status review meeting is one of the most important strategies that you can use in driving team performance and accountability. The significant benefits of the status review meeting are that it:

✔ **Influences positive peer-group pressure.** Everyone commits to getting work done and reporting their results at the next meeting. No one can run and hide in the background. As a result, peers know who's contributing and pulling their weight and who isn't. Team members often talk informally with one another between meetings, a type of exchange that helps everyone follow through and meet their commitments. At the same time, the status review helps you recognize who the reliable people are.

✔ **Keeps you in the loop without having to micromanage.** Status review meetings enable you, the manager, to watch team and individual members' progress without chasing people around and bugging them to find out. In addition, you can find out which people need your individual attention to keep them on track.

✔ **Develops planning skills.** The status review meeting teaches team members how to plan and how to make realistic commitments about what they can get done between meetings. After a few meetings, newcomers to this process usually become better at estimating so that they can present a more accurate picture of what they can truly get done. At the same time, they discover how to plan ahead and not just live day-by-day in their work — a valuable skill to develop that drives team performance.

✔ **Provides focus.** You *do* remember the focus cornerstone, don't you? Everyone knows who's responsible for what work, because everyone has a copy of the team's tracking sheet. Everyone knows the priorities, because they helped establish them.

✔ **Identifies issues for resolution.** When difficulties arise, the status review meeting becomes a forum for identifying them. The meeting helps you avoid situations in which team members struggle on their own in isolation. You hear what the issues are, and you involve the team in addressing them. No one is shot down for bringing a problem forward that affects the way an assignment gets done. And because problems are flushed out, the team makes progress.

✔ **Builds accountability.** Better accountability is, of course, the bottom line.

Your role in the status review meeting is to ask questions, clarifying what has or has not been done related to the team's action items. No public flogging is necessary when something doesn't get done. Team members know the situation and often are back on track by the next status review meeting. You can deal individually and privately with people who continually do not pull their weight.

Maximizing your meeting mileage

Because meetings are their lifeblood, teams need to hold themselves accountable for having productive meetings. I say more about meetings in Chapter 12, but, briefly, I suggest that you take the steps outlined in the following two sections to build productivity into your meetings.

Deciding what goes into an effective meeting

At one of its initial meetings, the team, with your guidance, establishes the criteria the team must meet for a gathering to be effective. Here's a handful of factors that you can use to score how you're doing with your team meetings:

✔ Meetings start and end on time.

✔ Members actively and constructively participate.

✔ The meeting has a defined and useful purpose.

✔ An agenda is prepared and distributed in advanced to meet the purpose of the meeting.

✔ Members come prepared for the meeting and are ready to act on their own action items.

✔ Everyone stays focused on the agenda.

✔ The meeting accomplishes results.

✔ Minutes are produced and published.

Talking about how the meeting went

At the first few team meetings and periodically thereafter, conclude the gathering by asking team members for their comments about how the team meeting went as determined by your success factors (see the previous section). Include the results of the discussion as part of the minutes.

Making meetings work

I once was asked to work with a group of four people who were trying to become a team. Their team meetings, however, were quite unfocused and sometimes contentious — "like cats and dogs fighting" as the manager put it. None of the members of the team saw the meetings as productive, yet each wanted meetings to work better.

So in the first of the meetings that I attended with the group, we listed the criteria of an effective meeting, beginning with having a clear purpose for meeting and an agenda. I provided some training about how to make meetings work productively.

After that, at the conclusion of each meeting (usually once every two weeks), the team routinely assessed how well it had met its effectiveness criteria. The first few times they barely met even half of the items. But they stuck with it, and after a short period of time, they were meeting every one of their criteria. They were addressing issues, reviewing progress and results, and carrying on a focused and constructive discussion.

The difference between their first, floundering attempts at meeting and these highly productive sessions was simple: They'd fashioned a measuring stick and could assess progress, which they did with pride. Conducting productive meetings became their expectation — accountability at its best.

If the team has trouble meeting more than a few of the items on the list of effectiveness criteria, use that shortcoming as an issue for future problem-solving with the team. Seeking improvements to the point where the team is effectively meeting all its meeting success criteria is the idea.

By closing meetings with a few minutes of assessment, you build accountability into your team meetings.

Reporting Results Outward and Upward

People outside the team, like management above you and groups affected by what your team does, may sometimes wonder, "Just what are you folks accomplishing?" You can answer that question with two strategies that add to the accountability cornerstone and help meet the needs of interested parties outside your team. Those strategies are outlined in the next two sections.

Publishing a summary report

A summary report is a written progress review of your team's work. The report isn't only for the team's use. It also is for broadcasting the team's progress and results to those outside the team who want or need to know. Generally, you want to publish the team's summary reports at reasonable intervals — once a month to once a quarter often works best.

A good summary report gives those outside the team a picture of its progress. So stick to the highlights and avoid globs of detail. Keep the length reasonably brief. Here's the sort of content you can include:

- Status reviews of important work issues
- Progress reports against key performance measures or indicators, if relevant
- Overview of any significant results
- Plans for the next period of time
- Other relevant news, business- and personnel-related

Because a summary report displays the team's performance, everyone on the team needs to play a role in putting the report together. Don't fall into the trap of being the only one who prepares and compiles the report every time. Your role as manager is best accomplished when you review the final draft. Make the report part of the team's work and ask team members how they want to do the work. Depending on how involved your report needs to be, each member can contribute in part to the report while one or two people are responsible for tying it all together.

How to sell anything to management

Mike led a cross-functional task team whose purpose was developing and proposing new personnel policies for the company. About once every quarter, the team presented its policy recommendations to the senior management group.

While preparing for the presentation, the team outlined the content and order in which its recommendations would be presented and decided who would speak when. The usual routine was to define the problem, talk about research, highlight the proposed policy, and finally describe the benefits of the recommendation and how to implement it. Team members took time to rehearse — every one of the eight team members had a speaking part. Mike usually handled the opening and any transitions that were needed. During a period of a year and

a half, the team presented proposals half a dozen times, and every one of its recommendations was accepted, although sometimes acceptance included modifications. Many members of the senior management group made a point to thank the team for its hard work and thoughtful presentations.

Mike, reflecting on the experience, sometimes joked that his task team could have sold management dirty socks if they had tried. Management was so impressed by how well organized and thorough the task team came across. It was something they seldom saw in the company. Management also said that the substance of what was presented mattered less than the way the team came across, which is what really sold the proposals.

When everyone on the team shares in reporting progress, everyone becomes accountable for results.

Making a team presentation

The second useful strategy for "spreading the wealth" about your team's progress is making presentations to management above you or to other groups that are interested in your team's work. These are live, face-to-face events — teleconferencing is fine, too — where the entire team gets involved. A presentation is most useful when you want to:

- ✔ Provide recommendations
- ✔ Explain plans for upcoming special events
- ✔ Share important research findings
- ✔ Report results from significant work

Presentations help other people, especially those in management, understand what your team is doing. They build support for the team. Presentations also serve as forums where your team receives feedback for revising or fine-tuning its work, which sometimes is a way of testing the waters before plunging forward with a plan.

Because the stakes are high, you want to make sure that your team looks good when it delivers a presentation. Here are a few tips:

- ✔ **Getting everyone into the act.** Even though some team members may prefer having root canal to standing up and speaking before a group, the presentation is far more impressive to an audience when all members of the team contribute. Whenever you or only a few do all the talking, the rest of the team looks like useless furniture.

  But not everyone has to be a soloist. You may want to create some reporting "duets," matching more confident presenters with others who aren't so confident, thus helping people overcome stage fright.

- ✔ **Organizing like crazy!** With your team, you can plan the key information that you want to present and the supporting materials you need, such as slides and charts. Be sure to determine the order that you and other speakers will follow when making key points. The time of the presentation also is important. Generally, shorter is better in formal group presentations. Whenever you're planning to go longer than an hour, you'd better have a good reason! To be on the safe side, tell the meeting sponsor in advance how long your presentation will be — and make adjustments if necessary.

When you organize, think what the intended audience most wants to hear and what work bests for that audience. One choice is making the presentation in chronological order — from past to present to recommendations for the future — explaining what issues you've encountered and how you propose to resolve them. Or, you can start by showing the positive results that have already been gained and then revert to the beginning as a means of showing how you arrived at those gains.

Remind your team that you're seeking to gain the interest and support of others, not to bore them to death. Significant points need to stand out sharply with only necessary details added as supporting information. You want your team members to show that they know what's most important in their work — audiences are impressed when they see that your people understand that point.

✔ **Assigning parts.** Determine with your team members who will present what parts of the presentation, factoring in personal areas of interest or expertise. Having a formal introduction and conclusion makes you appear more organized. You have a part as manager — possibly the opening, or the close, or both, but you want to make sure you're not dominant. You want your entire team to be on display for the presentation. They're the musicians; you're the conductor.

You also need to determine how and when you want to respond to questions so that the team is prepared to field any challenges that come its way. Asking the audience to hold its questions and comments until after the presentation is a good way of avoiding interruptions to the flow of the presentation that can send you off track.

✔ **Rehearsing.** Of course, allow time for a rehearsal or two. Rehearsing not only provides team members with the practice they need to give a polished presentation, it also familiarizes everyone with the entire presentation and not only their individual parts. In fact, you want your team members to be ready to cover for one another in the event someone isn't there on the big day — state this expectation upfront and make it standard practice going forward.

Evaluating Team Performance

Your journey toward strong team performance and a sense of shared accountability continues. Two checkpoints lie ahead and both are about evaluating overall team performance. (Evaluating *individual* performance most likely is your job exclusively as manager.) Buckle up for the tour.

Conducting postmortems (without a body)

In medical jargon, a postmortem is an examination of a body after the person has died. For teams, death isn't involved (at least you hope not). A team postmortem is an evaluation of performance after a project or special event has concluded. The idea is to learn lessons from the past (using hindsight), the pluses and minuses, and then to apply them to future performance. A project postmortem is most relevant when your team knows it will take on similar projects in the future.

When you don't stop long enough to evaluate what's going right and what's going wrong, you're doomed to repeat your mistakes and squander your successes.

A postmortem is best conducted as a team meeting. Reviewing the past and then planning for the future is a good method to use.

  ✔ **Reviewing the past.** Ask team members for individual comments on two questions: What went well in the team's performance? What didn't go as well? Record individual comments on a board or flipchart as they're offered by team members, but hold off on discussion until everyone has contributed. Then discuss and draw conclusions. You can highlight all the good outcomes as guidance for future performance and all the bad outcomes as opportunities for improvement.

  ✔ **Planning the future.** Ask the team members to brainstorm ideas that will be most useful to apply in the future. Chapter 9 gives you specific tools that help you facilitate a brainstorming session and evaluate the ideas that are put forth.

Make sure that you document the postmortem so the team has some history (or basis) to apply when the next performance evaluation comes around. That's how an evaluation tool becomes a tool for planning and improving the quality of team performance — accountability at its best.

Conducting a performance evaluation

A team performance evaluation is similar to a postmortem. It's an evaluation of the team's overall performance at the end of a given cycle, generally at the end of a quarter or six-month period. It's a scheduled event, and the team is responsible for making it happen, evaluating results against established performance criteria that are selected in advance. This isn't you (the manager) evaluating the team but rather the team evaluating itself, including your input.

You have two jobs as manager:

✔ Making sure the team selects criteria for evaluating its performance and knows where data is coming from.

✔ Gathering all relevant data, such as computer-generated statistics and similar documentation and possibly surveys of external and internal customers, asking them to evaluate the team's performance in delivering its services.

With data in hand, your team is ready to start the evaluation meeting. Remember that focusing on total performance, instead of the work of particular team members, is important. As you facilitate the meeting, do the following:

✔ **Compare results to performance criteria.** With team members, go through each performance factor, such as goals or standards, that's being evaluated and have them report the data that describes the results. Enable team members to include their own observations but keep the focus on measurable results. Remember to have someone taking notes.

✔ **Solve problems; plan for the future.** This second part of the meeting needs to be as long as, or longer than, the first. When critical issues or problems affecting the team's past performance arise, use this time for generating ideas for solutions and establishing performance plans that help you move forward. You may have to set new goals, update performance standards, or modify other performance criteria. As always, take notes so that the team's plans aren't left only to memory.

Reflecting on past successes helps a team learn from what it has done well.

Peer Feedback: Rating Each Other's Performance

For any team that's going to be together for an extended period, *peer feedback* is one of the stronger strategies for building accountability among individual team members. Don't be surprised, however, if some team members are scared to death of the idea, because they may be used to complaining about others behind their backs (and even enjoying it, maybe). That means they're not used to talking openly and directly about matters of behavior and performance when everyone is present. So be careful. Avoid plunking everyone down around a table and declaring open season on personal assessment. That's a formula for disaster. You can, however, set the stage for a productive peer-feedback session in which everyone is comfortable and from which everyone profits, simply by educating your team, using a good feedback questionnaire, and following certain ground rules during discussion.

Educating the team

The key to educating your team is making sure that everyone understands that *constructive feedback* means describing what you observe about another person's behavior — what you see that person doing — as opposed to voicing an opinion or an assumption about what he or she is doing or why he or she is acting a certain way. In short, constructive feedback focuses on observations, not interpretations, and it is far more factual and objective than an employee opinion survey. Constructive feedback is the same as *describing*, a communication tool that I describe in detail in Chapter 10.

You can show your team members the meaning of constructive feedback and familiarize them with the process of a peer-feedback session by:

- **Performing a written assessment.** Team members fill out a feedback questionnaire (see Figure 7-2) about each of their fellow team members, including you (when you're an active part of their day-to-day interactions).

- **Summarizing the findings.** Data gathered from the questionnaires is summarized into individual composite reports for each team member. This needs to be done by a neutral party, such as the company human resources staff, a department administrative staff member, or an outside consultant.

- **Openly discussing the findings.** In a team meeting, each team member, speaking one at a time, shares his or her feedback results from the summary reports. You encourage other team members to offer comments to help provide insight to the individual team member, who then establishes goals for moving forward based on the feedback.

Designing the questionnaire

For guidance when designing the content of a good feedback questionnaire, take a look at your team guidelines (Chapter 5). Team guidelines are expectations and commitments developed *by* everyone on the team *for* everyone on the team. They define behaviors — how team members perform and work with others, helping the team achieve its targets.

Figure 7-2 shows you the first page of a sample team feedback questionnaire. As you can see, each question requires you to choose a number that describes the frequency the behavior occurs and to provide a brief statement of observations to back up your rating. (Do you see why educating team members on the difference between observations and interpretations is so important?) Insist that team members write observations for all the questions. Remind them that they can also do a self-assessment to keep for comparison.

Team Member Feedback Questionnaire
(A few sample questions)

Feedback for _____

Part I

A. Based on your experience with this team member, rate the frequency each action described has occurred according to the following scale:

5 = Frequently
4 = More often than not
3 = Some of the time
2 = Occasionally
1 = Seldom

B. Then provide your observations NOT interpretations to explain the basis of your rating.

1. This team member communicates with others in a clear and constructive manner.
RATING: _____
OBSERVATIONS:

2. This team member listens to others in a respectful manner and shows understanding of what others have to say.
RATING: _____
OBSERVATIONS:

3. This team member shares information openly that keeps others well informed.
RATING: _____
OBSERVATIONS:

4. This team member works with others on the team in a helpful and cooperative manner.
RATING: _____
OBSERVATIONS:

Figure 7-2:
Team member feedback questionnaire.

Having team members assess eight to ten key teamwork-related behaviors often works well. In Part II of the questionnaire, you can ask for comments on two open-ended questions like the following:

- ✔ What does this team member do well in his or her interactions and performance with this team?

- ✔ What should this team member work on to improve his or her effectiveness as a positive contributor to this team?

Allow plenty of time for team members to complete these questionnaires. On the first occasion, giving the instructions and having everyone complete the questionnaires right on the spot is best. Place their finished work into envelopes and pass them along for the neutral party to prepare the summary reports. Give the neutral party ample time; a few weeks to a month usually is sufficient When the summaries are back, hold a feedback meeting as soon as possible; you don't want this stuff to get stale.

Running the feedback session

The peer-feedback session is a special meeting that may take up to half a day. At this meeting, you want to enforce ground rules that assure constructive participation and respectful listening. Remind team members that the focus is on the content of observations rather than on the person who made the observations — on *what's* being said rather than *who* is saying it. Here's a good agenda to follow for facilitating the meeting:

- ✔ Have team members silently read their own feedback reports, asking them to note two important factors as they read:

    - Points that need clarification

    - Key messages they're getting from the feedback, from positive to negative

- ✔ After providing everyone with copies of the composite reports so they can follow along, take turns — one person at a time in the discussion phase — having each person present his or her own feedback summary. Everyone starts by asking for clarification on points where needed and then offering their own take on key messages they observe in their own reports. Encourage other team members to reinforce or add to those messages. Open and honest dialogue is what it's all about.

- ✔ Ask the person who's in the spotlight to develop and work on at least one personal goal that improves teamwork, having other team members assist in this effort. Then move on to the next person and the next. How long does this all take? My experience is that feedback discussion can run from 20 minutes to an hour per person.

- ✔ When everyone has finished, including you, do a quick debriefing: Ask members of your team. How did peer feedback go? When will you do it again?

Peer feedback in the executive suite

One of the more interesting peer-feedback sessions that I've ever facilitated was with a company president and his five vice-presidents. The president was trying to build an executive management team, but he faced some working relationship problems that affected team dynamics, and he thought a facilitated feedback session might help.

Each executive first filled out a feedback questionnaire calling for observations about other team members, following a set of guidelines dealing with cooperation and communication for effective team dynamics. I assisted team members, as needed, ensuring that they each provided complete feedback comments. I also compiled the summary reports.

On the day of the feedback session, the six executives were as anxious as any team I'd ever seen. When I handed out their individual summary reports to read and analyze, they looked like honor students churning away at the final exam.

The president spoke first — we had set this structure up in advance, hoping to break the ice.

He summarized the key messages in his report and turned to other members of the team for discussion. His openness in admitting his shortcomings, which were identified in his feedback report, set the tone for the rest of the meeting. Each person was received with lively dialogue. Issues among team members that had been simmering below the surface finally were recognized and discussed, and everyone set a goal to make improvements. When the session ended, you could feel a great sense of relief in the room. People remarked how, although initially painful, the experience had been positive and fruitful.

The high point of this peer-feedback session, I thought, was when the last vice-president spoke. He had received the most positive report of anyone. And with great humor, his teammates complained that they had nothing to complain about with him. In the end, he was recognized as the executive role model — the one who had built collaborative and respectful working relationships.

Some team members may find the initial peer-feedback session quite a challenge. It's important for you to set and enforce ground rules that support active listening and constructive dialogue. You don't want team members reacting defensively to their feedback reports.

Conducting peer-feedback sessions on a quarterly or half-yearly basis provides the full benefit of this accountability strategy. Conducting these sessions right after a team evaluation sometimes is a good idea (see the "Evaluating Team Performance" section earlier in this chapter). Ideally, as peer feedback becomes a normal practice for the team, you can skip the part about compiling composite reports. When you reach the stage where team members openly give feedback to one another on the criteria, you have a mature team.

Realizing the benefits of peer feedback

When you design a peer-feedback session as an observations-based, criteria-driven sharing of information related to effective teamwork, you and members of your team stand to gain several important benefits, including:

- **Reinforced individual accountability.** Peer feedback involves everyone in the process of assessing individual actions that help or hinder the team's performance — shared accountability at its best.

- **Open and honest dialogue.** Peer-feedback sessions help you discover how to give and receive open, honest, and constructive feedback and to validate the practice as a routine part of good management practices. Quite often after only one or two sessions, you can see team members informally exchanging feedback with one another.

- **Positive peer-group pressure for individual improvement**. Peer feedback doesn't relieve you of responsibility for dealing with individual performance problems. But the process helps you identify where improvements are needed with each individual. Performance issues come to the surface and people are asked to do something about them. The message to individuals is: Take steps to improve your teamwork and performance — we're all watching and expecting it from you.

- **Recognition of outstanding team members.** When team members are pulling their weight, working cooperatively with others, and interacting respectfully with fellow team members, just to give a few examples, those behaviors are reported in peer-feedback sessions. Recognition among your peers is a great motivator.

Teams that can provide supportive and challenging feedback to one another, without depending on you, the manager, can push themselves to the highest performance levels.

Reinforcing Good Performance

An old line about motivation that I frequently use with managers and executives says, *Behavior that's rewarded is repeated.* This maxim applies to individuals and teams. Elsewhere in this chapter I talk about the importance of team evaluations, team presentations, and postmortems as sources of positive reinforcement. A few more strategies that reinforce good team performance include:

✓ **Assessing team success.** Sometimes in the midst of working hard to achieve good results, the reasons for your success are overlooked. So take time to assess why you and your team are successful, recognizing good team and individual performances.

✓ **Celebrating with an outing.** Chapter 6 goes into detail about celebrating. But briefly, you can plan to go off-site for a celebration marking the team's success — a dinner, a movie, a ballgame, a trip to an amusement park, a night at the theater, whatever the team finds rewarding, and at company expense, of course.

✓ **Getting some ink in the company newsletter.** Without gloating too much, highlight your team's achievements with an article in the company's newsletter. An article in the newsletter also lets others (who may not have a clue) know exactly what your team does and can lead to further informal recognition via conversations with other employees prompted by the item appearing in the company newsletter.

✓ **Sending letters upward.** Writing a letter to your boss about the team's accomplishments can work even better than your routine reports of progress and results. The idea is to tell management above you about the good things your team is achieving. And if the boss doesn't get the hint, encourage him or her to drop by to express a little of that good old-fashioned appreciation.

A little clapping of hands by you at the right moment goes a long way in motivating and reinforcing high standards of performance. Your team will catch on and join the applause. Your bosses will, too.

Teams are made up of individuals, and you want to recognize individual good work — without creating resentment among others. A key strategy is to offer this positive reinforcement one-on-one, not in a public forum. Here are a few ways to do it:

"The Recognizer" enforces recognition

Making sure that no good work by an individual goes unrecognized, one team that I know of created a rotating role they call "The Recognizer." This person — you can think of him or her as an *enforcer* of sorts — serves as the eyes and ears of the team, with plenty of backup from everyone else. When a team member makes some form of positive contribution to the team, The Recognizer's job isn't to issue the recognition, but rather it's his or her job to speak with others working with that individual and to make sure that *they* publicly recognize their teammate's good efforts.

✔ **Giving positive feedback.** Behavior that's rewarded is repeated. (Yeah, I know, I've said that before, but it's important.) When you notice and acknowledge what individual team members do on an ongoing basis (their own work and their contributions that enhance teamwork), you reinforce that behavior. One of the simplest and most powerful ways of reinforcing good performance is giving *positive feedback,* verbally acknowledging an incident of good performance with specific observations, not general statements — which is the difference between positive feedback and praise. So you say, "What I noticed you did well on that assignment was *(fill in the specifics)*." That's a lot better than simply saying, "Great job!"

✔ **Passing feedback to the individual's manager.** When you're leading a project team or a task team, you're usually managing people who aren't your direct reports or regular staff. But reinforcing accountability with them doesn't mean that they have to be your direct reports. So tell them periodically that you'll pass on significant news about their performance to their managers — and you hope most of it is *good* news. Remember to copy team members on whatever you pass on about them electronically.

✔ **Encouraging team members to acknowledge one another's performance.** You're not the only one responsible for providing recognition. Team members are, too. They're in the trenches everyday and they know what's happening. Let them know it isn't only okay but it's expected that they pat each other on the back — and tell them to let you know, too, when it's an exceptionally good performance they're recognizing. See Chapter 10 for more on this topic.

Part IV
Developing Tools for Productive Team Players

The 5th Wave   By Rich Tennant

You ever get the feeling some of the deputies are beginning to lose focus?

In this part . . .

Part IV contains tips and tools for developing strong team members and explores the critical team skills that help team members to work effectively together.

Chapter 8

Communicating: Listening and Speaking at Your Best

. . . .

In This Chapter

▶ Recognizing what listening is all about

▶ Developing a talent for skillful listening

▶ Getting better at *assertive* speaking

▶ Polishing your speaking style — using *all* of you

. . . .

*T*he skills that team members need to work together effectively begin at a simple level: listening and speaking. Interpersonal communication is the core of a team's ability to function and perform and usually makes the difference between success and failure.

The scary part is that most people become a part of teams without the tools they need to speak and listen really well. The reason is that they've never been educated. Think about it: What do school kids spend most of their time being taught? Listening and speaking? Reading and writing? Or daydreaming?

Okay, daydreaming isn't a part of the curriculum. So, the answer is reading and writing, the skills that provide you with basic literacy. But speaking and listening — the interpersonal channels of communication — seldom are taught. Through no fault of their own, most adults who enter the workforce — and become part of your team — are functionally illiterate when it comes to interpersonal communications.

This chapter provides you with insights and tools that you need to empower your team members to communicate well with one another — listening well and speaking to be heard and understood.

Listening Effectively: There's More Than Meets the Eye and the Ear

Ever play the telephone game as a kid? You remember how it goes: A group of people stand single file and the first person whispers a message to the next person, who passes it to the next person, and so on down the line until the message reaches the last person. When I use this activity with the teams that I help, I like to start a second and different message moving from the other end of the line. That way, two messages are going at the same time through the line, crossing one another. As you can imagine, the messages that emerge at the ends of the line don't much resemble the messages that started out at the beginning of the line.

The telephone game is a pretty good way to describe how communication often works in teams. Interactions can be rife with miscommunication and misunderstanding — the twin enemies of teamwork.

Tuning in to the full message

To listen effectively, you must know what to listen for — and what to watch for. A speaker's message to you contains three pieces:

- Words
- Tone of voice
- Body language

Words are the verbal component of the message. They tell you *what* the person is saying. Tone of voice and body language are the *nonverbal* components of the message. They're *how* the message is being said, and they greatly influence the overall meaning of the message. Body language consists of facial expressions, hand gestures, and the other movements people use when they speak.

To show how nonverbal components affect the overall meaning of a message, stand in front of a mirror and say this message in an upbeat tone:

> **"You've been a positive contributor on this project."**

Now say the same words but this time with a sarcastic tone. What happens between the first and second messages? Is your smile replaced by a frown or maybe by rolling your eyes? (By the way, this is a fun and insightful activity to do with your team.) Although the words stay the same, the message is totally different in meaning.

An entire message contains verbal and nonverbal components. You can remember with this formula:

Content + Emotion = *The Meaning of a Message*

The *content* of a message is expressed through the words the speaker chooses — the verbal component. The *emotion* in a message usually is expressed nonverbally by tone of voice and body language. People at times state their emotions — I'm happy, I'm sad — but more often they exhibit their emotions instead of actually telling you what they are.

Capturing a person's total message involves listening as much with your eyes as with your ears. It's called reading the message. When you're on the phone with someone and can't see the other person's body language, tune in to the tone of voice to pick up on the emotion that is being expressed with the content.

Tuning in to the message requires concentration — your attention focused totally on the speaker. This is how you do it:

- ✔ Turn and face the speaker.
- ✔ Provide steady eye contact.
- ✔ Show a sincere, interested facial expression.
- ✔ Maintain an open and alert posture.

As you can see from this little list, tuning in and capturing the speaker's full message depends greatly on *your* nonverbal behavior.

Sometimes as listeners you and I turn off the person who's speaking to us by:

- ✔ **Looking away.** When you look at other people, your watch, or other distractions, the person speaking to you begins to think your attention has strayed.

- ✔ **Doing two things at once.** This kind of behavior is rampant in offices across the country today, and it's a real conversation wrecker. You may get a rush out of multitasking — for example, keyboarding or answering the phone while someone else is trying to speak directly to you. However, the message you're actually sending is: "I'm rude, dude." As one person recently said to me, "It's top of the list for how to royally irritate a fellow team member."

- ✔ **Showing looks of disapproval.** Scowling, rolling your eyes, furrowing your eyebrows . . . without saying a word, you put up a barrier that usually startles and turns off a speaker.

- ✔ **Fidgeting.** Tapping fingers, pens, and pencils; twirling paper clips and hair; pulling on chains and other jewelry . . . Can't you sit still?

✔ **Slouching.** Nothing is wrong with listening in a relaxed manner, but slouching, leaning way back in your chair, putting your feet on the desk . . . Look, that's just too relaxed. Your posture sends the message that you don't consider the conversation important, even when you do.

✔ **Reacting with sharpness in your tone of voice.** When your tone shows that you're reacting strongly in any negative way — sarcasm, defensiveness, or disdain to name a few — most speakers won't try to continue communicating with you.

Tuning in and fully reading a speaker's message begins when you become open and receptive with your nonverbal behavior.

Role-playing is an entertaining way to reinforce the importance of listening attentively. Divide your team into pairs and give each pair a few minutes to plan a conversation that shows bad nonverbal behavior in:

✔ Eye contact

✔ Positioning yourself in the conversation

✔ Facial expression

✔ Movement

✔ Posture

✔ Tone of voice

With each pair, one person is designated the speaker and the other is the listener. As they act out their conversation, the audience shouts out which bad habit is being demonstrated. You can have the pairs follow up by demonstrating the opposite, good nonverbal behavior.

Finding your level on the listening scale

People learn to listen in four different ways. The most effective way is *active listening*. But the default mode for many people is *passive listening* or *selective listening*, and neither one works well. When people really make an effort to listen, they can ratchet up and become *attentive listeners*.

But the highest and best level of listening is called active listening. And wouldn't you know, it's also the least used method. Setting you up to be an active listener is my goal in this section. Look at these definitions to find out what kind of listener you are right now:

✔ **Passive listener** He shows up for a conversation but you'd hardly know it. He sits there quietly but does little more. If the conversation is on the phone, you may hear a few uh-huhs but that's about it. Maybe you can blame passive listening on a person's upbringing — some kids never forget a scolding about being seen but not heard. As adults they continue to sit quietly in a conversation, passively listening, and frustrating a speaker who wonders if anything is getting through.

✔ **Selective listener.** She hears what she wants to hear. When what you're saying doesn't interest her, a selective listener almost ignores you — glancing away, looking down at her watch, or focusing her attention elsewhere. You may get a perfunctory, "That's nice," out of her but nothing to suggest that she's actually listening. On the other hand, when something you say doesn't please her — and it can be almost anything, she isn't that particular — a selective listener may become quite hostile, interrupting you with critical remarks and turning judgmental. In both patterns of selective listening, the listener isn't hearing the full message. The result places stress and strain on a conversation, promoting divisiveness rather than the cohesiveness that a team needs.

✔ **Attentive listener.** He maintains eye contact with the speaker and asks questions to draw out the speaker's message. This usually makes the speaker feel free to express the message. But an attentive listener often doesn't go all the way. He deals with the tangible part of the speaker's message — the content — which is expressed verbally. But he may overlook the nonverbal components of the message, failing to acknowledge or explore the emotional side of the message. So an attentive listener can tell you what the speaker is talking about but may fail to capture fully what the person means.

✔ **Active listener.** She captures the speaker's full message — the facts and the feelings, the verbal and the nonverbal components. Active listening is about listening with care and respect and verbally acknowledging what the speaker is saying. Sometimes called *responsive listening* or *reflective listening,* active listening is the only form of listening that checks out what the speaker's message means from the speaker's point of view and without passing judgment on it. That's *empathy.* An active listener provides verbal feedback to the speaker, clarifying and confirming that the message expressed is understood — the opposite of passive listening. Active listening helps speakers because they know they are being heard and understood.

Making Active Listening Work for Your Team

Active listening — I define it in the previous section — is a skill that you and your team members can perfect and use every day for better interpersonal communication. This section lays out tools and techniques that everyone can adopt to become better at active listening, plus a few warnings about what pitfalls to avoid. The five tools of active listening are:

- Door openers
- Probes
- Reflections on feelings
- Paraphrasing
- Reflective paraphrasing

Opening the door to a good conversation

Door openers are signals that you give to a speaker that let her know you're paying attention, both nonverbal and verbal signals. Here are examples of *nonverbal* door openers:

- Stopping whatever you're doing, turning, and facing the speaker
- Maintaining steady eye contact
- Looking interested or concerned as appropriate
- Nodding your head
- Looking patient
- Leaning forward slightly in your chair
- Maintaining a relaxed but alert posture

Here are examples of *verbal* door openers:

- "Uh huh" and "Um hum"
- "I see"
- "Okay"
- "Right"
- "Really?"
- "Sure!"
- "Yeah"
- "Yes!"
- "Wow!"

Door openers mean nothing more than you're showing an interest, following along, and wanting to hear more. Your tone of voice with verbal door openers needs to be sincere and nonjudgmental. Otherwise, door openers may have the opposite effect — they may be door closers!

Drawing out a speaker with probing questions

Probing with questions is a listening tool that you can use to draw out and add depth to the speaker's message. By asking open-ended questions you can move the speaker beyond short answers and help him reveal more details about his topic.

Open-ended questions often begin with words like *what, how, tell me, describe,* and *explain.* Here are examples:

- ✔ What are the key findings of your report?

- ✔ How did you come to the conclusions mentioned in the report?

- ✔ Tell me more about the idea that you think will help the team.

- ✔ Please describe an example to illustrate your point.

- ✔ Please explain your thinking behind this recommendation.

When asking a speaker for these responses (using your probing tools), you shouldn't lead the speaker toward answering in a prescribed way but rather toward communicating freely. In other words, open-ended questions have no right or wrong answers.

When you probe, you're being inquisitive. You're *not* conducting an inquisition or interrogation!

Reflecting feelings that you hear and see

When you *reflect feelings* that you are picking up in a message (they're usually nonverbal cues), you're acting like a mirror. You reflect back, or run a check, on the emotions that you think you sense which carry significant weight to the meaning of the message. You do it by saying things like:

- ✔ You're feeling excited about what happen?

- ✔ Sounds like that was a frustrating situation. Is that right?

- ✔ I sense you've become worried. Is that so?

- ✔ Seems like you had a fun time, correct?

Your reflection is phrased in a question-like manner, because you're inviting a response from your speaker, confirming or clarifying what you think you heard. That's understanding gained right on the spot! And you avoid the cross-examiner style. Thus the wording, as in the examples, is meant to be soft and easy — the reflective nature of the tool.

Paraphrasing to capture the content

Paraphrasing means summarizing the main idea of the speaker's message, not all the details, so you can check whether you understand its content.

Similar to when you reflect feelings, a paraphrase is one sentence to which you sometimes tag on an ending like "Is that right?" to show that you're seeking confirmation. Showing that you're truly paying attention, the paraphrase is in your own words, not the words that the speaker is using. Often a paraphrase begins with starter phrases like, "What you're saying is that (such and such) is important to you. Is that right?" Here are some variations:

- ✔ "So what you mean is . . ."
- ✔ "In other words . . ."
- ✔ "As I understand your point, it's . . ."

Reflective paraphrasing: Checking content and emotion

Reflective paraphrasing is a combo version (but please hold the pickles and the lettuce). As the name implies, it combines the tools of reflecting feelings with paraphrasing when both carry important weight in the overall meaning of a message.

Reflective paraphrasing occurs all in one sentence. Here are a couple of examples:

- ✔ "You appear to be feeling frustrated because none of your proposals have received any comment from management so far. Is that so?"
- ✔ "Because you were able to find out so much, that experience turned out to be rewarding for you. Is that right?"

Dodging pitfalls

As your team members begin applying the tools of active listening, check their verbal responses, making sure that in their enthusiasm for gaining an understanding of the speaker's message they're not, in fact, creating barriers for the speaker. That can happen oh-so-easily when team members slip into bad habits like:

✔ **Criticizing.** The rule is: Don't become a critic until you thoroughly understand what the speaker is saying. It's amazing how a solid understanding sweeps away hasty criticism. So remind team members to hold off passing judgment and, instead, go for understanding first and foremost.

✔ **Reacting defensively.** You don't have to like or agree with everything someone else says to be an active listener — not at all. But when you react with verbal counterattacks or agitated responses, you show only that you can't listen and understand anything at all.

✔ **Debating.** Some people get a kick out of sparring with the speaker, challenging and debating nearly every point the speaker makes. But when a speaker thinks he must defend his message, he may be inhibited from getting the full message across, and that blocks understanding.

✔ **Giving advice.** Although many people like to give advice, it is best received only when it is requested. Not every concern expressed by a speaker is a problem looking for a solution. Active listeners do far better when they show understanding first, which is also the first step for good problem solving when a problem truly does exist.

✔ **Shifting the focus to yourself.** When your responses to someone else's message concern mostly me, myself, and I, you're no longer listening. You're dominating the conversation. No, thank you!

As your team members get into the swing of active listening, you may see them begin to kid one another when they spot a listening tool being applied — or ignored — on the job. Don't be alarmed when they joke around this way, because they're mastering a new skill, and humor helps them get through their initial discomfort. It's okay for you to join in the kidding and share in the laughter.

Speaking So That People Listen — and Get Your Point

This section is your reference for guiding team members to become better at expressing themselves to others. Just like training for active listening, training for interacting effectively as a speaker mostly is ignored in school. People seldom are taught how to convey important messages positively and work through issues and differences constructively with others — keys for team functioning and success. So as you initiate this work with your team, work on building people's awareness, beginning with rooting out bad habits.

Changing old speaking habits

I won't ask for a show of hands, but if one of the following three kinds of speaking behaviors describes you, you know what to work on. But don't worry — you're not alone, and the only way to measure progress is to see where you are at the outset.

These three speaking approaches — aggressive, nonassertive, and passive-aggressive — seem to pop out in times of great challenge and stress. Teams certainly can be a Mecca for challenge and stress, so building awareness of these habits is a good way to introduce new and better habits.

The aggressive approach

Aggressive communication is a hard-charging approach with a manner that often comes across as harsh, controlling, and dominating. Some common behaviors you see when people express themselves with the aggressive approach are:

- Demanding and ordering
- Raising the voice to a loud volume to push a point of view
- Being blunt with words and sharp with tone in expressing a message.
- Taking the my-way-or-the-highway stance for dealing with a disagreement.
- Blaming the other person when a problem occurs.
- Using profanity and making personal insults.
- Using intimidating body language such as finger pointing, hovering over someone, and invading someone's personal space.

As you can see, nothing is subtle about the aggressive approach. It's a push-hard tactic for getting what you want. But this approach often invites confrontation or avoidance by others who dislike or are intimidated by harsh mannerisms, and neither of those responses spurs good teamwork.

The nonassertive approach

Nonassertive communication comes across as passive, and because the speaker makes little effort to state a point of view, others are likely to take control. These behaviors are what you see when people express themselves in a nonassertive way:

- Sitting quietly in a team meeting and barely offering a thought
- Speaking hesitantly and softly
- Beating around the bush while trying to make an important point
- Avoiding dealing with tough problems or issues of concern to others

✔ Sounding helpless and remarking that nothing can be done about a problem

✔ Devaluing his contributions with words like, "I'm not sure this is a good idea"

✔ Showing withdrawal in body language and making little direct eye contact

✔ Offering little verbal response in listening to a speaker

As you can see, the nonassertive approach is a sit-back-and-blend-in-quietly form of communication, which isn't helpful when you need team members to contribute ideas and tackle problems.

The passive-aggressive approach

Passive-aggressive communication is negative in effect but subtle in manner. It tends to inflict damage without leaving a trace, or at least that's what the receiver feels. Look for these kinds of behaviors:

✔ Appearing to agree with and accept a commitment yet not following through or doing something entirely different, and even later denying that an agreement ever was made.

✔ Using sarcasm or subtle put-downs concerning ideas or people.

✔ Talking behind a person's back.

✔ Sending venting-type messages — "flaming e-mails" — to other team members (and copying third parties) rather than speaking directly and personally to the other person.

✔ Rolling the eyes or sighing in disgust or displeasure when someone else is speaking.

✔ Second-guessing, saying in effect, "I knew that wouldn't work," or "I told you so," after the fact.

✔ Inflicting revenge by withholding information or ignoring someone — otherwise known as the silent treatment.

✔ Expressing a message in words that sound positive yet displaying a facial expression or a tone of voice that gives the opposite impression.

The passive-aggressive approach usually stirs anxiety and turmoil — behavior that can be divisive in a team situation.

Stressful and challenging situations bring out the worst in all of us from time to time. Keep in mind that unproductive communication is about *patterns of behavior* and not about people. The idea is for every team member to be aware of his or her own behavior in exceptional circumstances. That's how you know where to begin making improvements.

Adopting the productive approach: Assertive speaking

Assertive speaking means expressing yourself in a positive and confident manner and allowing others to do the same. This manner of speaking is far more effective than the aggressive, nonassertive, and passive-aggressive approaches, because it promotes a two-way conversation and a collaborative effort to communicate.

When you speak assertively, you are

> ✓ **Being direct.** You get to the point of your message, clearly and tactfully.
>
> ✓ **Listening actively.** You hear and understand what others have to say. You're willing to have two-way conversation.
>
> ✓ **Making the sense of importance clear.** You leave the listener in no doubt about how important the topic is to you.
>
> ✓ **Taking initiative and responsibility.** If a call needs to be made, you'll make it. If dialogue needs to begin, you'll begin it. You accept responsibility, neither making excuses nor blaming others.
>
> ✓ **Expressing confident nonverbal behavior.** You look people in the eye, you speak to be heard easily with energy in your voice, you gesture appropriately to emphasize a point, and you have a sincere tone.
>
> ✓ **Collaborating to address concerns and problems.** When you have an issue to resolve with someone else, the assertive approach is to go to that person first and express the issue, listen to the other person, and work out a solution together. Avoid the issue? No. Attack the other person? No. Complain to others but not to the person? No. Go to the other person no matter how uncomfortable you may feel, and discuss the issue to work out a solution? A great big YES.

Anyone can become an assertive speaker — no special communication style is required. You can be low key or high energy; it makes no difference. What matters is dealing with situations and people in a positive, straightforward, and action-oriented manner.

To reinforce understanding of these four speaking patterns, try this: Pair up your people and have them role-play each of the four approaches — aggressive, nonassertive, passive-aggressive, and assertive. These demonstrations can serve as a springboard into group discussion of effective ways to express a message.

You can create scenarios related to the workplace, or use these:

✔ A team member has expressed an idea that is unclear to you, but what sense you can make out of it, you totally disagree with.

✔ As part of a joint effort, another team member agreed to perform an important task. Now as the deadline approaches, the task is not done and both of you thought the other person was going to handle it.

✔ You sent an e-mail message to someone in another group requesting some important information. A week later, you've received only half of what you need and you have little time to wait any longer.

✔ You need another team member to join you for a critical meeting and being on time is important.

✔ You need to tell another team member about a delay you've encountered with your part of an important assignment that is going to affect the other person's part.

For some extra fun, take one member of a two-person team aside and assign him to demonstrate the assertive approach and one of the less productive approaches — first one, and then the other. The other member of the team and the audience have to guess which approach is which.

Making Assertive Speaking Work for You

This section provides you with two sets of tools for showing your team members how to express their messages assertively. One set is designed for nonverbal communication — how a person speaks — and the other concerns the verbal side — words themselves. As you and the team become skilled at using these tools, you can expect to see much improvement in communication.

Special delivery: Using nonverbal tools of assertive speaking

The nonverbal tools of assertive speaking help you deliver messages in a positive and confident manner and make others to want to listen to you.

Here are some of the more important nonverbal tools:

✔ Looking at the audience.

Your eyes are like a magnet, attracting attention and interest. They also give you credibility and your message believability.

✔ Projecting the voice and varying its inflection.

Speak to be heard easily. Especially in group situations, if you're too soft, people tend to ignore what you say. Also, put some variety in your voice. Don't squeak like a church mouse or drone in a monotone; people will tune you out.

✔ Being sincere.

A tone that blends honesty and consideration of the audience commands attention in positive ways. Guard against sounding frustrated, angry, or sarcastic.

✔ Looking animated.

People prefer to listen to others who appear confident and full of life. So forget that blank look, rigid posture, and hands jammed in the pockets. Smile, stand alert like you're ready for action, and use gestures to make your points.

✔ Adopting a good pace.

Not too fast, not too slow, but *just right*. How do you know what's right? One trick is adjusting your pace to your listener's normal pace. But avoid speaking so fast that you slur words or so slow that your listeners lose patience with you. And don't forget to pause now and then. Pauses — silence — help refocus the listener's attention on what you're saying. Pauses help you minimize the overuse of boring, empty words like *uh, um, like,* and *you know*. Pauses also help you think before you speak, and that's much better than the other way around.

Edward speaks up

Edward was a soft-spoken man who often shied away from saying much, especially in group settings. As a result, his team didn't expect to hear much from Edward at team meetings.

Then Edward and the others received training in communication. With encouragement from his manager and the instructor, Edward took to heart what he discovered about assertive speaking. Technically, he knew his work well and did a good job, and now he applied the same diligent approach to mastering a few communication tools.

Over time, Edward began speaking up more in team meetings and in everyday work situations. He managed his speaking pace carefully so that his accent didn't make his words hard to understand — he had mastered English as an adult. He projected his voice and gestured when he talked.

Although still low-key in his style, Edward soon caught the team's attention with his thoughts and ideas. Bolstered by his newfound confidence in speaking, he became known as a valuable contributor to the team.

Speaking in the positive — verbal tools at your disposal

How you speak is one set of tools for assertive speaking. *What you say* — word choice — is the other set of tools. Your objective when speaking assertively is to phrase your message in the best way possible. By that, I mean honestly, directly, and constructively — all three at once. The following list of tips can help keep you on track.

Say what you can do

Part of everyone's work is responding to other people's requests and inquiries. When someone asks you to do something, focus on what *can* be done. De-emphasize what *can't* be done. No one says you must act at once on every request or do things you aren't able to do. But most of the time, *something* can be done, so make that fact the focus of your response.

The language of can-do communicates helpfulness.

To show you what I mean, compare these two different responses to the same request:

> ✔ "Based on the requirements involved, I can have that request fulfilled in three days."

> ✔ "With all that you're asking for, I can't possibly fulfill your request in any less than three days."

The first example says what *can* be done. The second example says can't be done and even leaves some doubt about whether it will be done in the allotted time. Can-do language shows that you can act and plan to act. It shows that you're prepared to get work done and to provide service — a focus that helps teams perform well.

Say what you will do

When someone, for example, suggests Friday as a deadline for certain work, and you say, "I'll try to get it done by Friday" or "Maybe I'll get it done by Friday," the other person walks away with little confidence the job will be done by Friday. Compare that to the firm commitment, "I will have it done by Friday." Of course, if you have grave doubts that you can deliver, you need to negotiate the deadline. Will-do language communicates commitment and certainty.

Remember: Less is more

Everyone's busy, so remember to give the main idea and the important points, but don't overload people with all the details. You can always add more when an interest is expressed, but you can't go back and delete what you've already said when you've already bored your listeners with too much information. Enough said.

Speak in language that your listeners understand

Avoid jargon and abbreviations when you talk with people who may not speak your language — especially customers. Translate your technical terms and acronyms whenever they are vital to your message. Otherwise, use lay terms or common language.

When dealing with problems, use the language of solutions

To acknowledge "we have a problem" isn't a terrible thing; problems are business as usual for teams. But be sure to pay attention to the words that follow. When your language focuses on defining problems so that you understand them and then developing solutions for those problems, you engage others to work with you in the effort. Certain words can help you focus other people on working with you to develop solutions. Those words include:

- Recommendation
- Option
- Idea
- Suggestion
- Alternative

These are positive words that point toward solutions. They are not negative words that dwell on finding blame and putting people on the defensive.

Bring issues to closure

A big part of assertive speaking is bringing discussions to a clear end — to closure. You don't want people walking away from a conversation wondering what happens next or who's doing what. So, make sure that important points stand out, agreements are confirmed, and action items are clear to everyone. Language like this can help:

- "To recap, what I'm stressing that is important for us to do is . . ."
- "Just to make sure, we've agreed that you'll do such and such and I'll do this and that. Is that correct?"
- "Let's set some action items for what needs to be done before our next meeting."

Reviewing a team's written communications inside the organization and with outsiders, reinforces the importance of choosing the right words and determines how well the team is following the good practices that I outline in this section.

When you're equipping your team with language tools for assertive speaking, don't forget to warn them away from language that switches people onto the negative track. Here are a few examples:

- **Trigger words.** They aren't negative by definition but often trigger a negative response in the recipient. Examples:

    - **Not, can't, won't, don't** — the language of being unable and not helpful.

    - **Should, need to, must** — the language of demands and directives.

    - **Policy, code, rule** — the language of inflexibility and mindlessness.

    - **Always and never** — the language of absolutes.

    - **Try, maybe, perhaps** — the language of doubt and uncertainty.

- **Loaded language.** Comments that others find instantly upsetting or offensive. (Don't try these at home either.) Profanity, slurs aimed at someone's personal background such as race, religion, gender, or age, and labels like "stupid" and "idiot" are but a few examples of loaded language.

- **Mixed messages.** They are *yes-but* messages. A mixed message may begin with what sounds like a sweet comment, but it turns sour after the "but" or the "however" in the middle of the sentence: "That's a good idea, *but* I don't see how it will help this team or why we'd want to do it." The real point is expressed at the end of the sentence, and it reduces to nearly zero the sincerity of whatever was said before. My advice: Being direct and sincere tends to work far better than saying nice things that you don't really mean.

- **Statements that negate your message.** Look for them in the opening phrase of what you say — and get rid of them. Statements like these tune listeners out; that's the opposite of what you want.

    - "Now don't take this personally."

    - "I hate to have to tell you this."

    - "You may not want to hear this."

    - "I don't know if you'll understand this."

    - "This may not be a good idea."

Enable your listeners to evaluate your messages for themselves. Don't bias them. Be direct and sincere. Get to the point and say it with a sense of importance. That way, you use the verbal and nonverbal tools of assertive speaking for maximum effectiveness with the team.

Chapter 9

Problem-solving and Planning: Adding Method to the Madness

In This Chapter

▶ Looking at skills and benefits for more effective planning

▶ Examining behaviors to avoid and models to use for effective problem-solving

▶ Gaining techniques for developing solutions

*P*lanning is all about looking to some point in the future and figuring out how to get there. Problem-solving is about removing obstacles, making improvements, and tackling challenges — some big, some small — that pop up as you're carrying out your business.

You don't have to be a genius to make good plans or solve tough problems. But you do need to pay attention and think — think, then act, not the other way around. When teams are reactive to problem situations or just jump into work with nothing organized first, chaos and inefficiency reign.

Planning means thinking about what you're going to do before you do it. For teams to perform well, planning needs to become a routine part of the work. Quite simply, you stand a better chance of reaching your destination when you make a plan for getting there.

The same is true of problem-solving: You don't have to be a giant to push problems out of the way (remember David and Goliath?), but you do have to have a problem-solving approach so you know what to do and what *not* to do. This chapter shows you the way.

Planning the Work, Working the Plan

Teams are all about getting work done and dealing with problems as a normal part of doing the work. This section gives you tools and tips for guiding your team toward using planning as a function of everyday work, for helping you recognize what you need to plan for and what benefits you can expect, and for developing strategies for creating plans.

Teams also need their leaders or managers — that's you — to model the behaviors that make for effective planning. So, when you want your team to perform efficiently and not chaotically and to have a sense of direction and not be lost, applying the tactics in this section is well worth your while. Just *plan* to do so.

Don't rely on memory for your plans — write them down. Until a plan is committed to writing, it doesn't exist.

Understanding what you need to plan

Why does a team need plans? The answer is: for many important activities, such as the following:

- ✔ **Setting goals.** Goals define the outcomes or results that the team seeks to accomplish. Taking time for determining what those goals are is crucial for developing a team's proper focus.

- ✔ **Developing work plans.** Work or action plans often support goals. They define what needs to be done to achieve the desired outcomes of the team's work.

- ✔ **Managing projects.** When you manage a project team, as Chapter 14 examines, developing a project plan with the team is one of the first steps you want to take before launching into the work of the project. The project plan becomes the team's road map for guiding the work and the people doing the work from start to finish.

- ✔ **Defining priorities.** Deciding what issues or activities come first helps move team members in the same direction.

- ✔ **Solving problems.** Planning helps define how solutions are implemented and evaluated.

- ✔ **Mapping out work schedules.** Planning helps teams determine who's going to work when so that coverage is maintained even when people take time off.

- ✔ **Organizing short-term work assignments.** Planning can help determine what work each team member does from day-to-day and week-to-week. That, in turn, helps the team achieve its longer-term goals.

- ✔ **Addressing training needs.** Planning helps determine what skills need to be mastered and when time can be taken for learning them — especially important when cross-training is needed.

- ✔ **Guiding individual performance.** Planning in the form of *time management* helps individual team members outline their tasks and stay on top of them.

Two crazy, mixed up managers

Let me tell you the stories of Patty and Billy, two managers.

Patty often works like this: On one day she tells team members to work on Assignment X. The next day she tells them not to worry about X but, instead, tells them to focus their attention on a new area, Assignment Y. Two days later (she skips a day because at the last minute she decides to join an off-site management meeting), she dashes in and tells the team to do Y in a different way, and, by the way, get going on X.

If you worked for Patty, how would you feel? Confused, bewildered, frustrated? Many Patty-type managers are running loose in organizations. They live day-to-day and react to the issue or crisis of the moment. Because of these constant twists and turns in their priorities and a general lack of overall direction, Patty-types can drive their staff members nuts.

So can the Billy-types: Billy has never met a problem he didn't like. Whenever he sees or hears about a problem in operations, Billy jumps in and tells staff what to do. Billy doesn't waste time. He's out in the middle of the work area, shooting orders from the hip: "Here's what you need to do," or "Here's what you must do."

If you worked for Billy, how would you feel? Confused, bewildered, frustrated? Billy-type managers also are on the loose in many organizations. They constantly chase problems, giving directives to staff (just trying to be helpful). When Billy senses a problem, does he get people involved in discussing whether a real problem exists and defining it? No. Does he tell people how to do their jobs (a major turnoff)? Yes. Does he reduce teams to chaos and make team members feel disempowered? You know the answer.

People support most that which they help create. Your job as manager is working with the team members to ensure that everyone affected by the team's plans is involved in developing them.

Counting the benefits of good planning

Why bother planning? What's the payoff? Your team members may wonder at times, and you may, too. After all, planning takes time and nobody has time to spare in a fast-paced work environment. You need to get to work! Right?

Before plunging into planning as standard practice, spend a little time reviewing the benefits that teams can expect to see from the planning process. My list includes:

> ✔ **Providing direction.** When employees have a sense of where their group is going, or even where their entire organization is going, they have a greater sense of clarity in their work and commitment to their jobs. Many of the strategies of the focus cornerstone for team discipline (see Chapter 5) involve planning to establish direction. When a team knows where it's headed, its focus is clear.

✔ **Creating alignment.** *Alignment* means that everyone is headed in the same direction. The benefit is obvious: When team members have differing priorities and agendas that aren't sorted out, divisiveness often results. Setting plans collaboratively ensures that everyone is on that so-called same page and that everyone is connected and moving forward together, which is key to achieving cohesiveness and ultimately improving productivity.

✔ **Measuring progress.** The plan is an instrument for the team to use for checking its performance, which is part of accountability (see Chapter 7).

✔ **Organizing activity.** Plans organize work so that everyone knows what needs to be done, by whom, and when. The opposite of organization is chaos, and in the contest between organization and chaos, organization wins every time. It uplifts team morale, gives clarity, builds unity, and creates efficiency.

✔ **Saving time.** Yes, even though the planning process consumes time, good planning nevertheless comes with a good *ROI* — return on investment. Your upfront investment in planning time saves time down the road — in team performance. With less confusion, fewer tasks overlooked, more cohesiveness, and more efficiency, a team makes better use of its time. Time, often more than money, is the team's greatest resource and the one that it can have the most control over. Planning is step one.

✔ **Adapting to change.** Plans give teams the flexibility they need to incorporate change into their work by laying down a baseline as a guide. When changes come in (as they always will, from small to large), repositioning your team is much easier when you know what your present bearing is. Making adjustments without a reference bearing is like setting a new course while sailing without a compass.

✔ **Driving performance.** This last benefit is the sum of all the rest. Creating plans as a team strengthens its performance. Plans provide focus, pulling people together and serving as yardsticks to measure progress and results. Say hello to the three cornerstones for achieving high performance with teams: focus, cohesiveness, and accountability. Planning strengthens each of these three cornerstones.

Making plans, step by step

Planning is a skill that you learn best by doing. But you don't need to reinvent the process every time you plan something. One all-purpose outline and set of questions can successfully lead you through the planning for practically any work assignment. I recommend the following outline and questions as your step-by-step guide.

- ✔ **Objective**
  - What do we need to accomplish?
  - What are the outcomes we need to achieve?
- ✔ **Milestones or key steps**
  - How do we get from where we are today to the conclusion of our plan?
  - What are the main actions that need to be taken to reach our destination?
- ✔ **Schedule**
  - When does the objective of this plan need to be accomplished?
  - On the key steps that need to be taken along the way, when do we need to accomplish them?
- ✔ **Resources**
  - Who's going to serve in what roles for the team to achieve this plan's objective successfully?
  - What materials do we need to do the work?
  - Who outside of the team might we need to call on for assistance or support?
- ✔ **Contingencies**
  - What obstacles or challenges might we face along the way?
  - How will we deal with obstacles?
- ✔ **Checkpoints.** When will the team meet along the way to review progress on its plan?

Your team can use this checklist as a guide for developing work plans, taking care to establish the steps sequentially in one of two approaches:

- ✔ **Going-forward approach.** You start with where you are today, mapping each key step and point in time as you move toward the target.
- ✔ **Backward-planning approach.** You start at an end point (at some point in the future), the target, and working in reverse, setting down each step your team needs to accomplish until you work your way back to the present. This planning strategy is particularly useful when your team faces a hard and fast deadline — because the one thing you know for certain is the date you *must* meet.

The length of time that a plan covers depends on the nature of the work. Major projects may go on for months requiring months-long plans. By comparison, a week-to-week plan may be more helpful in accomplishing ongoing work. The idea in either case is to apply issues and questions from the checklist as a guide to the development and redevelopment of the team's ongoing plans.

Whatever you do, steer clear of seat-of-the-pants, spur-of-the-moment plans. That's what you call chaos.

Going-forward approach

Figure 9-1 shows how a work-unit team, responsible for an ongoing function, plans its weekly output flow. This is the six-member team that handles customer order fulfillment.

Order Fulfillment Team Work Plan
Week of May 1 - 5, 2002

1. Monday – Estimated 90 orders to fulfill for week.

ASSIGNMENTS:

- Picking orders – Jim and Sue.

- Packaging orders – Jose and Lou.

- Handling customers issues – Maria, Jose backup.

- Vacation – Sam.

2. Wednesday – Progress review and adjustments. meeting

3. Friday – Prepare report of results for the week. meeting

Figure 9-1: Weekly work plan for the order fulfillment team.

As you can see in Figure 9-1, the order fulfillment team has established a process for planning work and getting it done. On Monday, team members estimate how many orders they're going to fulfill that week and assign two-person teams to the three main functions. In the example, they also plan to cover for a team member who's on vacation, to meet midweek to review progress and make any needed adjustments, and to meet Friday to prepare the week's report. Come Monday, they're ready to plan for the new week of production.

Because of the ongoing nature of their work, the order fulfillment team finds it useful to plan weekly and keep the plan simple. Each week, using the going-forward strategy, they factor in contingencies such as vacations, training and the volume of work they expect to handle. No need to make the plan any more complicated than that.

Backward-planning approach

Figure 9-2 illustrates the backward-planning approach. In this case, Team Y has been asked to make a 30-minute presentation on its key accomplishments for the past year and its goals for the coming year. The team has one month to get ready.

Figure 9-2 shows how Team Y plans to meet the drop-dead, no-excuses date when it must be prepared to stand up and deliver its report before a management group. The team starts with the delivery date, July 1, and steps backward, noting in reverse order everything that must be done, all the way back to the present. Note also that people are assigned specific responsibilities.

Figures 9-1 and 9-2 illustrate that a good team plan is

✔ Simple

✔ Clear

✔ Hits the important stuff but skips little details

You don't need to go into fine detail in the plan. All that does is confuse people and create a document that no one uses. Details can be worked out at each step along the way.

For longer-term plans, you may want individual team members to keep track of their own details in a *to-do list* that's perpetually revised as tasks are completed and new ones come up. (Chapter 5 covers the planning process to meet longer-term goals.)

Planning with a team is more than merely setting up the plan. Planning also means living the plan, using it as a guide for doing the work. You can help make that happen by:

✔ **Making the plan visible.** Everyone on the team receives a copy of the plan, either paper copy or online version.

✔ **Reviewing progress regularly.** Individual team members come to the review meeting ready to report on what they've done to help the team achieve its plan. (Chapter 7 explains this *accountability* strategy of status review.)

✔ **Updating the plan.** No plan is carved in stone. Teams cannot afford to be that rigid. The farther a plan reaches into the future, the more you need to expect it to change as you move forward.

Team Y
Special Presentation to Management

Objective: Deliver a presentation within 30 minutes for the special July 1
              management meetings that positively highlights Team Y's past
              year accomplishments and projected goals for the next fiscal year.

MILESTONES	DATES
• Presentation to upper management.	July 1
• Rehearsal of presentation.*	June 28
• Slides and materials for presentation set.* Presentation organized.	June 24
• Projected goals for next year set.*	June 20
• Data finalized on past year's accomplishments.*	June 15
• Assignments set for execution of plan.	June 1

      * Checkpoint meetings for whole team.

ASSIGNMENTS

• Data gathering – Rosie, Kevin, and Arlene

• Presentation materials – Don and Rachel

• Taking issues to management,
  setting outline for presentation – You (the manager)

• Delivering presentation – Whole team

Figure 9-2:
Planning
backward
from a
target date
of July 1.

Solving Problems (Rather than Making Them Worse)

Problems are not the problem. They're a routine, normal part of any team's work. But the way a team goes about solving problems — ah, that's sometimes a problem.

In this section, I talk first about team member behavior that only makes problems worse, listing a few pitfalls to avoid. Later, I describe a couple of problem-solving models that your team can use in an organized or systematic approach to finding real solutions to work-type problems.

Avoiding the pitfalls

When a problem surfaces, certain kinds of team member behavior may pop up, making the problem worse. Stay alert for bad behavior like these five classic examples:

- **Finger-pointing and blaming.** Finding fault with other people is one of the all-time great aggravators of problem situations. The verbal barrage of accusations may sound like: "Why do you always mess things up?" or "Why did you do you that?" Although problems sometimes can be upsetting, blaming others for them doesn't solve a thing and only builds resentment and anger in others.

- **Dwelling on the problem.** This behavior wins first prize in the *woe-is-me* category. It means constantly talking about how things are wrong, wrong, wrong. After awhile the negativity of doom and gloom begins creating a really bad stink.

- **Getting defensive.** Reacting in sharp tones, attacking others, and taking everything personally are characteristics of someone who's on the defensive. Defensive reactions shut down dialogue at a time when what's needed most in a problem situation is for dialogue to increase.

- **Avoiding the problem.** Problems can't be wished away. Yet people sometimes try to wave the magic wand and do just that. What usually happens? Chaos and frustration occur among team members, and you can say goodbye to positive morale and high productivity.

- **Developing a solution without understanding the problem.** Rushing in with a solution before you have a thorough understanding of a problem often simply compounds that problem. This kind of bad behavior may be based on good intentions — a team member's eagerness to be helpful, for example — but that doesn't excuse it. Sometimes a *quick fix* is, in fact, a solution to a problem that doesn't exist, making a complicated situation even harder to untangle.

Bad behaviors sidetrack a team that's trying to solve problems. What can you do as manager? Certainly you can lead by example, as I explain in Chapter 3, and you can coach individual team members away from their bad habits, as Chapter 4 explains.

Demand that your team's behavior generates positive energy and creativity, the kind of behavior that helps to solve problems. Encourage your team to:

✔ Be patient and stay in control.

✔ Follow a systematic approach.

✔ Listen actively to one another (see Chapter 8).

✔ Understand the problem first and then focus on developing a solution.

✔ Solicit everyone's input.

✔ Be persistent, sticking with the work until you resolve the matter.

Revving up your problem-solving machine

This section walks you through two problem-solving models for the team to use as it works through issues. Like all good problem-solving models, these two ask you to understand the problem first before you work on developing a solution.

The S-T-P Model

In this three-step model, the *S* stands for Situation, the *T* for Target, and the *P* for Proposals. If the initials remind you of a certain well-known engine additive, that's a great way to remember this problem-solving model. Figure 9-3 is a visual reminder.

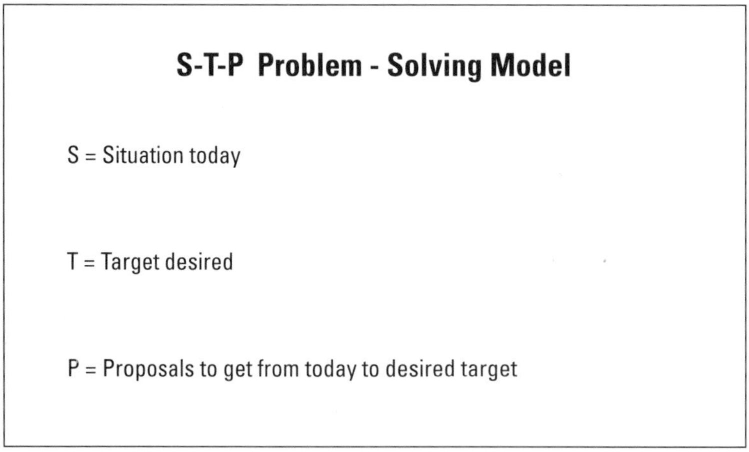

S-T-P Problem - Solving Model

S = Situation today

T = Target desired

P = Proposals to get from today to desired target

Figure 9-3:
The S-T-P problem-solving model.

Here's what happens at each step of the S-T-P Problem-solving Model:

✔ **S = Situation:** The team defines the current situation concerning the problem or issue:

   • What's working well? What isn't working well?

- What are the facts as we know them today and how do people feel about the situation?

Ask each team member to answer these questions and write what they say on a flipchart for all to see. Discuss the issues until everyone has answered.

Everyone seeing the current situation exactly the same way isn't as important as the team seeking the common sense of present conditions so that it can pinpoint the problem areas that are most in need of correction.

✔ **T = Target:** The target is the situation that you want in the future. When the present problem is resolved and everything is working well, ask what the team's future looks like? The target serves as the goal.

Have your team develop a target statement by following these steps:

- Ask each team member to write a one-sentence statement that defines the desired future state.

- Post the sentences for everyone to see.

- Using common themes from the posted sentences, collectively craft a target statement for the issue at hand. Try saying everything in only one sentence — make it a big-picture statement, skip ping the details (they come next).

✔ **P = Proposals:** The gap between your situation today and your target for the future is what the P step is designed to fill — how you get from here to there. The proposals are the ideas for the solution to reach the desired target.

You can illustrate your words with an appropriate gesture. Try this: Hold your left hand at waist level, palm facing upward, fingers out, to indicate "where the team is today." Holding your right hand at the top of your head as if you're blocking the sun out of your eyes, show that you're looking toward "how high the team wants to go." The right gesture adds a nice bit of visual reinforcement to the idea that you want to communicate.

Follow the same routine that you use whenever you want the entire team to engage in problem-solving: Ask team members for ideas that they think can help solve the problem. Take enough time for everyone to contribute before you begin discussing the issue, evaluating it, eventually reaching consensus on the proposals that will help most, and talking about the plans you need to make to implement the proposals.

The S-T-P model often works best when a team has a fairly good understanding of the current situation and a well-defined and desirable target in mind. It's usually the quicker of the two problem-solving models presented in this chapter.

But some issues are more complex or require more analysis to get a good handle on them. In such cases, the second model is good to use.

The Six-Step Model

No, don't confuse this with your dance lesson! But I do intend to "lead" you through a problem-solving model that works well when the issues are complex or require more analysis than usual. Figure 9-4 gives you an overview of the Six-Step Problem-Solving Model.

Six-Step Problem - Solving Model

<u>Step</u>

1 Identify the problem

2 Analyze the problem

3 Explore alternatives for a solution

   A. Brainstorm
   B. Evaluate

4 Project results of main alternatives, including how they would be implemented

5 Select and agree on a solution; present recommendations as needed

6 Finalize and execute the implementation plan

Figure 9-4: The Six-Step Problem-Solving Model.

Here's how it works:

Step 1: Identifying the problem

Reach *consensus* with the team about what the problem is and describe it briefly — in one sentence, if possible. (For details on the consensus-building process, please see Chapter 11.) Consensus is important because reaching it ensures that you're all tackling the same problem.

Aim to define the problem in *problem* terms: for example, "Many customers' orders are currently being shipped with errors and are going out past their scheduled ship dates." *That's* a problem statement and much more precise than, "The team needs to do a better job at fulfilling customer orders accurately and on time." The problem with the second sentence is that it looks more toward the solution and doesn't zero in on what's going wrong in the present.

Step 2: Analyze the problem

You want to gain a clearer understanding of the circumstances surrounding a problem, so answering these questions will facilitate this analysis:

- How long have we had the problem?
- What factors caused the problem?
- How often does it occur?
- What's the difference in performance between now and before the problem began?

Team members may find it necessary to research these questions so they can gather the data they need to answer them adequately. You're looking for root causes and patterns that explain recurring circumstances. People who like to use charts and graphs in problem analysis have an opportunity to put their talents to use.

Step 3: Exploring alternative solutions

The third step, searching for alternative solutions, has two substeps:

- **Brainstorming.** Team members generate all the ideas they can think of for solving the problem.

- **Evaluating potential solutions.** Team members discuss various possible solutions that have bubbled up during brainstorming, selecting a few that probably will work best. Sometimes more study and fact-finding is required for an improved understanding of how potential solutions actually can help.

In a later section of this chapter, "Brainstorming — Developing Ideas for Solutions," I provide more tips on facilitating the brainstorming and evaluating potential solutions with your team.

Step 4: Discussing how to implement a potential solution and forecasting the results

Sometimes a team hits on a solution that looks great, but when they examine what is needed to implement it and what probably can be expected to happen over the long term, they realize that although the idea may have sounded good, it isn't feasible. Other times the opposite occurs: What looked like a lame idea at first, upon further review, turns out to be the one that works well.

Certainly you want your team members to remain creative and open to new options. They may have to run a possible solution through some trials to determine whether it's feasible.

Beware of the quick fix. Remind your team to be patient, following a systematic approach. Establishing good problem-solving habits is your objective, not repeating the slipshod ones that other people indulge in.

Step 5: Agreeing on a solution and presenting your recommendations

Agreeing on a solution may be the easiest step in the six-step model. A good solution often is a combination of several alternative solutions rather than one original idea. Remember, you're seeking consensus: Everyone on the team must agree to support the solution. So take your time in getting everyone on board.

The other part of Step 5, presenting a recommendation, comes into play when the designated solution requires support from people outside the team, including other groups or management above you. When you do need to make a recommendation, I suggest this routine:

- ✔ **Getting the entire team involved.** Members of your team are the knowledge experts just as much as you are. In addition, when a team presents together on a problem the members have worked hard to solve, you usually add a powerful punch to the presentation — strength in numbers.

- ✔ **Finding out how much time you have.** Key members of your audience may tell you how much time you have, but you may also be able to negotiate the time. Either way works as long as you touch all the bases while presenting your recommendation.

  Less is generally more in formal presentations. That means, taking less time is better than taking too much time. So plan to cover all the main points but skip the little details. Leaving your audience interested and eager to ask questions is better than boring them out of their minds.

- ✔ **Using the problem-solving model as your agenda.** Using the model as your made-to-order presentation guide, or agenda, shows your audience the thought process and work that was done arriving at the recommended solution and demonstrates how thorough and organized your team is — traits that can really woo the crowd.

- ✔ **Defining everyone's role.** Decide who will deliver what parts of the presentation. Everyone needs to participate, including team members who'd rather go to the dentist than make a public presentation. You can pair up your reluctant presenters with more eager participants — not everyone has to present equally in time. But avoid bringing a team member along who just sits there like a mummy. That looks bad.

Remember to assign someone to prepare and distribute any printed materials that the audience needs. Again, rely on people's strengths. If a team member or two are good at creating graphics and making PowerPoint slides, cut them loose on it.

Consider making your role the master of ceremonies. You can kick off the presentation, wrap it up at the end, and handle transitions from one presenter to the next. Working as an emcee gives you freedom to jump in and help a team member if an unexpected challenge comes from the audience.

✔ **Rehearsing.** Practice makes perfect definitely applies when your team must make a formal presentation. Don't forget to set aside plenty of time to rehearse.

Don't lose sight of your main focus — making a recommendation that others will support.

Step 6: Finalizing and executing the implementation plan

Take care to communicate with everyone who needs to know about the solution that you're rolling out. When a solution affects other people and they're not included in the loop, you often create a brand new problem, one characterized by confusion, resentment, and even resistance. So make sure that you decide how to spread the word — in writing, face to face, or a combination. When the solution doesn't affect anyone outside the team, implementation is simpler: Just clarify who's doing what, and away you go.

Brainstorming — Developing Ideas for Solutions

Brainstorming is a group activity aimed at producing ideas — ideas about solving problems, for example. In some problem-solving situations, a few main ideas or options for solutions are obvious from the beginning, and you don't need to brainstorm. But in many other cases, quite the opposite is true. Your team is short of ideas and needs to be creative.

The goal in brainstorming is simply generating ideas, as many ideas as possible, but not yet evaluating them. That takes place after brainstorming ends. In this section I cover how to make brainstorming work — and in the next section, what to do with all those ideas.

Here's how to get the best out of your team's brainstorming efforts:

✔ **Set ground rules.** You want an uninterrupted flow of ideas coming in at a good pace, so remind everyone that no comments or judgments are allowed until you reach the discussion stage. Only when someone's brainstorm is truly unclear can you permit a quick question for clarification, but try limiting even those instances. Otherwise, permit no discussion whatsoever as ideas are volunteered. On the other hand, you can encourage team members to take a *what-if* approach in their thinking — if anything were possible and no limitations existed, what would you suggest? This kind of thinking opens people's minds and truly enables them to be creative. Remind team members that no such thing as a bad idea exists when they're brainstorming.

✔ **Decide how long to brainstorm.** If you're under time constraints, set a time limit for brainstorming of, say, 10 minutes or so. But when time is not an issue, brainstorm until the team runs out of ideas. In either case, state up front whether you're watching the clock.

✔ **Select a brainstorming process.** You have two choices: *free-for-all* and *go-in-turn*.

- In the free-for-all process, people shout out ideas as they think of them. This fast-paced approach often generates a great deal of creative energy.

- In the go-in-turn process, the team follows a set order, like a batting order in baseball. The first person in line states an idea, then the next, and so on. If a person has no idea when his turn comes up, he just says, "pass" so the process keeps moving at a good pace.

  Using the go-in-turn approach, you can give an idea only when it's your turn. And one idea per turn, not five at once.

Unless a team has been together for long time and is therefore skilled in the art of brainstorming, I recommend using the go-in-turn process. It equalizes participation and involves everyone on the team in generating ideas. Go-in-turn also works better with less-developed teams where the free-for-all process tends to push quiet members to the sidelines while more vocal types dominate.

✔ **Warm up if necessary.** It may be useful for team members to think about ideas silently for a few minutes and write them down into notes before brainstorming begins. This can prepare them to participate more easily when brainstorming begins.

✔ **Record ideas for all to see.** A flipchart works well and can be retained for future use as needed.

Whoever is responsible for recording the ideas must be careful to capture the exact words without editing them. Rephrasing ideas may be well meaning, but it can be a drag on the process and irritating to brainstormers. Be sure, however, to permit the recorder to participate by adding his or her own ideas to the list in turn with the rest of the team.

✔ **Limit long-winded statements.** As team leader you serve as its Doppler radar, remind team members when their brainstorming suggestions have been on the scope for too long Keep the thoughts short and sweet. Go for the big idea. Save the details and explanations for the discussion stage.

✔ **Let people add on to ideas.** In the language of brainstorming, this is called *piggybacking* — adding on to ideas that already are on the list. Nothing is wrong with enhancing a brainstorm with a bolt of related lightning.

Brainstorming can be used for situations other than problem-solving. Think about using this technique whenever you're seeking ideas. For example, when you're leading a task team to develop key personnel and operational policies in a company where few exist, one of the first meetings with your team can be a brainstorming session to generate a list of issues for policy development. Or when you're leading a discussion about ways to recognize outstanding team and individual performances, brainstorming can jump-start the conversation.

Guiding Discussions After the Brainstorming

I remember the members of one team that I taught how to brainstorm. They loved the exercise and began using it for all sorts of situations where they wanted to generate ideas. They became good at generating a quantity of ideas but, like many teams, found that paring the list down to a workable few was challenging.

Brainstorming is a great process for helping people see new and different possibilities but also is frustrating when you produce a number of worthy ideas but can't possibly act on all of them. Getting down to the workable few is important.

Narrowing down the idea list

Here's a five-step process to follow as you guide your team through the discussion phase after brainstorming.

1. **Clarification.** Go down the list with the team, asking if any of the ideas need clarification. For those that do, let the idea-givers provide an explanation but avoid discussing the merits of ideas.

2. **Quick elimination.** Look at the list and ask whether any ideas can be eliminated right away. Prime candidates for the brush-off are ideas that

sound interesting or creative but everybody knows they're not feasible, as well as platitudes lacking any specific action to them. You may be talking a handful of expendable items at most. Be sure to get consensus agreement before you cross them off.

3. **Consolidation.** Combine similar ideas. This step, plus the first two steps above, shouldn't take more than a few minutes.

4. **Theme identification.** Look for common themes represented by the ideas and label and group them by those themes. Doing so helps streamline the final step — evaluation.

5. **Evaluation.** Discuss the merits of each idea. How will the idea help the team get to where it's going? What will the team need to implement the idea? Use questions like those to stimulate the evaluation effort and push the team to scrutinize each idea thoroughly. Remember: You can't implement all the ideas at once — even when you like them all.

Allow enough time for discussion of the merits of each idea, but don't get into discussions of personalities. Who proposed an idea is of no consequence. When an idea seems to gain favor among team members, check with each one to see whether he or she supports the idea before you discuss the next idea. (Please see Chapter 11 for details about forming a consensus.)

Some ideas that fall off the list during evaluation still may be worthy of discussion at a later time. Make sure those ideas are documented so they can be reconsidered.

I worked with one team that made this discussion tool work really well. In a previous meeting they had defined the problems they faced. I was asked to come in and facilitate them through the developing solutions.

At first, I had the team of ten do brainstorming in turn. In just over ten minutes, they came up with over 40 ideas — and were quite pleased at their effort. Then we started the discussion phase by doing the clarification, possible elimination, and consolidation of ideas. This took a few minutes and narrowed the list of ideas by a few.

Then in examining the list, five themes could be seen among them. Those themes were labeled and the ideas placed accordingly with each category. The discussion then proceeded evaluating the merits and feasibility of each idea per category. In the end, the team agreed to act on a half-dozen ideas.

This whole solutions-developing work, from brainstorming through discussion, was completed in less than an hour and an half. The team members walked out of the meeting quite pleased that they had created some very action-oriented ideas and had done so in such an efficient manner.

The dysfunctional executive team

Early in my career as a consultant, I learned a lesson about how *not* to brainstorm. I was asked to facilitate a problem-solving session with an executive group. It was a routine request and an interesting assignment. At least I thought it was, because I knew most of the executives individually from my leadership development work for the client. However, the human resources director warned me that the executives tended to be somewhat dysfunctional when they tried to work as a team. Oh boy was she right!

On brainstorming day, I began by explaining the ground rules and was barely into my spiel when a couple of executives interrupted, telling me that they knew all about brainstorming. Oh no, I thought, a bunch of know-it-all's. I asked them to humor me for a moment, so I could finish explaining the procedure and get the order set.

As the brainstorming began, so, too, did the attacking. Before I could finish recording the first person's idea on the front board, two others jumped in and sharply criticized the idea. I reminded them that no discussions or judgments were to take place until we finished getting all the ideas out. "Oh yeah, we forgot," the attackers acknowledged. And yet three or four more times during the next few minutes, more ideas were shot down in midair. I felt like a referee at a basketball game, calling fouls every few seconds. All I needed was a striped shirt and a whistle!

When all the attacking subsided, the executive team managed to produce only about half the number of ideas that I normally expect — in about twice the time. Some of the ideas seemed to have potential for solving the problem, and I was happy about that. But I walked away from this meeting with a much better understanding of what "dysfunctional team" really means.

Voting for winners — democracy in action

If, after discussion, the team still has too many ideas and can't narrow the list down to a workable few alternatives, you can get the job done by employing the technique that's called *multivoting*. This technique is no more complicated than casting a ballot on Election Day, except it's done in the open. Here's how:

- ✔ **Set the number of votes.** Decide how many votes each person can cast. Obviously, the number has to be much smaller than the number of candidate ideas you're voting on. Three to five votes per person can be just about right when you're looking at a list of 20 or more ideas.

- ✔ **Hand out markers and let the voting begin.** Team members put a check mark by the ideas that they favor most. But don't permit *gang-voting* — one person casting all five votes for one idea. If the agreed upon number of votes per person is five, then each person casts a single vote for five different ideas they see as most important to act on.

✔ **Select the top vote getters.** When voting is finished, circle the ideas that received multiple votes — I usually look for ideas that received three or more votes. The top few vote getters are the ideas or priorities for the team to implement.

If, after one round of multivoting, you still have too many ideas, conduct a second round of voting. For the second round, reduce the number of votes each person has in proportion to a shortened list of ideas.

Multivoting is used only after adequately discussing your team's ideas. Don't cut short the discussion simply to start voting and get the problem-solving effort over with. When multivoting is used at the right time, team members often find it helpful for setting priorities.

Chapter 10

Resolving Conflicts on the Team

*A*re conflicts a normal part of work places, even places where people don't work in teams? You betcha.

Are conflicts even more inevitable in team situations? You betcha.

Do team members often act in ways that aggravate conflict situations? You betcha.

Can team members learn to apply tools that help them to deal with conflicts in constructive ways and to reach resolution? Very much — you betcha.

I'm going to say something that may surprise you: When you want to build a high-performing team, you *want* conflicts. That's right — conflicts are *good* for the team. How come? Because you don't want everyone thinking the same way all the time, and you certainly don't want people agreeing just for the sake of peace and what appears to be harmony.

As your team searches for better ways of handling the work or resolving business issues, you want different perspectives to come out. When they do, conflicts sometimes arise. But that's good because of what can be gained. Conflicts can spark creativity, promote richer exploration of an issue, build more meaningful solutions, and strengthen teamwork.

This chapter helps you work with your team to identify the sort of behaviors that steer conflicts in a constructive direction — and to beware of behaviors that lead down a destructive track. I lay out the communication and problem-solving tools that you need for resolving conflicts. In addition, I offer tips for those times when a conflict puts a strain on team members and facilitating a constructive solution to it is a role you can play.

Streamlining Toward Solutions

The fact that conflicts among team members occur from time to time isn't unusual. The fact that team members may struggle to positively resolve conflicts that arise — that isn't unusual either. Finding out with your team members how best to deal with conflict situations begins when you recognize positive team behavior and negative team behavior.

Staying off the destructive track

In my seminars, I ask what kinds of behavior make conflicts worse, and people find that ticking off a bunch of examples is quite easy. Here are some of their examples:

- ✔ **Finger-pointing.** Finding fault or blaming someone else does nothing to solve the problem, but it's great for building unhealthy tension in a team.

- ✔ **My way, or the highway.** When you push and push for your point of view and show little interest in considering someone else's, you only increase the volume of debate, which drowns out any prospects of settling debate.

- ✔ **Insults galore.** Name-calling and other personal insults are not invitations for resolving a conflict.

- ✔ **Verbal threats and ultimatums.** These sound like, "I'm going to get you," or "This way or else!" Such outbursts intimidate some people, turn off others, and they're not exactly the best way to promote good teamwork.

- ✔ **Defensiveness.** Justifying your action instead of listening to what someone else is trying to tell you builds a wall between you and the other party, making agreements nearly impossible to achieve.

- ✔ **Avoidance.** Running away from the problem and hoping that it goes away — avoidance at its best — seldom resolves an issue.

- ✔ **Beating around the bush.** One of my all-time favorite examples of counterproductive behavior is when someone attempts to address the concern at hand, but all the rambling and talking around the point simply clouds the issue so much that it's left unaddressed.

- ✔ **Telling others and not the source.** Complaining to others about what someone else has done and not talking directly to that person is a great way of stirring divisiveness on a team. Many people place this behavior at the top of the destructive-behavior list.

- ✔ **Flaming e-mails.** This means blaming and complaining electronically about the source of your concern and not talking directly to that person. Sometimes the perpetrator makes this unacceptable behavior even worse by copying others with the disruptive e-mail.

✔ **Focusing on perceived intentions.** Making assumptions about another person — and, of course, assuming the worst — is not a great frame of mind for dealing with team members about your concerns.

Running on the constructive track

Because disagreements and differences are inevitable with teams, your best strategy is encouraging team members to learn behaviors that help them work through conflicts and maintain respectful working relationships in the process. If you want to realize the benefits that can come out of conflicts (creativity, richer solutions, stronger teamwork), put these constructive behaviors into practice:

✔ **Stay in control.** Being in control of your own emotions is where you begin when you're working out a concern with another person. Venting your frustration, spewing your anger, or throwing sarcastic barbs only shows that you're out of control and prevents you from inviting the cooperation of others.

✔ **Be direct, factual, and sincere.** You have to express your concern or problem clearly and constructively so that others understand where you're coming from. Getting to the point, stating the facts as you know them, and speaking with candor and respect are the best ways of getting to a point constructively and increasing the likelihood that you'll be heard the way you want to be heard.

✔ **Go to the source.** A conflict is best resolved by addressing it face-to-face with the other party. Telling a third party or communicating by e-mail cannot replace the person-to-person conversation that's required for conflict resolution to work. Despite the discomfort you may feel with this direct method, a good old-fashioned talk still is the tried-and-true method for resolving conflicts.

✔ **Get into problem-solving.** So you have a conflict with another team member. Big deal! And you've worked out a solution with the other team member? Oh, now, that *is* the big deal. The whole idea is not the fact a difference or disagreement exists between two or more people, but rather that actions are taken to hammer out a solution. When you're able to work out solutions with other team members, now that's the big deal that teams need to have for resolving conflicts.

✔ **Actively listen.** Chapter 8 shows you how to listen effectively. Active listening is all about showing that you care and working to understand what someone else is saying and what that person truly means. Understanding that efforts to actively listen are greatly needed during conflict situations isn't difficult. Those efforts are greatly needed so that the parties can work out their concerns.

Putting the team to the test

As a preamble to this little story you need to know that the characters, Joe, Frank, and Sue, are members of their company's Investment Operations Team and that they have received training in constructive conflict resolution. One day, Sue was accidentally copied on an e-mail that was going back and forth between Joe and Frank. They were venting their displeasure with Sue because of some of the ideas she raised during their last team meeting. They questioned whether what she was asking for would do the team more harm than good.

Sue, of course, reacted to this private correspondence very personally. She went to the team manager and asked for a team meeting to be called right away. Frank and Joe were talking about live team plans, Sue said, and it's better for all seven team members to be involved. The manager agreed.

At the special team meeting, Sue took charge. She handed out copies of the e-mail messages between Joe and Frank and stated in a firm and controlled manner what bothered her most about the situation. Her teammates were talking *about* her and not *to* her, she said, and they were expressing concerns about a plan that the entire team was developing but not raising those concerns for everyone on the team to discuss.

Joe and Frank immediately apologized, recognizing they had gone against the team's formal guidelines concerning conflict resolution. And the team then discussed Joe and Frank's concerns about the pending plan and worked through that issue.

This special meeting of the Investment Operations Team became a turning point. It opened up team communications and underscored the importance of dealing directly and constructively with conflicts. Sue's constructive, yet firm, behavior in dealing with her concerns became the model for the team to follow.

✔ **Assume that the other person means well.** This assumption is the safest that you can make when you're working with someone else, especially when you're dealing with a conflict. When you assume that the other person means well, you don't have to worry that someone's out to get you. You're free to deal with the actions and issues at hand. What a relief!

Reaching for Some Handy Tools to Fix Conflicts

Later in this chapter, I present some problem-solving models for constructive conflict resolution. Each one has special features, but common to all of them is a set of communication tools that supports all problem-solving efforts. This section introduces you to three such tools.

Showing understanding through active listening

Conflicts often sound like *The Great Debate,* with the parties trying to outtalk each other and pushing their differing points of view. Before you know it, their disagreement escalates into a full-blown argument and nothing is resolved. (Don't even try this at home.) What's happening is that no one is truly actively listening.

Showing understanding first is part of active listening. Chapter 8 covers the tools of active listening that your team members need to perform well together. In this active listening effort, you do the following:

✔ **Shift your attention to the speaker.** Instead of thinking about how to rebut what the other person is saying, you give your full attention to capturing that person's message. Whether you agree with the message is not your focus. You want to understand exactly what the person means.

✔ **Provide verbal feedback to check your understanding.** After you've fully heard the other party's message, you can employ the active listening tools of *paraphrasing* or *reflective paraphrasing* to find out whether you actually understand the message. You put the main idea into your own words, which is paraphrasing, and you can also account for the emotion you have detected with the main idea, which is reflective paraphrasing. Here's an example:

 • *Paraphrasing:* "So is your point that we should look toward doing some process improvements rather than training?"

 • *Reflective paraphrasing:* "You've been feeling frustrated because, from your view, I haven't been responding to your requests for help. Is that right?"

 Notice that each example is only one sentence and each is phrased as or followed by a reaffirming question — your voice rises at the end of the sentence, and you may tag on, "Is that right?"

✔ **Gain confirmation before proceeding:** By *checking* your understanding of the other team member's message, you're inviting that person to instantly respond with something like "Yes, you got it right," or "No, let me clarify." In either case, you're avoiding misunderstanding and you're gaining a picture of where the other person is coming from.

To enable the confirming process to work, maintain a sincere and nonjudgmental tone. When it's timely to ask more questions for gaining a deeper understanding of the other person's thinking, remember to recheck your understanding with paraphrasing or reflective paraphrasing.

When one person shows he is able to truly listen, tension subsides and discussion can proceed in a civil fashion.

After you've shown the willingness and ability to listen first, ask the other person to summarize your message. When two people are actively listening to each other, the conflict is moving down a constructive path.

Describing — getting into observations

The communication tool known as *describing* is extremely useful during discussions aimed at conflict resolution. You use this tool to report the concerns or problems that have been seen or experienced, in other words, to gain understanding. That's the foundation of a good problem-solving process.

For an understanding of what describing does for you, compare these two statements, one that's opinion-based and the other that's observations-based:

- **Opinion-based:** "You were not much help on this project, and what help you attempted to give was ineffective."

- **Observations-based:** "I have a couple of concerns regarding your work with me on the Alpha Project. First, I noticed that when I came to you with questions, the response that I usually received was for me to come back later because you were busy. That meant I usually had to go to you two or three times before I could get answers to my questions. Second, the parts you were responsible for and passed on to me were incomplete and had to be given back to you each time to be fixed, which led to delays in getting my work done on time." (Notice the tool of describing in use.)

As you can see in the first example, the message is general, personal, and an expression of opinion — altogether judgmental. In the second example, the message is specific, issue-focused, and based on observations — that's describing. It's the difference between being subjective rather than objective in expressing a concern — objective being the way that people best receive the message.

Here are key guidelines to follow using the communication tool of describing:

- **Focus on the issue.** State the issue or topic upfront, preferably in your first sentence of the description, so that it's clear what the information that follows is about.

- **State observations.** Explain what the person did as if you were watching it on a video monitor. Don't judge or interpret someone else's actions. Stick to reporting what can be seen.

✔ **Provide specifics.** Give a concrete description of the behaviors that occurred. Avoid being general or vague. You're seeking clarity, so provide the necessary detail.

✔ **Be straightforward.** Be direct and sincere. That's the best way to give a message when you're dealing with a conflict. Don't beat around the bush; get straight to the point. And avoid mixed messages, such as, "I know you've been working hard, but you haven't been helpful on this project." The *but* negates the sincerity of the earlier part of the message.

Feelings — nothing but feelings

The third communication tool that is useful in conflict situations is called *stating feelings* — describing the emotions that *you* feel about a situation. The best time to say how you feel is right after you've described your concerns about a work situation. Your objective with this tool is to create awareness and the sense of importance surrounding your concerns — not blaming someone or making someone feel guilty.

Guidelines to follow when using the tool of stating feelings:

✔ **Own the feeling.** *Own the feeling* means that you use the words *I, me,* or *my* to indicate that the emotion being felt is yours. "I was annoyed by that action," or "When that event took place, it made me feel excluded."

✔ **Identify the emotion.** Name the emotion that you felt in a given situation. Whatever the emotion or emotions were, say what you felt — frustrated, disappointed, annoyed, excluded — and make sure it's an emotion and not a thought. For instance, "I'm *happy* about that new idea," identifies an emotion — happy in this case. But the statement, "I felt that was a good idea," even though it contains the word *feel,* actually is only a thought or an opinion, without any emotion identified. In stating feelings, as the name of this tool indicates, you're identifying the emotions that you had at the time in question.

✔ **Be constructive.** Your feelings often appear in the first thing that you say, so choose your words carefully. For instance, "I was frustrated by what happened," is far more constructive than, "I hate when you do that." Being constructive also means being sincere. And there's no room to vent or whine.

✔ **As needed, explain the basis of your feelings.** Be brief, explaining your feelings in two to three sentences at most. Providing a little background that gives context to your feelings is okay for the sake of clarity, but try not to repeat the problem: Stating your feelings comes after you've described the problem, and revisiting the problem is counterproductive.

One good way of stating your feelings is to follow this format: "Because of (*what happened*), I felt (*your emotions*)." Here's an example, with the blanks filled in: "Because you went ahead with the marketing event without consulting me, I felt excluded and that my input was no longer valued on the team."

Stick to issues and actions when you explain your feelings. Avoid making assumptions about the other person's attitude or motives. Attitude isn't the same as behavior. Attitude is how someone thinks or feels — what's going on inside the individual's head. You can't see it. But behavior is action. It's observable.

Resolving Conflicts the Old-Fashioned Way

Ultimately, when resolving a conflict, you have to do it the old-fashioned way. You have to sit down with the other person, put the issue on the table, and work out a solution together. That's the behavior — the kind of attitude — that you want to teach your team members to use with one another. To do so constructively, you need problem-solving models, and this section covers two such models that I've used through the years. One of the models is particularly effective with conflicts of an interpersonal nature; the other is designed to help resolve differences about work matters.

When a conflict is an isolated, one-time event, I suggest that you keep your response simple and follow this three-step approach when meeting with the other person:

1. **Describe your concern or the problem as you see it.**

2. **Together, work out a solution.**

3. **Close by recapping the agreement that the two of you have reached.**

But when a conflict is more involved or repetitive, you may be better off using one of the two models explained in this section. They're intended for use in one-on-one team member discussions, but they also can be applied at the group level.

Resolving interpersonal conflicts

When two people have an interpersonal conflict, the stress and strain between them prevents them from constructively and cooperatively working together. This model for resolving interpersonal conflicts has six steps:

Step 1: Introduction

Whoa, Nellie! Don't just dive into the details of the problem. You want to set the stage, preparing the other party to hear what you have to say, and your script announces these three topics:

- ✔ **The general purpose of the meeting.** This usually is a broad, one-sentence statement, for example:

  "As you know, I asked you to meet with me today so we can address some issues that I have related to how we've been working together."

  Highlighting the importance of the meeting is the purpose of this opening statement.

- ✔ **Your positive intention.** In a one- or two-sentence statement, emphasize the point that you *mean well*. That tells the other person that your actions in the meeting — the only part the other person can see — are meant to match your good intentions. This statement needs to be sincere and positive. For instance:

  "Sandra, what I want to accomplish in this meeting with you is a solution that helps us work together in a constructive and productive manner."

  Setting a tone that promotes dialogue and problem-solving rather than one that provokes defensiveness and debate is the idea.

- ✔ **The agenda.** Here you outline how the meeting will flow:

  "Sandra, I want to first describe the concerns that I've been having and their impact. Then I want to hear from you about these issues. Most important, I then want to work out a solution with you that helps both of us."

  Announcing the agenda shows the other person what to expect and helps her understand that the meeting is a two-way problem-solving session.

Step 2: Describing the concerns

Using the communication tool of describing that I presented in the section about "Describing — getting into observations" earlier in this chapter, you briefly state what you have noticed about the other person's actions and provide an example or two of what you're concerned about without becoming overly detailed. Making sure that you communicate coherently and concisely, you may want to come prepared with some notes to remind you about the main points.

Remember that you're stating only what you have seen and not offering any interpretation.

Step 3: Expressing your feelings or explaining the impact

Tell the other person how you feel (see "Feelings — nothing but feelings" section earlier in this chapter). Or explain how the concern has affected your performance or your working relationship with the other person.

Focus what you say only on job-related issues. Doing so helps you steer clear of making the concern into a personal matter. And keep in mind that the purpose of this step is to create a sense of importance — not to push guilt or blame. So, be sure that your language is constructive, your tone is sincere, and your message is brief — no more than a few sentences — so that the importance comes across.

Step 4: Letting the other person respond

Now it's time for you to listen — truly listen. Hold the debate and arguments; in fact, when you feel an urge to respond in those directions, throw that urge into the trash. The other person may have concerns with what *you've* been doing. He may agree with you or disagree with you. What he says doesn't require a rebuttal; it requires only that you show you're open to listening.

If you do anything, plug in one of the active listening tools such as *paraphrasing* or *reflective paraphrasing* so that you can check your understanding of what you're hearing. The meeting isn't about who's right or who's wrong. Focusing on that only stirs debate and argument. The meeting is about resolving a conflict.

Step 5: Developing a solution

Plan to spend the most time on Step 5, because it's the key to your success. Here's a three-step process for creating the solution:

1. **Establish a desired goal.**

   The goal is your target — the point that you want to reach with your solution. For conflicts of an interpersonal nature, the goal statement describes a working relationship, for instance:

   Develop and maintain a working relationship where we provide the support, cooperation, and respect to one another that help us achieve the team's goals.

   Write a draft goal statement and ask for the other person's feedback. Limit it to one sentence, stated positively, and make certain that it connects both parties. Agreements are best made when both parties are part of the solution.

2. **Develop ideas collaboratively to meet the goal.**

   Share ideas. Look for two things: what you want the other person to do to meet the goal and what *you* will do to meet the goal. That's right. Both parties need to contribute and take action for the goal to be reached.

3. Evaluate ideas and set the working agreement.

Get all ideas on the table before you begin discussing their merits. Then evaluate what you have, focusing on ideas that will be mutually benefi-cial and most helpful in attaining the goal. Work the ideas into specific actions so steps forward occur. Generalities produce little action.

The working agreement is a *written* document containing the goal and the action items assigned to each person. This document must be writ-ten simply because you don't want to leave an important discussion to memory. Everyone involved in the original conflict and in its resolution needs to receive a copy of the working agreement, including you, the manager, when you're playing a supporting role.

Step 6: Closing and setting follow-up

Recapping the working agreement and making certain that it's clear to both parties is a good way to close your meeting. Schedule a follow-up session within a month so that you can check your progress and reinforce account-ability. End the meeting on a positive note.

Figure 10-1 shows you all six steps in a nutshell.

Figure 10-1:
The six-step model.

**Resolving-Concerns
Conflict Resolution Model**

<u>Steps</u>

1 – Introduction

- State general purpose of the meeting
- State your positive intention
- Announce the agenda

2 – Describe the Concerns

3 – Express Your Feelings or Explain the Impact

4 – Let the Other Person Respond

5 – Develop a Solution

- Establish a desired goal
- Develop ideas collaboratively to meet the goal
- Evaluate ideas and set the working agreement

6 – Close and Set Follow-up

Resolving work-related, needs-based conflicts

Sometimes team members have conflicts over work procedures, or ideas for solving a work problem, or strategies for executing a work plan. Differences of opinion about work issues can pop up unexpectedly — even when you're meeting on a totally unrelated topic. But you can deal with them by applying this five-step, needs-based model:

Step 1: Defining the problem

First, develop a one-sentence statement that defines the problem or issue. Limit it to only one sentence so that the central issue is clear to everyone.

Second, clarify what the differences are. What are the perspectives of the parties involved? Are the differences based on methods, ideas, goals, styles, or some other factor? Use questions like these to analyze where the differences are, but don't spend too much time at this point or you may fall into the pit of overanalysis and possibly more conflict.

Step 2: Identifying the needs of stakeholders

Moving away from people's positions — your way versus my way — and looking, instead, at people's needs is a critical step. Consider needs extremely important because they explain *why* you want what you want.

For instance, when you go car shopping, you can easily haggle with the sales representative about the price that you want to pay — that's your *position.* But a good sales representative seeks out what's important to you in buying a car, whether it's gas mileage, style, how you'll use the car, your budget, or what not, before attempting to talk price with you. Meeting all your needs so that your purchase gives you *value* is key.

The same idea applies in this second step of the conflict-resolution model. Identifying needs moves everyone to a higher level, where seeing what is truly important is easier.

Stakeholders are parties affected by the issue and the outcomes. Certainly the list of stakeholders includes the team members involved and quite often the team as a whole. Stakeholders also can be people outside the team who are affected by what the team does, including other departments, management above you, and customers. What you do in this discussion is identify each stakeholder and then list the critical needs each one has. What you often find is that stakeholders have some needs in common or at least complementary needs.

Step 3: Developing options for resolution

Using your brainstorming skills (see Chapter 9), generate ideas for meeting the needs of the various stakeholders — without passing judgment on any idea they have. As people volunteer ideas, write them down for all to see, together with the needs that they address.

Step 4: Evaluating options against needs

Evaluating is the step where conflicts really get worked out, so spend the most time with it. You want to focus discussions on ideas or options that work best to meet stakeholders' needs. Avoid backsliding into the problem. Drill the ideas down into specific actions so what's to happen going forward is clear and concrete.

The key in conflict resolution is spending more time working on the solution than dwelling on the problem.

Step 5: Confirming and implementing the agreement

Recap the agreement that you reach making sure that it's clear and understood by everyone. After that, discuss how to move forward — who's going to do what and when — in the implementation phase. Set a date to review progress, and don't forget to put everything in writing.

Figure 10-2 shows all five steps of the needs-based conflict resolution model.

Figure 10-2:
The
five-step
model.

Needs-Based Conflict Resolution Model

<u>Steps</u>

1 – Define the Problem

2 – Identify the Needs of the Stakeholders

3 – Develop Options for Resolution

4 – Evaluate the Options Against the Needs

5 – Confirm the Agreement and Set the Implementation

Mission possible: Settle these conflicts

The best test of your conflict-resolution skills is, of course, putting them to work in a real-life conflict. However, until one comes along, you can stay sharp by working on these fictional cases. It's amazing how lifelike fiction can be.

Case 1

The team recently implemented a new work procedure that everyone is supposed to follow. But Julio hasn't bothered. Every time he passes his part to Maria, she has to do what Julio *should* have done to fit in with the new procedure, and that slows Maria down. She returned the work for Julio to fix a couple of times, but he didn't. A third time, she told Julio that he needed to follow the new procedure, but he snapped that he *was* following the procedure and that she doesn't need to be his boss. Obviously, a conflict is brewing. Applying the model for resolving interpersonal conflicts, what should Maria do and say to settle this problem with Julio?

Case 2

Customers have been rejecting their orders at a higher rate than normal, and the Order Fulfillment Team, your team, is feeling the heat. Various kinds of errors in fulfillment are occurring, causing more and more customers to be upset with your company. The marketing department is annoyed about your team 's decline in performance.

At the first team meeting at which you first attempt to figure out this problem and solve it, team members appear to form two factions led by Sue on one side and Bill on the other. Sue and her group say that better training is the answer; Bill and his faction argue that streamlining the work process is what's needed the most. Tensions are growing as discussion bogs down. Your assignment is to resolve the issue by applying the work-related conflict-resolution model.

Coaching a team to settle conflicts on its own

Your ultimate goal when conflicts arise in your team is for team members to settle the issues themselves. You want them to take responsibility for their behavior and for developing their own solutions.

When the team depends on you to resolve all its conflicts, here are some outcomes that you can expect:

- ✔ You become complaint central, the place where team members constantly come to complain about one another — tattling on each other like siblings whining to a parent.

- ✔ You become the almighty monarch, making all the decisions and preventing your loyal subjects from thinking and doing for themselves.

- ✔ You become the *source* of many conflicts. Team members who don't like what you decide criticize you, often behind your back.

- ✔ You have little time to focus on the important issues that you need to attend to as the team manager or leader.

To avoid creating a dependent team and, instead, facilitate the growth of a self-sufficient and responsible team, remember these tips:

- ✔ **Lead by example.** Never complain about other managers or other groups in front of your team. When you have issues with other people, go talk to them directly (don't use e-mail). When team members know that you address concerns and conflicts timely and directly, they have a role model: you.

- ✔ **Teach.** One reason that many team members dodge dealing with conflicts is that they don't know how. Most have not had role models for conflict resolution (have you?). That's why you show your team how to use the communication and problem-solving tools outlined in this chapter. The sooner they learn, the better.

- ✔ **Coach with questions.** Questions are good coaching tools because they prod staff members into thinking issues through and working them out for themselves. When you provide answers instead of asking questions, you deny that benefit to team members. See Chapter 8 for tips about asking questions in an open-ended, nonthreatening fashion.

When one team member comes complaining to you about another team member, use questions like these to lead the complainer to take responsibility for himself:

- ✔ What have you done so far to address your concern with (the other person)?

- ✔ What would be your objective if you talked to (the other person)?

- ✔ How would you express your concerns constructively — what would you say?

- ✔ What would you propose as a solution to this conflict for each of you?

- ✔ What did you learn in the training that can help you deal with this situation?

When team members understand that you turn their complaints into queries about what *they* intend to do in resolving their own problems and concerns, they'll get the idea and start figuring things out for themselves, sparing you the trouble. But you can take full credit for that breakthrough.

Raul changes the Rauls

Raul's city government team provides permit and inspection services to contractors and real estate developers. The work can be stressful at times, but that doesn't excuse shabby behavior by some team members toward other team members. Raul used to hear about this when someone came in griping and moaning about someone else. He hated to see a complainer coming because he had set himself up as the go-between and reconciler of conflicts. (Not a good move, Raul!)

But Raul was smart enough to schedule training sessions for his team on the communication tools of active listening and assertive speaking, and he included training in conflict-resolution tools, too. Even better, Raul took the training along with his team. (Good move, Raul!) He learned that he didn't need to be the one resolving the conflicts — that his team members could settle conflicts themselves.

Sure enough, a few days after the training ended, Sarah was in Raul's office complaining about Brent. The way Sarah told it, Brent wasn't following through on a certain permitting task that affected her. Raul checked his impulse to act as the grand conciliator. Instead, he asked Sarah, based on what she had discovered in the recent training, how she planned to address the matter with Brent?

The question surprised Sarah at first — this didn't sound like good old Raul. But she recovered quickly and outlined a simple plan that she could follow with Brent. Raul asked her to come back afterward and let him know how it went.

Later that day, Sarah checked back in with Raul. With much delight, she reported how she had quickly and positively resolved her problem with Brent. The training in conflict resolution really helps, she said. "It sure does," Raul thought.

Asking for commitments and follow-up

When team members figure out how to constructively address a conflict, you want to hear a firm commitment. Ask: "So, when will you address that issue with (the other person)?" Then say: "Check back with me after you've had the meeting and let me know how it works out." Those statements ensure accountability, and the best part is that the team member is addressing the conflict without your intervention. Your good coaching pays off.

 When a team member doesn't want to take any action himself — let the choice be his to address his problems — you can still ask him what he's going to do to remain respectful and cooperative with the other team member. Addressing the situation that way tells him that you expect him to remain a professional and a helpful team member. Telling you about his issues with another team member changes nothing as far as what's expected in his behavior with the other party and everyone else on the team.

Addressing performance problems

A *performance problem* is not the same as a *conflict,* and I want you to remember the difference. Team members have their clashes and differences sometimes — those are the *conflicts* that you coach them to handle themselves. But when you see a team member whose behavior has become disruptive in the team, who isn't pulling his weight, or who remains uncooperative after good-faith efforts by other team members to address concerns, then you have a *performance problem,* and stepping in as coach to work things out with the problem team member is your responsibility as manager. Chapter 4 offers you some tips about how to take corrective action with performance problems.

When team members know that you expect them to handle their own conflicts but that you're always there for performance problems, you're building a high-performance team.

Serving as the third-party facilitator

Occasionally, a third party must step in to help the first and second parties settle their differences. Observing when a third party is needed is easy: The other team members continue their clash; the tension between them grows so thick you can cut it with a knife. Clearly, they can't constructively resolve the conflict themselves and your intervention is needed. This section contains tips for working as a third-party facilitator.

- ✔ **Decide which players come to the table.** When the conflict involves only a couple of team members, the meeting is between them. When a number of team members are involved, then everybody comes to the table. Don't use a group setting to address a conflict that involves only two players — unless, that is, you prefer fighting fires with gasoline.

- ✔ **Select a problem-solving model.** Decide what you're dealing with — whether it's a personality clash or a dispute over a work-process matter, or a little bit of both. Remember that you can mix and match methods from the two models that I present in the "Resolving Conflicts the Old-Fashioned Way" section earlier this chapter.

- ✔ **Write an agenda and set ground rules.** You need an agenda so that you can hand it to participants in advance of the meeting. The agenda doesn't have to be any more elaborate than the numbered steps of the problem-solving model you want to use. When the meeting begins, set a few ground rules to govern the professional conduct that you expect. Stick to the agenda; insist on professional conduct. When the meeting involves the whole team, you may want to appoint a team member who understands the conflict-resolution models to serve as facilitator. You attend to provide guidance and support as needed.

✔ **When the clash is interpersonal, prepare the individuals separately.** Common sense tells you not to throw the combatants together without giving them a chance in advance to sort out their thoughts and emotions. While you prepare the team members separately, ask them to write out their concerns and their ideas about what each person should do to reach a solution. Doing so helps to move them from simply venting anger to focusing on being constructive and gives everyone a script, increasing the likelihood that the meeting will stay on track.

✔ **Put the agreement in writing.** Don't leave an agreed-upon resolution to memory. The written working agreement defines the solution, and everyone gets a copy.

✔ **Meet later to review progress.** Set a time for everyone to return to the table and review progress — perhaps a few weeks or a month out. At the follow-up meeting, use the working agreement as the agenda. Ask the parties to talk about how things are going with respect to the agreement. Don't forget to provide your observations, too. If the agreement needs to be modified, do so. If the team members are making progress, let them run the next follow-up session themselves and just keep you informed about their progress. But if things are not progressing, stay directly involved. If you don't see progress at follow-up meetings, set consequences such as disciplinary action and carry them out.

If you observe at the first follow-up meeting that both parties are sticking to the agreement, don't hold back on positive feedback. Your reinforcement of their good efforts to resolve differences encourages them to do even more of the same.

Chapter 11

Making Decisions as a Team

*W*henever you're asking team members to pull together in helping to get the work done, having them help you make decisions about day-to-day work is part of the plan. In fact, leading your team effectively as a coach involves utilizing some form of shared decision making on a regular basis. How come?

People support most what they help create. Getting your people involved in making decisions about issues that affect the team gives them a sense of ownership. In addition, teaching them the decision-making process makes your team less dependent on you for every single decision. That's good!

Furthermore, if you're the leader of a group of people who do not report directly to you, such as a cross-functional task team or a project team, making all the decisions for the team by yourself is certain to cause rebellion. Team members grumble, "Who are you to think that you can be our boss for this team?"

In this chapter I show you how you can provide useful group decision-making tools for your team members, so that the next time you say that such-and-such an issue lends itself to using a *consensus approach* or a *consultative approach* in reaching a decision, they'll know what you mean and how to work with you.

Contrasting the Ways that Decisions Are Made in Groups

In Chapter 1, I point out that teams are work groups but that not all work groups are teams. In fact, many more work groups are *not* teams than are teams. But all work groups, team or not, rely on the same kinds of decision-making processes.

Decisions are made in groups by one of five main methods:

- Unilaterally — by the boss
- Unilaterally with some input from others
- By simple majority vote
- By consensus — everyone agreeing to support the conclusion
- By the consultative process — one primary decider with help from members of the group

No one type fits best for all situations. This section weighs the pros and cons of each type.

The unilateral mode

In unilateral decision making, one person takes responsibility for making the decision for the whole group. Usually that person is the boss. As boss, you decide and announce your decision, and the others are expected to carry it out. Here are the pros and cons of the unilateral mode:

Pros

- **Enables you to move fast.** If you're willing to assert yourself and not be wishy-washy, unilateral decisions are quick — the fastest of the five main decision-making methods. Just make a decision and roll. Next issue, please!

- **Takes care of the small stuff.** Not every issue that you face in a workday requires a group to meet for discussion. Many such issues only require someone to act.

- **Works well in emergencies.** When the patient is in grave condition, everyone on the medical team wants the lead doctor to direct the surgery. When the building is on fire, everyone on the fire crew wants the fire captain to decide how to get water on the blaze. You simply don't have time to organize a meeting and have a group discussion.

Cons

- ✔ **Leaves some people scratching their heads.** When you're the only one doing the thinking, others may not understand your decision and thus may fail to implement it well. People can become confused by things that don't make sense to them.

- ✔ **Leaves you short of vital information.** No one person is all-seeing and all-knowing . . . not even you. When you make unilateral decisions, you shut the door on vital information that affects the way you make the final call. But, because you don't ask around for input, you don't know what you're missing. On the other hand, members of the group *know* what you're missing and may remark on your lack of common sense as they complain about you behind your back.

- ✔ **Generates less support.** People support most what they help create. If they're not present at the creation — well, you get the point. Especially true with issues that have a deep and broad impact on the group; the less they're involved in making the decision, the more they're inclined to resist the decision. You may have the greatest idea since the wheel, but when others who are affected by it are not consulted in any way, they have little motivation to buy in and support you.

The unilateral mode with individual inputs

Similar to the unilateral mode, one person, usually the person in charge, makes the call — but only after talking individually with others on the team, bouncing ideas off of them, and getting their thoughts. Here are the pros and cons:

Pros

- ✔ **Moves fast.** As decision maker, you can consult with as few or as many people as you desire. You get the input you need, and you act.

- ✔ **Gives you more information and insight**. The advantage is obvious: When you're speaking clearly to your team members about an issue and listening well to what they say, you're bound to be better equipped to make a decision than you are unilaterally without their input.

- ✔ **Creates more support and understanding.** The people with whom you consult usually understand your decision better and usually go along with it more readily than in the unilateral approach without input.

Cons

- ✔ **Gets little support from those who are left out of the process.** Individual consultation takes time, and some people may be left out. You can't count on support from people who are left out.

✔ **Short-circuits true discussion.** When it's just you and the other guy talking, neither of you reaps the rich benefit of a good group discussion, where differing perspectives can mix, creative sparks can fly, and good ideas germinate and grow.

✔ **Can make explaining your decision difficult.** Because you consult with individuals individually, you alone hear a variety of views. No one else has the complete transcript, so to speak. So, if along the journey the things that you hear cause you to make quite a different decision than what seemed apparent in your first one-on-one, or if you just change your mind along the way, others may not understand why you did what you did and may initially oppose your decision. Explaining your decision after all that can be quite a challenge.

The simple majority mode

Making a decision by simple majority means half of the group plus one agrees with an option, and that becomes *the group's* decision. For example, five members of a nine-member group choose option A, and the other four chose option B. Option A is the group's decision. Here are the pros and cons:

Pros

✔ **Easy to administer.** People know how to vote — it's the democratic process. You can do it by raising hands, shouting out choices, or by secret ballot.

✔ **Promotes group participation.** Unlike the two unilateral approaches, decision making by majority vote usually includes group discussion. Options are presented and discussed, and a selection process takes place. Everyone is present and can participate in making the final decision.

✔ **Helps in managing large groups.** When dozens or hundreds of people are in a common work situation, majority vote on decisions works well. The process is efficient and familiar.

Cons

✔ **Breeds a winners/losers climate.** Quite often, people on the minority side feel like losers. Even when those in the majority don't gloat, the losers often turn into the opposition and don't support the decision. (See the United States Congress for examples of this gridlock.) This *con* tends to be the biggest problem with simple majority decisions in work group situations.

✔ **Lessens creativity and flexibility.** The first objective in majority decision making is deciding what choices to present to the group for a vote.

If too many options are put on the proverbial table, a simple majority becomes much more difficult to reach. (See the Italian Parliament for examples.) Consequently, groups often try to artificially limit the number of choices by dumping them into categories. That process, in the name of efficiency, tends to turn off discussion and the possible discovery of even better options through the creative process of combining factors — for example, concluding that the best decision for the team is neither Option A nor Option B but a combination of the two as Option C.

The consensus mode

The word *consensus* is often misused. It doesn't mean a majority or a large majority agreeing to the terms of a decision. It doesn't mean that all agree — that's being *unanimous*. A decision made by consensus is one that everyone agrees to *support*. Support is the key word. Some group members individually may not agree with the group's conclusion, but they're willing to support it. Consensus is reached through collective participation. Here are the cons and pros.

Cons

I've unilaterally decided to start with the *cons* so that you understand the potential difficulties before you see the plus side of decision making by consensus.

✔ **Takes the longest.** Decisions made through consensus often involve a great deal of back-and-forth, give-and-take collective discussion. Reaching outcomes doesn't happen quickly. All it takes is for one person not supporting the decision everyone else does, and the work for achieving a decision is not done yet.

✔ **Requires the highest level of communication skill.** When I mention this factor to groups, some people wonder why it's not in the *pro* column. The reason is that people in group situations often don't bring communication skills to the table — the ability to actively listen and to speak up and express themselves constructively. They can get stuck arguing positions and never offer ideas to resolve the differences. These kinds of behaviors can swamp the consensus process.

✔ **Doesn't work for large groups.** The more people involved in the group, the harder reaching a consensus is. This especially tends to happen when a group size grows to ten or more. In groups of that size, it's hard for everyone's ideas to get a good hearing, and the likelihood of opposing points of view can often rise as well.

Pros

✔ **Builds the strongest buy-in.** Decision by consensus requires more participation than any of the three modes that I have presented so far. The group is not finished with its work until every member expresses loudly and clearly her willingness to support the outcome the group reaches. That's buy-in.

✔ **Makes for the quickest implementation.** Unilateral decisions usually are the quickest to make but the slowest to implement. By comparison, decisions made by consensus usually are the slowest to make but the quickest to implement. Because everyone in the group participates in making the decision, everyone is onboard and understands what needs to be done to implement the decision.

✔ **Develops a group's problem-solving skill.** Reaching consensus involves sorting out differences and resolving concerns — problem-solving at its best. The more that groups, and especially teams, make decisions by consensus, the more their problem-solving skills develop.

The consultative mode

In the consultative mode, one person — the primary decider — makes the decision but does so with the help of the group. In a collective forum, group members provide input helping to shape the decision to be made by the primary decider. Later in this chapter, in the section about "Following the Consultative Route," I show you how to use this decision-making method.

Here are the pros and cons:

Pros

✔ **Builds strong understanding about the decision.** Because group members are part of the collective work helping to shape the decision, they definitely understand what the decision is when it's reached. They're present to hear what the final outcome is and the rationale for it, and they know how it evolved during the discussion to which they contributed. You'll find no better way of gaining a strong understanding. In fact, the depth of understanding usually leads to group member support for the decision.

✔ **Mines rich input for the decision maker.** One big value of the consultative route, more so than the unilateral approach with individual consultations, is that the decision maker has the entire group together. Discussing the issue as a group generally produces to a richer variety of points of view as the participants bounce thoughts off one another and the primary decider. In essence, more ingredients are thrown into the mix than typically are in one-on-one discussions.

Qualified consensus: The deadlock buster

A sixth decision-making method exists, but I tend to share it only with management groups that recognize a primary decider. The method is called *qualified consensus,* and it may come into play when a group has exhausted all efforts to reach a consensus on an issue. At that point, the primary decider makes the decision and explains the rationale for it. You can think of this process as consensus with a consultative feature.

The pro side of qualified consensus is that it enables a team to overcome stalemates. On the con side, when a primary decider steps in too soon to end a discussion, or when he uses this method too often, the team may feel that an exercise in decision making is just camouflage for a unilateral approach and not worth their participation in the future.

I've used the qualified consensus mode a few times with management and executive teams that were involved in tough personnel and organizational decisions, but I made sure going in that the teams understood what qualified consensus is and how it works. As an outside facilitator, I was authorized to hand the decision over to the primary decider when consensus could not be reached.

One executive team that I worked with made more than a dozen decisions on organizational strategies and other issues during a single day — all by consensus. Team members mentioned that they were motivated to reach consensus by the fact that their top executive could be asked to step in and make a unilateral decision, whenever necessary. That day, they said, was the most efficient experience they had ever had in making decisions by consensus.

Another management team, this one at a small company, had the task of calibrating annual performance reviews. Their objective was making sure the appropriate overall rating was given on each review — no inflated ratings and no undervaluing of good performers. More than 50 performance evaluations were reviewed and decided upon in one day by this management group, and only once was the president asked to make a decision to break a deadlock.

The consensus of this management team: Qualified consensus keeps you focused and working hard to reach conclusions.

✔ **Provides a structure for maximizing group participation.** The consultative mode follows a four-step process in reaching a decision (as I explain a bit later in "Following the Consultative Route"). This organized process helps you gain full group participation in the decision and makes it clear who in the end makes the call. No one is left out nor does the group have to keep going until consensus is reached. The structured process enables you to have good discussion and a relatively efficient way of reaching a decision.

Cons

✔ **Requires good listening and facilitation skills from the primary decider.** When you're the decision maker and your mind is fully made up on an issue, don't try using the consultative mode simply to gain the blessing of your group. It won't work. People see through this tactic. They can usually tell when you aren't genuinely open to differing points of view. You can save everybody's time by using the unilateral mode (described at the beginning of this section).

✔ **Requires recognition of someone as a primary decider.** In some team situations, such as task teams, project teams, and self-directed teams, no one person has the recognized authority to serve as a primary decider. Team leaders usually exist but their roles generally are as coordinator or facilitator but not as manager. So, unless the team designates someone as the primary decider of an issue, the consultative mode of decision making can't be used.

Because teams need collective efforts to succeed, they periodically need to employ collective forms of decision making, in particular, the consensus and consultative modes. But the key in showing team members the decision-making process is acquainting them with all five main methods so they're aware of possible approaches when an issue requires a decision.

Reaching a True Consensus

Earlier in this chapter I talk about using *consensus* as a tool to reach a decision, and it's defined as everyone agreeing *to support* the conclusion of the team. Reaching a consensus may sound like the most natural thing in the world, but it isn't. Teams get derailed on their way to a consensus. But that doesn't have to happen when your team understands the steps that make the consensus tool work. That's the topic of this section.

Following the Yellow Brick Road to consensus

Your team can reach a decision by consensus in five steps. Show them all the details so that the next time you want to settle an issue by consensus, they'll know exactly what to do.

Step 1: Identifying all options or views.

Get all the options and viewpoints out in the open. Write them on the board or flip chart, but hold off on any discussion until all points of view have been discovered. Groups sometimes derail their own efforts by jumping on the first idea or point raised and that tends to cut off further input.

When your team has more than one issue to decide, take them one at a time through all five steps.

Step 2: Building on common ideas.

Look over your list of options or views to find out what thinking is in common. By piecing together commonalties before sorting out differences, teams build support for agreement easier and faster.

Step 3: Discussing the differences.

By identifying the commonalties first (Step 2), you often begin narrowing the number of differences anyway. But before evaluating individual options, let people explain their thinking. You want team members to actively listen to various perspectives so that everyone truly understands the choices. Achieving this understanding makes the next step in the process so much easier.

Step 4: Proposing alternatives or compromises to settle differences.

The best way of settling differing points of view is first to listen and gain an understanding (that's Step 3), and then to ask team members for ideas to resolve the differences among various points of view. Make sure that everyone feels free to be creative. Sometimes a good alternative is a compromise crafted from elements of two different viewpoints.

Reaching consensus with "E.F. Hutton"

Once while I was helping a group develop various team skills, members of the group ran into a tough problem and asked me to facilitate a meeting to work through the issue.

This team had 12 members, including its manager. One of the team members was what I like to call an "E.F. Hutton" person. You remember the old television commercials for this investment firm: The tagline was: "When E.F. Hutton talks, people listen." The idea was that when you have great expertise that others desire, you don't need to shout to get those people to pay close attention. The E. F. Hutton member of the team was a person with a great deal of expertise who was greatly respected by other members of the team. However, he also had a quiet and reserved communication style and tended not to speak up much in group situations.

On the day I served as facilitator, the team had worked through its tough problem and seemed to have reached a solution. Vocal members were quite excited and ready to close the discussion when I reminded everyone about testing consensus — polling the members individually and asking whether they supported the decision, and, if not, to explain why and offer an alternative, if possible.

As I went around the room, checking consensus, I received 11 strong responses of "Yes." But the 12th person at the table, "Mr. E.F. Hutton," surprised everyone by saying, "Not really." He explained the problem he had with the proposed decision and presented an alternative. For the next five minutes, a lively discussion ensued, and in the end, the team's decision was slightly modified incorporating the new and valuable input from a soft-spoken but respected member. When I checked consensus a second time, it was unanimous: 12 strong affirmations.

Sometimes the best question to ask team members when they wrestle with differences is: "What would you suggest?" Doing so pushes everyone to think in terms of solutions instead of getting stuck on positions.

Step 5: Testing consensus when you seem to have a conclusion.

As a team works through the first four steps of the consensus process, a potential outcome and a potential decision may appear on the horizon. But appearances can be deceiving, because group dynamics can fool you. Sometimes in group situations more vocal people actually reach an agreement on an issue while quieter folks just sit there, smiling at best. That's when you must test consensus with each individual not by asking, "Do you agree?" but by asking:

> *"Will you support this decision?"*

Consensus doesn't mean that you're seeking everyone's agreement with the decision or conclusion. You're seeking everyone's *support.* People sometimes may not personally agree with an outcome, because it wouldn't have been their individual choice, but by being part of the discussion, they're willing to go along with or support the conclusion that the group has reached. Asking for someone's support is far different from asking for agreement. When you have every team member's support, you also have his or her commitment — that's true consensus.

In testing consensus, ask each team member the "Will you support . . ." question one at a time. I like to set up this part of forming a consensus by instructing team members to give a clear *Yes,* or a thumbs-up sign, if they support the conclusion or a clear *No,* or thumbs down, if they don't; moreover, I insist on them explaining why and offering an alternative if they can.

Checking consensus lets you know if you have true support and offers you the opportunity to pull out any dissenters when you need to hear their concerns. This opportunity opens the door for naysayers to express and explain their doubts and even to lobby for changes in the agreement. It reinforces the point that exploring concerns is part of the consensus process — and that team members are *expected* to express any concerns they may have. After concerns are worked through and everyone gives clear affirmation in support of the decision, the team has reached consensus.

You may want your team to practice using the consensus mode before applying it to any real issues. Doing so shows team members how well they work together and how well they follow the key steps of consensus. You can make up an issue that lends itself to good discussion, or create a checklist by consensus on the guidelines to follow for having productive meetings.

Games that I have used with good success include "Lost On the Moon," "Lost At Sea," and "Stranded on a Desert Island." In these survival-type exercises, team members first must individually rank a number of action options in order of importance. Then the team collectively ranks those same items through consensus. More often than not, the team score is better than any individual scores after they are compared with rankings made by experts. That shows you the power of consensus: Two or more heads together are better than one head alone.

Dodging the potholes that throw you off Consensus Road

Sometimes when teams try to reach consensus on issues, they take shortcuts that stymie the formation of a true consensus and undermine the decision. Pitfalls that you want to avoid are

- **Jumping to majority vote.** When a team is getting stuck in its discussion to reach consensus, abandoning the path and settling the differences by taking a vote doesn't help at all. Team members in the minority often walk out in opposition to the decision. Informal voting can be useful as an interim step to determine how people are thinking about an issue, but you need to immediately return to discussion to sort out differences in a true consensus mode.

- **Striking a deal.** Making a deal sounds like this: "If you support me on this issue, I'll support you on some future issue that's important to you." Sorry folks, trading favors doesn't build support for a decision needed now and it may create animosity later when the favor isn't returned. So, don't make political bargains when you're working to reach consensus.

- **Using tie-breaking methods to end a stalemate.** Tossing a coin or drawing straws is okay for settling kids' disputes, but those tactics have no place in the consensus process. The problem is that you wind up with winners and losers and not a decision that everyone can support.

- **Browbeating a lone dissenter.** When one team member doesn't support a decision that everyone else favors, avoid launching a verbal barrage at the dissenter just to make consensus happen. Doing so intimidates some dissenters and causes others to argue even more. Neither outcome builds support but rather only stirs resentment. Differing views need to be welcomed and their proponents made to feel safe if a team ever is going to develop the skill of consensus decision making.

> ✒ **Accepting appeasement in place of affirmation.** As discussion drags on, some team members may conclude that they agree with a decision just to get the session over. Or they may say they agree simply to avoid expressing a difference and causing a conflict. You can hear it in their half-hearted "That's fine with me," or "Whatever you folks want." Don't let appeasement substitute for affirming support behind a decision, because, if you do, the appeasing team members sometimes walk out after the meeting is over and immediately criticize the decision — a surefire way to produce a false consensus and a decision that eventually is undermined.

Differences of opinion are natural and expected. Seek them out and involve everyone in exploring alternatives to settle the differences. Stick with it. That's how you work through discussions to reach consensus.

Following the Consultative Route

In the consultative approach to collective decision making, the team helps the primary decider, most often the manager, to make the best possible decision. Here's how this four-step process works:

Step 1: Primary decider establishes a starting position or clarifies an issue to be decided.

After giving the team a brief background about the issue to be decided, the primary decider announces his or her position and supporting rationale. At this point, the primary decider is leaning toward his stated position but hasn't settled on it, which is why the team is being asked to help. Sometimes, however, the primary decider may not have formed a starting position; or the decision may concern only a few options, such as deciding which person to hire, and the primary decider doesn't state an opening position so as not to bias the team. In those instances, the primary decider simply tells it like it is and the process moves to Step 2.

If your mind is really made up on what you want to do about an issue, don't use the consultative approach. People can see through a facade of participation. Being sincere and using the unilateral mode is much better, and then you just explain your decision.

Step 2: Team members provide input on the issue individually.

The primary decider plays the role of a facilitator and hears from each team member one at a time. The decision maker records each member's input on the front board or flip chart for everyone to see. Doing so helps reveal ideas in common. Team members are welcome to state their views about the decider's opening position, add suggestions, and raise questions. But no discussion takes place during Step 2.

Step 3: General discussion.

You want a give-and-take discussion about the issue to occur between you (the primary decider) and team members and even among members themselves. As primary decider, you may want to pose other questions so that your team can explore matters at a deeper level. You may want to test your ideas to determine what they think.

The discussion stage is the longest stage of the process, so let it run its course. Check in with team members along the way to see what they're thinking. You're not seeking their support as you do with consensus. Here you're seeking their input and understanding.

Step 4: The primary decider states the final decision and supporting rationale.

When discussion concludes, the primary decider makes the call and explains why. But if the primary decider isn't ready to make a decision, that's okay, too. Sometimes you simply need time to mull it over before making the final call on an issue. If the primary decider defers at this point, however, setting a time when the decision and supporting rationale will be announced and explained is critical to do and is to be done live and *with* the team.

The consultative decision-making tool is used when team members are working together, not when they are apart. If, as the primary decider, you ever feel unready to make the call at the end of the meeting's discussion, then come back when you are ready so that you complete Step 4 properly. Don't wait long because you brought the issue forward to make a decision in the first place. Remember, too, that you're not seeking consensus or total buy-in from everyone on the team. Instead, you're using the consultative approach because you want team members' input and understanding so that you can make a final decision — which is especially useful on more sensitive issues for which a consensus is difficult to achieve — as the next section explores.

Having shown teams how to use the consultative mode and having led them through its application, I've seen two outcomes more than any other. One, the primary decider is leaning one way on an issue at Step 1 but changes positions by Step 4. Two, the primary decider's original position is unchanged but acquires added depth through consultation, making it a better decision. In each case, rich input gained from the process helps the decision maker immensely. The key to success is that the primary decider comes across with a willingness to listen that is receptive to the team's input, which greatly pleases members of the team.

In some cases, team members are greatly relieved that a tough issue has been decided and that they don't have to wrestle with it any more.

Selecting the Right Decision-making Tool for the Situation

Earlier in this chapter I show you how to teach your team to apply two collective forms of decision-making tools — the consensus approach and the consultative approach. But how does a team decide which one to use? Equally important, how does a team know when the issue requires a formal process for resolution? If you use these shared decision-making approaches for every little issue, your team won't have much time left for work!

This section provides you with answers and guidance so that the team makes the best use of its time.

Taking a moment to plan

Before deciding whether team participation is needed in decision making, you need to figure out a few basics. Here's your to-do list:

✔ **Define the issue first.** Clarify for yourself what the issue that needs a decision is. When you do that first, you begin discovering whether you need team involvement.

✔ **Clarify the role of the team.** When you have an issue for which team involvement can be beneficial, clarify the role that you want the team to play. Sometimes that means a decision-making role with you using the consensus or consultative modes. Other times you may want the team playing only an advisory role. You can avoid confusion and misunderstanding by making sure that team members understand what role you want them to perform.

✔ **Set parameters for the team's involvement.** Parameters are boundaries. They determine how far a team can go in deciding an issue, measured by factors like:

- Budget

- Time

- Responsibility or authority

- The objectives of management above you

Avoid misunderstanding and havoc: Let your team know this pertinent information as you involve them in the decision-making process.

✔ **Determine the decision-making mode.** The choice is totally yours, and that's the way it should be. Acting decisively and independently is appropriate for you as coach of the team. No hard-and-fast rules exist to help you with deciding when to involve the team in making a decision — the consensus and consultative approaches — or when to handle the issue yourself — the unilateral and unilateral-with-consultation approaches. (Wouldn't life be so much easier if there were rules?) But a few factors may influence your judgment one way or the other, such as:

- The extent that an issue directly affects your team's day-to-day work

- The scope of an issue beyond the team's direct work level

- The importance to you of garnering team-member support behind an issue

Even when the factors that I list above are present, *don't* involve the team in making the decision if your mind is strongly made up on what you want to do concerning an issue. You're better off explaining what you want to do and selling the team on why you think it's the best way to go rather than asking them to "share" in making a decision that you've already made.

If you seek consensus on every little matter, your team can be bogged down in a *paralysis by analysis.* Small issues that involve primarily you and management above you or other persons outside the team often are best decided by you alone. Sometimes you can get the team to agree to let a small subgroup handle an issue for them. In these cases, you, or the subgroup, need to report back to the team so that everyone is in the loop.

Running a few test cases for practice

This part of the chapter helps you think through the kinds of issues that routinely crop up with teams and the arguments for and against various decision-making modes. In each of the cases, determine first what decision-making mode you'd use and why; and then read my recommendation. You can also use this section as a learning activity to teach your team about decision-making tools.

The Budget

You need prepare the group's annual operating budget to submit for management approval. Do you involve your team in this work and, if so, what decision-making mode is best to use?

My recommendation: When you want your team actively involved in the financial management and execution of the operating budget, then involving them in shaping the budget makes good sense. Define the parameters upfront and coach team members to come prepared with all possible relevant data and work needs for the budget meeting.

Using the consultative mode of decision making works quite well on budget matters (better than the unilateral with consultation approach). You and the team members can hear one another's ideas and points. Because financial matters usually are tough issues where a final call needs to be made, the consultative mode enables you to do so. The team knows that you're the one who decides among the various priorities, but they gain a better understanding of your thinking because you've had them directly and collectively involved in the process.

Vacation schedule

You know that all team members including you are going to want to take some vacation during the year. The goal is a vacation schedule so that operations are maintained while people are away. Do you involve your team in this issue? If you do, what decision-making mode is best to use?

My recommendation: Because a vacation schedule affects everyone, by all means, get the whole team involved. In defining parameters to the team, spell out what you believe is needed for adequate coverage.

Use the consensus mode. That way, everyone can share equally in shaping the outcome. By letting all team members hear one another's vacation needs and desires, making a vacation schedule that everyone can live with is possible. This process also keeps you out of playing the role of judge and arbitrator on an issue that a functioning team needs to be able to work out for itself.

Hiring

You have a vacancy to fill on your team. You want to make a good hire who fits in well and contributes positively to the team. Do you involve your team in the hiring process and, if so, what decision-making mode is best to use?

My recommendation: Definitely involve team members in the hiring process. They help on two important levels. First, they help by defining the job requirements — the important skills and qualities that you need in the right person for the role. Second, the team helps in interviewing and evaluating the top candidates.

With roles already defined for the team, the consultative approach works well in a hiring process. On the other hand, making hiring decisions by consensus is sometimes difficult to achieve because not every interviewer sees every candidate the same way. As manager of the team and the person to whom the new employee reports, you need to hire someone that you think is best. At the same time, involving the team members in shaping the role, interviewing, and giving their input to a final decision builds their support and enriches the input you receive for making a good decision. Usually, having the team members interview only the top two or three candidates works best for managing the amount of their input and utilizing their time efficiently.

At the meeting when you start the consultative approach for making a hiring decision — after the interviews are finished — avoid biasing the team by saying which candidate you're leaning toward. Instead, after each team member has offered observations on the candidates, promote a lively dialogue with questions and your participation. This enables you to gain insight into what your team members saw and thought about the job candidates and to test your own thinking with them.

Performance problem

You have a team member who isn't doing his fair share of the work and who's clashing with other team members because of this shortfall. You know it's a performance problem that needs to be addressed. Do you involve your team in this performance issue and, if so, what decision-making mode do you use?

My recommendation: Go unilateral — handle this performance problem yourself. Among other things, you need to respect confidentiality when dealing with sensitive personnel issues. That's why handling a performance problem is the role of the manager and not the team members. One obvious peril of a collective discussion is that you risk humiliating the employee and limiting the possibility of working out a constructive solution for improving that person's performance.

Work assignments

The team knows its goals. But what it needs now is a plan spelling out who will do what work over the next few months to reach those goals. Roles and responsibilities for executing the work need to be set. Do you involve your team in setting the roles and work assignments and, if so, what decision-making mode do you use?

My recommendation: Definitely pull the team together in a meeting specifically for developing this work plan. They're the ones who make the work reach the goals; so by all means, let them help decide who's going to do what parts and when.

The consensus decision-making mode works well in this scenario. Everyone shares in getting the work done and needs to be aware of the whole enchilada, not only their own respective bites. Sorting out the roles and assignments together, and all agreeing to support the plan, makes for a work plan that will be executed well. You don't need to be the one who determines what team members do. But in your leadership role, you make sure that all the work is assigned.

Chapter 12

Making the *M* Word (Meetings) Meaningful

*W*hen you were a kid growing up, you learned some dirty words that were absolutely forbidden at home, right? Now that you're an adult and experienced in the world of work, you've encountered a dirty word that people say out loud in polite company. That word is *meeting*. Say *meeting* to employees at all levels and many cringe, grunt, and groan. Why do you think that is?

Quite simply, if you're like so many people that I've encountered, you've attended many, many business meetings that just weren't productive. More than once, you've walked out of a meeting feeling worse than when you walked in. You recall that many meetings were a total waste of time.

But now that you have a team to run, what's one of the key mechanisms that you need to use for pulling your team members together? Oh, no — *MEETINGS!* In fact, as I point out in Chapter 1, meeting at some level of frequency is one of the biggest differences between regular work groups and *interdependent* work groups that are otherwise known as teams. If they're going to be effective, teams need to meet regularly. Again — oh, no!

The good news is that teams can find the right tools and techniques to turn the dreaded "M" word into a clean and positive word, even a way of life. And no religious conversions are necessary, either. Just make sure to pass along the meeting skills that you find in this chapter and apply them often.

Meetings: Why Some Are Called #@!&¿§!

Before you show the team how to make meetings run productively, spend some time reminding yourself what you dislike about those many meetings that have been a waste of time. This section explores the factors that cause meetings to not be very productive — the pitfalls to avoid. For purposes of discussion, I define a *meeting* as a formal gathering of four or more people.

Nixing the two big meeting no-nos

Throughout the long and dreary history of meetings that went nowhere, two problems tower above all the others that were encountered. I think it's a smart idea to deal with them right at the top.

1. No clear purpose (or reason) to meet

Why are we meeting? What do we want to accomplish? The answers to these questions define the purpose of a meeting. Quite often meetings are called for no stated or clearly defined purpose. And, the funny thing is, people still show up!

Simply because the calendar says that it's time for the weekly meeting doesn't mean that you have a reason to meet. Conducting meetings for the sake of meeting certainly is not a reason for any group to spend time together. Even when you have something in mind to discuss, you still may have no clear purpose for meeting. Talk alone does not a meeting make. The question is: What are you seeking to accomplish by having everyone get together?

Laying the foundation of a productive meeting starts with a clearly defined purpose. Without a defined purpose that participants know about, meetings seem unnecessary and often become unfocused. Without a defined purpose, you can kiss their usefulness goodbye. And whenever your sole purpose is communicating news or passing along information, team meetings can be short — or even replaced by other means. Memos and e-mail messages quite often are worthy substitutes for the one-way distribution of information at a meeting.

Teams are most effective when they have *working* meetings. The next section of this chapter shows how.

2. No agenda

An *agenda* is a written plan that guides the flow of the meeting to accomplish its purpose. Jotting down a few notes to yourself does not fit the definition of an agenda. Starting the meeting by asking the group what the agenda should be doesn't fit that definition, either. And the ever-popular approach of just yakety-yakking on an issue is definitely not what an agenda for a meeting means.

What percentage of business meetings that you attend lack an agenda? In my consulting experience, more than half the group meetings that people attend — managers' meetings, in particular — don't have agendas. Yet people still come.

Without a written agenda, staying focused and trying to get something done become much harder. The meeting has no path to follow and therefore becomes vulnerable to participants raising issues that you haven't planned on addressing. Having no agenda for a team meeting is like building a house without blueprints. Good luck as you try to piece it together!

Exposing other factors that lead to meeting disasters

The lack of a clear purpose and an agenda are only two of the reasons that cause meetings to become nonproductive. Many more exist. When I work with groups in my team seminars, I often ask them to list reasons that make meetings unproductive. I've never encountered a group that came up with fewer than ten such factors in only a few minutes. You can do the same with your team — and compare your list to the one that follows:

- ✔ **Poor facilitator (or none at all).** Either no one is guiding the flow of the meeting, which is the role of the facilitator, or the facilitation is so passive that it's like no one is doing the job. As a result, the meeting rambles and loses its focus.

- ✔ **Starts late.** Starting after the announced time for a meeting only adds to the pressure of trying to get through the entire agenda. Starting late also sends the message that it's okay to waste people's time.

- ✔ **Runs too long.** A meeting that has no stated ending time is an invitation for nonstop monologues that turn out to be tests of endurance. Some people say the longer that a meeting runs the less that gets done.

- ✔ **Lacks the right people.** This means that key people who are essential to getting work done or making decisions are not present. Sometimes they pull out at the last minute or are simply no-shows without explanation, leaving the group knowing that it's going to have to cover the same issues all over again at some future date.

✔ **Includes the wrong people.** Who invited *them* to come? That's often a mystery, but they show up, offering opinions on subjects that are neither relevant nor any of their business.

✔ **Drags on without closure.** Some groups have the knack of talking issues to death but never bringing them to closure. No conclusion is reached, and no decision is made. Plenty of hot air gets blown around the meeting room, but little is accomplished.

✔ **Rehashes old issues.** Old issues keep coming up at some meetings, often because action items or decisions are not documented. Attending meetings where old issues rear their ugly heads is worse than watching a replay of a bad movie — when will this issue ever be settled and done with!

✔ **Lacks follow-up.** Some group meetings may appear to be getting things done, but, because no follow-up is done to check on what's been done with assignments and decisions, no real progress is made. The lack of action outside the meeting renders your meeting agenda meaningless.

✔ **Gets derailed by a dominant person or two.** They never stop talking and essentially take over the meeting. Others can barely get a word in and walk away feeling that their contributions won't matter anyway.

✔ **Plagued by constant side chatter.** Meetings during which people constantly are whispering and having side conversations with each other often become a great annoyance to everyone else who is trying to stay focused.

✔ **Loses focus because of tangents.** Meetings that lack an agenda often suffer this pitfall by permitting discussion to wander away from the main focus of the meeting. Something hits a participant's mind and off the conversation goes in yet another different direction.

✔ **Covers issues irrelevant to many attendees.** Some meetings make no sense at all. They get into issues that are relevant to only a few people on hand. Everyone else sits on the sidelines wondering why time is being wasted. The thing is, if you leave a meeting like this one, you're not being a team player.

✔ **Gets into issues that need to be handled offline.** A few people get onto topics that are personal to them and better handled outside of the meeting. Listening to such discussions, especially when they concern sensitive topics, often makes others on the team feel awkward.

✔ **Includes people who are unprepared.** Participants who haven't done their homework are great at killing a group's progress at work. And their excuses don't change the reality: They're wasting other people's valuable time.

> ✔ **Lacks participation.** People tend to show up for meetings to which they're invited — and that's all that some of them do. They sit by passively, enjoy the coffee, but offer few ideas or other meaningful contributions even when asked. Chair-warming doesn't make for productive meetings.

Just showing up isn't enough to make a meeting work well. Circulate this list — or your team's own list — as a reminder to everyone of the pitfalls to avoid at meetings.

Giving Your Meetings New Life

Meetings don't have to be a boring or frustrating waste of time. In fact, meetings are the lifeblood of teams. They're the place where individual efforts are brought together and coordinated into a collective effort. So to make team meetings run effectively, help your team members discover the basic elements of structure that meetings need to have and then put those principles into practice. This section covers the fundamentals of productive meetings.

Live on stage! The three stages of the meeting process

A good meeting has three stages. Here are looks at each of them.

Stage 1: The organizational period

Organization takes place before the meeting, encompassing all the planning and preparation that precedes the meeting, including any or all the following:

> ✔ Defining the purpose of the meeting
>
> ✔ Inviting the appropriate people
>
> ✔ Writing and distributing the agenda to participants
>
> ✔ Making advance preparations with individuals when necessary
>
> ✔ Taking care of logistics — meeting room and materials — and food if you're lucky

Stage 2: The meeting itself

The group comes together to conduct its business and execute the agenda. I get into the details beginning at the heading "Facilitating a Productive Meeting: Tools and Outcomes."

Stage 3: Postmeeting work

The final stage includes everything essential to following through on agreements made during the meeting, such as:

- ✓ Participants performing the action items they have agreed upon
- ✓ Communicating to other interested parties who did not attend the meeting
- ✓ Preparing the meeting minutes and distributing them to all participants and any other interested parties

Many meetings flop because of the lack of attention paid to the before and after stages. Building in the discipline for top team performance includes following through on all three important stages of a meeting.

Taking a minute for the minutes

Minutes are the written record of a meeting. You're going to want them for nearly every team meeting because they document what the team did at the meeting — much better than relying on memory.

A good set of minutes needn't be lengthy. You want the highlights of the meeting, not a transcription of every word each person spoke. Structure the minutes around the flow of the agenda and capture highlights by:

- ✓ Covering the main topics
- ✓ Noting the decisions made and agreements reached
- ✓ Describing action items given, to whom, and when they're to be done
- ✓ Listing work products that were created
- ✓ Discussing issues that are in the works for next time

Have the minutes typed up and distributed as soon as possible after the meeting. Retain a copy of them and the meeting agenda in the team's central file. This routine ensures that the team has a record of work completed during meetings and helps members to stay on track and see their progress.

Rolling in the meeting roles

For a team meeting to be a good one, three roles must be performed every time the teams meets and a fourth role is performed as needed. Here's a look at each role:

Facilitator

The *facilitator* guides the flow of the meeting by helping the group work through its agenda so that it accomplishes the purposes of its meeting. As manager or team leader, you certainly need to be able to facilitate your team's meetings, but you don't have to do it every time. Coach other team members to use the skills of the facilitator so that they're better able to take on this role and so that meetings can proceed in your absence. The last section of this chapter covers the skills of effective facilitation.

Scribe

The *scribe,* sometimes known as the *recorder*, takes the minutes, types a clean copy, and distributes them. This role can rotate among team members. The scribe needs to take good notes, but the focus of the minutes is on the highlights or key points of the meeting — a job that almost every team member needs to be able to handle.

Participant

Participants contribute to the work of the meeting and are expected to come to the meeting prepared to be active and positive members of the meeting. They play the most important role for a meeting to be a success. Team guidelines can help to cover expectations of meeting participants, so make sure that you included those expectations in your guidelines. (See Chapter 6 for guidance on team guidelines.)

Presenter

Presenters appear at team meetings as needed. They are people who report findings, share expertise, or relay other pertinent information that the team needs to have for its work. Sometimes a team member plays the role of presenter; sometimes the presenter is someone from outside the team.

Make certain that the presenter, especially when it's someone from outside your team, knows what to talk about and for how long. Also, don't forget to factor in some time for questions from the team.

Meaningful purposes for team meetings

Purpose tells everyone why the meeting is taking place. It indicates what you're trying to accomplish when your team comes together at the meeting table. The *lack* of a clearly defined purpose is a major meeting-killer. So, what are some of the good purposes for team meetings? That's easy:

- ✔ Planning
- ✔ Decision making
- ✔ Problem-solving
- ✔ Group conflict resolution
- ✔ Evaluating results
- ✔ Setting goals
- ✔ Setting assignments and schedules
- ✔ Training
- ✔ Recognizing and celebrating success
- ✔ Building working relationships — that *team-building* stuff
- ✔ Creating policies, procedures, and other work products
- ✔ Generating or testing ideas
- ✔ Reviewing status
- ✔ Making recommendations
- ✔ Conducting a postmortem

Good purposes lead to *working meetings*. A team coming together to get work done helps all its members perform better when they go back on their jobs — that's a working meeting.

Jan's having another (yawn) meeting

Jan likes to have her department staff meetings every Wednesday afternoon right after lunch. To her credit — and much to the disappointment of her staff — Jan seldom postpones or cancels these meetings. She uses them as communication vehicles.

Typically, more than half of Jan's meetings feature her passing along all the company news that she can think of. From big items to trivial items, Jan does her best to talk at her staff. She then goes around the table, inviting staff members to report what they're working on. Because Jan manages an independent-level work group and not a team, what one staff member reports has little significance to anyone else.

The communication of information tends to be the main purpose for all Jan's staff meetings. Staff members usually sit by passively while Jan lectures and others report. Occasionally, a remark sparks a question or comment from another staff member, but more often, drowsiness sets in.

Everyone who has ever attended one of Jan's meetings, please raise your hand.

Notice that *communicating news* and *sharing information* are not on the list of good purposes for meeting. Teams need news and information, of course, and some of that sharing occurs during all purposeful meetings. But making communication the primary purpose of a team meeting means that you don't need to meet very often. Communicating information frequently can be done just as well by e-mail and printed memos. For teams to perform successfully, they need to have regular working meetings.

Next on the Agenda: Developing Focused Agendas

Question: What's one of the million-dollar secrets for having a focused and productive team meeting?

Answer: A well-defined agenda.

An agenda is a written plan that guides the flow of a meeting toward accomplishing its purpose. That's right — a *written* plan for all to see. Not a verbal outline, not notes to yourself, and not a laundry list of topics with no order or purpose.

Developing a meaningful agenda for a team meeting takes planning. The team leader takes an active responsibility in helping to shape the agenda but also involves the team members so their input is included. Express to your team that everyone has responsibility to help make a good agenda for the team meetings. You can even periodically delegate to a handful of team members the responsibility to take the lead in planning the agenda.

Planning the meeting agenda pays off well: Walking into a meeting with a well-organized agenda greatly increases the likelihood for a focused and productive meeting. This section offers you some tools, tips, and samples for showing your team members how to create a purposeful meeting agenda.

Starting with five essentials

A good agenda for a team meeting, and for most group meetings, answers five basic questions about the meeting. The first four are simple and obvious, but the last one can be complex. The five answers that you're looking for are:

1. **Group involved in the meeting.** Who are we? What's the name of our group or team? This point of reference needs to be prominently listed at the top of the agenda, much like a title. For example,

   - Executive Staff Meeting

   - Operations Team Meeting

   - Policy Task Team

   - The Make It Happen Team

   - The Employee Fun Bunch Committee

   The right title helps everyone know who's supposed to attend. If you're part of the named group, come; and if you're not, don't bother. Knowing what team or group improves the odds that the right people are present and the wrong ones are not.

2. **Day and time.** When is the meeting to take place? Identify not only the date but also a start time and (drum roll, please) an *end* time that you've projected. People have their own schedules. A meeting without an end time doesn't respect the fact that participants have other things that they'd like to plan for and do. Worst of all, it tends to encourage meetings to drag on and on. Meetings can end sooner than planned; however, without a stated ending time, they may never end at all.

3. **Purpose or objective of the meeting.** Why are we meeting? What, overall, is to be accomplished at the meeting? A meeting can have more than one purpose, but without at least one good one, why meet?

4. **Topics.** What are the items or issues to be discussed at the meeting? List them on the agenda in the order that they're to be addressed. I usually recommend two standard agenda topics — an introduction and a close — giving you a kickoff point before you dive into the issues and a wrap-up point for making sure that closure is achieved.

5. **Process for working through each topic.** The *process* represents $900,000 of the $1 million secret behind effective agendas. It's the element that's generally least found in group meeting agendas. The process defines how the group will work through each topic from start to conclusion. Its two main points are:

   - The steps to follow in working through each main issue or topic.

   - The ways by which participation will be governed in working through each step.

To illustrate what a discussion process looks like, say that your team has been working on a customer service problem. Part of the team meeting today is devoted to developing a solution to the problem. Figure 12-1 shows how that part of the agenda can proceed.

The Customer Service Problem

I. Review of Problem Issue
    A. Recap of previous work - Team leader presents
    B. Other comments - Group discussion

II. Developing the Solution
    A. Brainstorming ideas - Individuals give ideas going one at a time in turn
    B. Initial discussion of ideas
        1. Clarification - Individuals identify ideas needing clarification, group discusses
        2. Consolidation - Group discusses if any ideas can be combined
        3. Elimination - Group discusses if any ideas can be easily eliminated
        4. Categorization - Group discusses if main themes exist among ideas and, if so, places them in identified categories
    C. Evaluation of ideas
        1. Group discusses merits of each idea one at a time
        2. Group consensus on ideas most applicable to use

III. Moving Forward on Solution
    A. Define next steps to do - Individual inputs listed
    B. Finalize next steps - Group discussion and consensus

Figure 12-1:
An all-purpose process for working through a team problem or issue.

As you can see in Figure 12-1, a problem-solving process answers the what, the how, and the who — *what* we're working on, *how* we're going to work through it, and *who's* going to participate in each step. Defining the process on the agenda makes keeping people focused and involved easy.

Other agenda parts to include as needed

Sometimes you may want a little more structure to the five agenda essentials than I describe in the previous section. Items in the following list describe some options that may be useful in a longer or more involved meeting than normal, or when you sense a special need for discipline in keeping participants focused.

   ✔ **A special theme.** On occasion, meetings may have a special theme or focus. When that's the case, state the theme just below the group name at the top of the agenda so that it becomes part of the meeting title.

Putting a process into the meeting

Chris managed a team of four people who performed public relations services for clients. He generally met weekly with the team, reviewing the status of client accounts and planning work for the week ahead. Chris usually prepared agendas for his meeting, more so than many other managers in his firm.

But Chris sometimes felt frustrated with his team meetings. Team members didn't always participate and, at times, wandered off on tangents. Chris felt that his team wasn't accomplishing what it needed to do in an efficient and participatory manner.

Then Chris received some coaching about how to structure a focused and participatory agenda and how to facilitate a meeting with such an agenda. The key, he discovered, was defining the process that he wanted to use for working through each main issue.

The first time that he applied his new skills, Chris outlined an agenda that defined how the team would work through each topic and how participation was to be governed along the way. His previous agendas typically had listed only topics for discussion, but the new one was much more descriptive. He distributed it to the team a day in advance rather than at the meeting.

By following the new process, Chris found the job of facilitating the meeting so much easier than before. At the same time, participation was lively, engaged, and focused. The group got through the entire agenda within the scheduled time. In fact, at the end of the meeting, members remarked to Chris that this meeting had been their best by far. They really liked the new agenda format.

Chris was hooked. He continued designing and running team meetings the same way. For him, planning the *process* piece of the meeting made a positive difference.

- ✔ **The location of meeting.** When your team meets in different places, naming the site of the meeting is important.

- ✔ **The names of attendees.** Naming attendees is helpful when you're bringing together a relatively new team or one that is cross-functional, or when special guests or presenters are part of the agenda.

- ✔ **The amount of time allotted for each topic.** Estimating the time required for each topic on an agenda helps you and the team to stay focused. But remember, the time frame is an estimate. Don't become so rigid that you move forward just because the time for an item has expired. Use the time schedule as a reminder for how you're doing. As you get to know your team and team members get to know one another's styles, you'll be better able to plan the time with more accuracy. Best of all, this planning helps prevent you from loading the agenda with so many items that you simply have to quit before you're really finished.

- ✔ **Break times.** For the occasional meetings that run two hours or more, plan break times and list them on the agenda. Doing so minimizes the distraction of people running in and out of the meeting at any old time.

 ✔ **Desired outcomes.** This part of the agenda describes what work products are to be created during the meeting or what other results are expected. Stating the outcomes alerts participants to the work that they need to get done during the session.

 ✔ **Participant preparation.** Reminding attendees about their homework or about action items that were set at a previous meeting often is a worthwhile addition to the agenda.

Adding a *meeting evaluation* piece to the agenda is an especially good idea for teams that are in their early stages, discovering the discipline needed for productive meetings. You can add a checklist for meeting effectiveness to the agenda — Chapter 7 talks about this strategy as part of building the accountability cornerstone. At the end of the meeting, you run down the checklist with the team and see how well you as a team did in achieving each factor. Checklist factors may deal with the quality and level of people's participation, starting and ending the meeting on time, quality of facilitation, whether you stayed focused on the agenda, and so on. Have the feedback from the evaluation included in the meeting minutes. Taking a few minutes for this evaluation helps build in the discipline that you need for having effective meetings.

Formatting the agenda

The two best agenda formats are what I call the *chart style* and the *outline style.* Figure 12-2 shows you the chart form, and Figure 12-3 the outline form.

What these two formats have in common is that they describe the topics to be covered in the meeting and the process for working through each topic. Which style you choose doesn't matter — use the one that you find most comfortable. As a facilitator, I've used both.

Getting the "dys-" out of functional

Once I was asked to work with a team that was very good at having dysfunctional meetings. Members of that team were great at arguing and not participating. In our first session together, I facilitated the team as it defined a checklist of factors for effective meetings. They came up with nine. At each subsequent meeting, we ended by going through the list together and evaluating the team's performance. It took only a few meetings for the team to advance from dysfunctional to very functional. Every factor on the checklist was being achieved and — no surprise — team members found that meetings now had value to them. They were now able to discuss issues without lapsing into catfights.

In most cases, a well-defined agenda, including all essential ingredients, can be written on one page. Remember, the agenda is a plan for guiding the meeting and not a detailed script.

Chart-Style Agenda

Group/Meeting Name: Special Project Team: Project Planning Meeting

Date: November 21, 2002 **Time: from** 9:00 **to** 11:00

Location: Building 1 Conference Room

Facilitator: John Doe

Purpose: Develop project plan for upcoming special ABC project

Desired Outcomes: Written project plan that outlines the following:
- Milestones
- Target dates
- Roles and assignments

What	How	Who	Time
1. Overview of agenda	Present	Facilitator	9:00 - 9:05
2. Background & expectations for special ABC project	Present Discuss as needed	Team Leader All	9:05 - 9:15
3. Determine milestones	• List options • Discuss, evaluate • Reach agreement	All	9:15 - 10:00
4. Set time frames for milestones	• Discuss • Reach agreement	All	10:00 - 10:15
5. Determine roles & assignments	• List options • Discuss, evaluate • Reach agreement	All	10:15 - 10:45
6. Set deliverables for first phase	• Discuss • Reach agreement	Team Leader All	10:45 - 10:55
7. Close	• Recap	Facilitator	10:55 - 11:00

Figure 12-2:
A chart-style agenda.

Outline-Style Agenda

Operations Committee Meeting Evaluation

November 21, 2002
(10:45 - 12:30)
Main Objective: To define the role of the Operations
Committee and shape ways to enhance
effectiveness with its meetings.

I.	Introduction: Overview of Meeting – Team leader presents	(10:45-10:50)

II. Current Meetings   (10:50-11:10)
   A. What's Working – Individual inputs
   B. What's Not Working or Needs Improvement – Individual inputs
   C. Main Conclusions – Group Discuss

III. Establishing The Purpose Of The Operations Committee   (11:10-11:50)
   A. Why Should This Committee Exist–People Write
      and Post Individually
   B. Group Discuss Views and Build off Common Themes
   C. Collaborate and Shape Into Purpose Statement

IV. Structuring The Meetings   (11:50-12:05)
   A. Frequency and Timing – Group Consensus
   B. Key Roles and Shaping The Agenda – Group Consensus
   C. Other Actions – Group Discuss

V. Issues To Tackle In Near Term   (12:05-12:25)
   A. Brainstorm – Group, going one person at a time
   B. Evaluate Ideas – Collective Discussion
   C. Set Near Term Priorities – Group Consensus

VI. Close: Next Steps   (12:25-12:30)

Figure 12-3:
An
outline-style
agenda.

A good agenda gives structure to a meeting. Don't be afraid that structure will inhibit free-flowing discussion. Just make sure that you include enough time for discussion on your agenda.

Facilitating a Productive Meeting: Tools and Outcomes

This section provides you with tools for facilitating meetings so that you have two overall outcomes:

✔ Attendees participate in the meeting

✔ The meeting produces results

These two outcomes together make for a productive meeting.

Making up the foundation of effective meeting facilitation are the interpersonal communication tools known as *active listening* and *assertive speaking,* which you can read more about in Chapter 8. *Facilitating* effectively means tuning in to what the participants are telling you verbally and nonverbally (active listening) and, at the same time, speaking positively and confidently so that the team moves forward through its agenda (assertive speaking).

The word *facilitate* means to make easy. That's the role of a facilitator at a meeting — helping to make a group's agenda easy to work through so that results are accomplished.

You can become an effective meeting facilitator by applying the six important facilitation skills — planning, summarizing, recording, focusing, stimulating participation, and gatekeeping — that I describe in the following sections.

Planning

Planning is what you do before the meeting. In other words, it means playing an active, if not primary, role in preparing the meeting agenda and, most important, defining the process that the team will use when working through each main issue. The process shows you how to guide the group through the meeting. Planning also includes having pre-meeting conversations with individuals to prepare them for the meeting and anticipating any possible challenges from participants and determining how you'll handle them if they should arise. For instance, if you know you have a controversial issue to work through with the team that some members have some strong feelings about, you can have pre-meeting discussions with these individuals so they come ready to be focused and constructive at the meeting.

Summarizing

Summarizing is the same thing as recapping, and it sometimes is used for capturing points that come out of a discussion. Summarizing is especially useful as a transitional tool from one topic to the next — recapping the key points or decisions made on one topic and then moving on to the next. Summarizing also is important to apply at the end of a meeting as a means of bringing closure to the session.

When summarizing, be brief. Generally a few sentences, at most, do the trick. After all, you're recapping the highlights, not all the details.

Recording

Recording means writing on a board or a flip chart the discussion inputs, group conclusions, ideas from brainstorming, and any other important information that comes up during a meeting. Recording is different from merely taking the meeting minutes. Recording happens live — in real time — and in front of everyone. It captures the activity and important points that emerge as the meeting rolls along, makes a discussion *visible,* and helps team members feel that their points are being heard.

When recording, capture what people are saying in their words. Don't interpret the messages and then record them in your own words. Not writing what people are saying *exactly* makes them feel that you're not really listening and, perhaps, that you're pushing your own agenda. But whenever you paraphrase someone's point out loud and confirm with that person that you heard it right, then recording the point in your own words is fine. The confirmation indicates that you understood. Many times, a participant will consider your paraphrase better than the original.

Focusing

The facilitation skill known as *focusing* pushes you toward stepping in and asserting yourself in running the meeting. In focusing, you summon the group's attention so that you are

- Maintaining order in a meeting.
- Extinguishing side conversations.
- Moving a team to the next agenda item.
- Moving a group past its seemingly endless discussion into taking some form of action.

The emphasis of focusing is on guiding the attention of participants to the agenda and to the issue at hand.

When you focus, project your voice, sound firm, and keep the message short. Here are a few examples of what to say when focusing team members during a meeting:

- ✔ "We covered everything we need to in Item 2. Let's move ahead now to Item 3 on our agenda."

- ✔ "Let's please have everyone's attention back to the front and let Sue state her point now."

- ✔ "We've discussed different options for quite awhile. Time now for us to make a decision on what's best to do going forward."

Stimulating participation

Stimulating participation means taking an action that gets team members involved in the meeting. Organizing your agenda in advance and defining the process for working through the issues help you stimulate your team's thoughts and actions because they outline the flow of participation. In addition, this tool relies on other efforts for promoting active and positive participation, such as the following:

- ✔ **Calling on people individually, including quiet people, to express their thoughts and ideas.** Don't wait for people to raise their hands and speak up. Make it a regular practice to call on people, including everyone. Ask good open-ended questions and wait patiently, enabling the person to think and respond. Using this tool tells team members that they're expected to think and contribute and not just passively sit by and eat the donuts. (But do make sure that someone brings the goodies.)

- ✔ **Probing deeper when someone's message is vague or unclear.** Probing an issue deeper helps people with fully explaining or clarifying their thoughts — sometimes it takes people below the surface level of their points. Probing gives team members enough space to truly speak their minds and be heard, which is encouraging for participation.

- ✔ **Paraphrasing when people make important points.** Paraphrase periodically, so that you make sure that what people are saying is what they really mean. You can ask and encourage participants to do the same with each other, too. Using this reflective feedback not only helps you check your understanding, but it also helps other participants receive the right message. Likewise, it helps the speaker realize he or she is being properly heard, which, in turn, encourages other people attending the meeting to speak up and participate.

✔ **Systematically problem-solving when differences of opinion arise.**
When discussions become lively, sparked by differences of opinion or
flat-out diatribes, moving the team into a problem-solving mode is sometimes a good idea. Guide team members through the steps, from defining
a problem to creating its solution. Better yet, plug in a known model:
Take a look at the problem-solving tools in Chapter 9 and the conflict
resolution tools in Chapter 10. If you must engage in problem-solving to
deal with an unexpected difference of opinion or strong concern, take
special care to involve the entire team and not just the few parties to the
dispute. Getting everyone involved avoids a situation in which two
people get stuck on opposing points of view.

Gatekeeping

Gatekeeping is a tool that helps you encourage full participation by gracefully
seeing to it that no one dominates any discussion. Gatekeeping comes in two
varieties — *gateopening* and *gateclosing.*

✔ **Gateopening** invites participation, giving people a chance to say something without having to speak the loudest. Sometimes, especially with
the more reserved individuals, you notice a facial expression indicating
that they're about to say something or that they're at least concerned.
Because these team members can easily be drowned out by the others
or ignored because of their soft-spoken manner, you have an opportunity to open the gate for them. By picking up on their nonverbal cues,
you can invite participation by saying something like, "Angela, you were
about to say something, right? Please go ahead."

✔ **Gateclosing** temporarily ends someone's participation and redirects
attention to a different participant or different item on the agenda. Keep
in mind, however, that the skill is gate*closing,* not gate*slamming.* You
don't put people down for what they've said or how much they've been
participating. ("Sharon, we've heard enough out of you for today!")

When gateclosing a long-winded person tactfully yet assertively, you sometimes can first paraphrase to acknowledge that person's point. Upon confirmation, you can move ahead. At other times gateclosing can mean deferring
what someone is saying because it more closely relates to another item later
on the agenda: "Andy, please hold that thought, because it ties in with what
we're going to discuss in Part 3 of the agenda."

Sometimes you close one gate and open another simultaneously: "Hold on,
José (gateclosing), Amy had a thought she was about to express (gateopening). Please go ahead, Amy."

Raising the meeting score

Dan took over a group of employees who were responsible for planning and executing capital-improvement projects in a municipality. They'd grown accustomed to working on their own, even though their different assignments truly needed to be coordinated, and they'd become used to sitting passively at meetings — at least the ones that they bothered to attend. Dan needed the staff to begin working as a team, so that all these critical, high-dollar projects could be organized and moved in the same direction. So, he instituted regular team meetings.

Dan designed focused agendas and brought his secretary to each meeting to take the minutes and distribute them. To spark participation at meetings, he wrote every participant's name on the front board, including his own. If someone came unprepared, without a writing instrument and paper, Dan marked a minus one next to that person's name. When someone spoke up and made a valuable contribution, Dan awarded a plus two (or more) next to that person's name. For every important kind of behavior needed for conducting an effective team meeting, from coming prepared with assignments to actively participating in discussion, team members received or lost points. The points were added up at the end of the meeting, and Dan always added a touch of humor to keep the mood relaxed.

His experiment worked. After a few team meetings, people starting coming prepared and actively participated. They laughed when scores were reported and started volunteering whether they thought plus or minus points should be applied. Dan even got a minus now and then for rambling off topic. More important, team members said that meetings had become productive and a good time to boot — no more the dirty "M" word for them.

You may find that you use facilitation tools in rapid succession when guiding a team meeting. For example, when you call on people directly for their thoughts on an issue, you record their inputs on the flip chart, you gateclose to keep people from rambling, you gateopen to invite others to join in, and you summarize the key points of discussion. That's the idea — plug in the tools for gaining good participation and moving the team forward toward results with the agenda.

Dealing with a few familiar challenges

Some challenges can arise in team meetings that may test your skills as a facilitator. This section presents some common challenges and helps prepare you for what to do and what not to do.

Use the four situations described below as a learning activity with your team.

As a facilitator, what do you do and say? Compare your responses with my don't-say and do-say suggestions.

A team member makes a point that doesn't make much sense.

Don't say (even though it would be fun if you did):

> *"Bill, that idea you're offering makes no sense at all. You'll have to do better next time. Let's move ahead."*

Do say:

> *"Bill, I'm not fully clear on what your idea is about. Please explain more what your idea means and how it will help us on this issue."* (Using questions to stimulate participation.)

A team member raises an issue that isn't relevant to the issue that you're discussing.

Don't say:

> *"Julie, we can't discuss that. It's not relevant to what we're working on right now!"*

Do say:

> *Situation 1: When the issue relates to a later part of the agenda, say, "Julie, we're going to get into that issue in Part 4 of today's agenda, so please hold the thought until we get there."* (Gateclosing.)

> *Situation 2: If the issue doesn't seem to have any relevance to the meeting, you have two useful and constructive options:*

> *You can post the point on a side board, which sometimes is referred to as parking an issue. Say you're doing this: "Julie, that issue sounds important yet different from our focus today. Let me post it over here so we park it for consideration in an upcoming meeting. Recorder please note this in our minutes." Parking the issue ensures that the thought is not lost so that it can be addressed at a future meeting.* (Recording and gateclosing.)

> *You can say: "Julie, I'm not clear how your issue relates to what we're working on today. Please briefly explain if there is relevance to it. Otherwise, we can move ahead and table it for a future meeting."* (Stimulating participation.)

The team has an issue that needs to be resolved.

Don't say:

> *"Team, here's what we need to do to resolve this issue."*

Do say:

> *Ask for a brainstorming effort by calling on each team member one at a time and including yourself.* (Stimulating participation.) *Resist the*

temptation to lead first with your ideas for solving a problem. As team leader, your ideas may sound more like directives and thus may make people less likely to offer any opposing ideas.

Two team members start an argument over what method to use to execute an assignment.

Don't say:

"John and Maria, you two need to pipe down. We're going to do this assignment my way because you two can't stop arguing about it." (This is another line that you should never use at home.)

Do say:

You can paraphrase, or ask the two people to paraphrase each other's points to make sure their respective messages are understood. Post the paraphrasings on the board. (summarizing, focusing, and recording tools.) Then invite team members to offer ideas about how to resolve the differences and even plug in a conflict resolution model to guide this discussion. (Stimulating participation.)

Juggling act: Facilitating and participating at the same time

Your biggest challenge in running meetings as the leader of the team is playing two roles simultaneously — facilitator and participant. That's a real balancing act! Whenever you get caught up in the content of the meeting, offering your many thoughts and ideas, you may end up dominating and not facilitating. On the other hand, whenever you remain a neutral facilitator, you're not providing the valuable input that your team needs as it works through issues.

In the truest sense of the role, a meeting facilitator is supposed to be neutral — the objective guide staying out of the content and helping to manage the process. But in teams, that neutrality usually doesn't work because your contributions are needed as a member of the team, especially as its leader. Here are some tips for handling the challenge of having dual roles:

✔ **Design your participation into the agenda.** As you plan how you want participation to flow through each main issue, factor in the places when you'll speak up; taking your turn with all others or as an identified speaker. Either way, just plan for it so that your participation doesn't disrupt the flow but rather fits in with everyone else.

✔ **Keep your self-awareness up and stay focused on the agenda.** Be conscious of what you're doing in the meeting at all times — self-awareness goes a long way in effective team leadership. Sometimes you can announce what role you're playing: "Let me put on my participant hat for a moment on this issue." Then step back into your facilitating role, following the agenda.

✔ **Finish speaking by directing a question to a participant.** This tip can work in tandem with the previous one. One technique to help prevent yourself from becoming an overzealous participant is developing the habit of finishing any comment that you make with a question to another participant: "Julio, what's your thought on this issue?" This enables you to spark the team's participation and to step back, guiding the flow of the meeting once again.

✔ **Delegate the facilitation to others on occasion.** Depending on the issues, you may want to ask someone else on the team to serve as facilitator. Ask the person in advance and indicate on the agenda what parts that individual will guide. Then that person can run the meeting, and you can participate to your heart's content without worrying how the discussion process is working. Bringing in an outside facilitator also can be helpful at special meetings, such as off-site retreats with your team — that's what managers call me to do sometimes. Make sure that you spend some planning time with the outside facilitator so that the issues and your objectives for the meeting are well known in advance.

Part V

Managing Some Tougher Team Matters

"A large part of our success is based on our ability to resolve conflicts before we get to work."

In this part . . .

Got a project team or task team to lead? Want to understand more about self-directed teams and how to make them work? Want to figure out a way to reward team performance, both financially and non-financially? You can find the answers in Part V.

Chapter 13

Managing Without Supervisors: Self-Directed Teams

*W*henever I mention the concept of self-directed teams to senior level managers and executives, I usually sense considerable interest. The idea of tapping into employee potential and enabling workers to take ownership of their jobs in reaching higher levels of productivity entirely on their own initiative without supervisors — well, that idea certainly catches attention among management folks.

When I tell a story or two about the success I've seen with self-directed teams (you can call them self-managed, same difference), enthusiasm really grows. And it grows for good reason: Who's going to argue with increased productivity, cost savings, and greater employee job satisfaction and commitment?

But when I remind managers that no magic wand exists for tapping into the employee potential of self-managed teams, some of the enthusiasm melts away. (See Chapter 2 for more about avoiding the magic wand approach in leading teams.) In fact, I must point out that self-managed teams aren't the same as *unmanaged* teams. You can't just one day decide to ditch an old supervisor-to-subordinate adversarial relationship (as bad as that *me boss-you worker* setup can be). Doing that is an invitation for disaster.

A *Dilbert* cartoon hits the nail of this challenge right on the head: A manager tells his group, "Okay, I'm turning you into a self-directed team." Then he predicts they'll come back begging to be micromanaged when chaos and frustration set in.

Dilbert aside, self-directed teams are successful in private and public sectors. But *batteries are required,* because making these special teams work takes a lot of energy. This chapter helps you understand what self-managed teams are all about, guides you through the transition, makes you aware of challenges by offering tips for overcoming them, and shows you how to develop a self-directed team to its full potential so that it flourishes.

Defining and Dissecting a Self-directed Team

This section defines a self-directed team, shows you where the concept comes from, describes the key roles in a self-directed team, and lists the common features of such teams.

An offline, non-Webster, but pretty good definition

You won't find *self-directed team* in the dictionary. But here's a commonly accepted definition:

> *A group of employees organized around an operation or a process of work who are responsible for managing themselves and the day-to-day functions of the work that they do with little, if any, direct supervision.*

Self-directed teams — sometimes called self-managed teams, empowered work units, or autonomous work teams — function in their truest sense without supervisory authority. Team members are interdependent, but the role of supervisor usually is missing. A self-directed team is as much a team as any others that I discuss in this book, but it has a unique management structure — no supervisor.

By comparison, a regular work group reports to a supervisor who is part of the group. In many such cases, the supervisor does much of the same work that the group members do, or he performs a higher level of the overall work that the group must accomplish. Self-directed teams, on the other hand, report to a manager, but generally no management personnel are part of the team's ongoing and daily operations.

The role of manager or supervisor, in the case of a self-directed team, is replaced by all the members of the team. Together, they plan and execute the work, day in and day out, carrying out the directions set by management above them. It isn't unusual for only one manager to oversee several self-directed teams.

Self-directed teams are, in most cases, work-unit teams that are ongoing in nature. By comparison, project teams and task teams often have qualities of self-management, but their time-limited nature generally doesn't enable them to fully develop as a self-directed team. On occasion, you may see a management team functioning as a self-directed team trying to run a department or division within an organization. Such a team has no designated department head and no top dog — only a group of unit managers trying to run the entire operation together. That's certainly no small feat, so I'm focusing primarily on work-unit teams that are functioning as self-managed teams in this chapter.

The premise behind the concept of self-directed teams is summarized in this formula:

Empowerment + Employee Involvement = Very Good Results

Empowerment means making people accountable for results by giving them timely and accurate information in addition to the authority, autonomy, and support that they need to do their jobs. In essence, management above says, "I'm giving you the freedom and resources to do the job as you see fit, within certain parameters, and you're then expected to produce good results and will be held responsible for doing so."

Employee involvement is about enabling people to participate in the management of their own work and having a voice in planning, shaping, and making decisions that affect the work that they do.

In brief, the core idea about self-managed teams is permitting the people closest to the work to organize, coordinate, and manage the work so that it gets done. They're all capable adults, so why not let them think and act as adults by providing them with the guidance, support, and direction that they need and then setting them loose to do the job.

The flipside, of course, is that if you permit a group of employees to manage their own work without close supervision, they're likely to do little of it. You're putting the inmates in charge of the asylum . . . so to speak.

If you like talking about *empowerment,* but your actions don't match your words, avoid talking about your interest in self-directed teams. Why damage your credibility? Managers who want to make every decision run into difficulties helping self-directed teams get up and running, and they probably won't make regular work-unit teams thrive well, either. Dictating and controlling can stimulate compliance among workers, but they also tend to kill off commitment, especially among adults.

From a manager's point of view, the idea behind self-directed teams is extending control without limiting responsibility or completely letting go. People need to know the boundaries within which to operate. Instead of the supervisor having primary responsibility for the group's performance, the team members together now have it.

No doubt, not every employee wants this level of involvement and responsibility, but I say more on dealing with such challenges later in this chapter under "Tackling the challenges."

Rolling out roles in a self-directed team

Of course, the biggest part of what every self-directed team does is identical to any team or regular work group — getting the work done. Whether that means making widgets, processing insurance claims, servicing customer calls, coding software, maintaining parks, producing books, or leaping tall buildings in a single bound, the work of the group needs to be done.

In addition, self-directed teams also handle many of the personnel, administrative, and operational responsibilities that a supervisor or manager otherwise handles.

When I work with groups on the concept of self-managed teams, I ask them to brainstorm and identify the kinds of responsibilities that group managers or supervisors usually handle. Here's a list:

- Setting group direction and goals
- Managing the group's budget, from forecasting to monitoring expenses
- Purchasing supplies and materials
- Exercising sign-off authority on timesheets and other personnel matters
- Writing and conducting performance reviews
- Making work assignments
- Scheduling when work is to be done and deploying resources to do it
- Monitoring and reviewing work progress
- Reporting group progress, issues, and results to management
- Enforcing policies

✔ Setting standards and developing work procedures

✔ Counseling employees on performance issues

✔ Carrying out discipline

✔ Hiring new members into the group

✔ Organizing and implementing staff training

✔ Tackling major customer problems

✔ Responding to management inquiries and requests

✔ Representing the group to management above and externally as needed

This list isn't exhaustive, but you get the point. Where self-managed teams are concerned, many of these so-called supervisory responsibilities are handled directly by the team. Generally, the longer a self-directed team exists, and the more mature it becomes, the greater the number of supervisory responsibilities it tends to handle. The team owns these areas and is accountable for them — in addition to doing its work.

The two most common roles in the day-to-day operation of a self-directed team are that of team member and team leader.

Team member

The team member is the worker bee on the team, and that means everyone. Worker bees do that which is necessary to produce the team's honey (not meant to be a stinging comment). That doesn't, however, mean everyone does exactly the same thing. Technical skills vary, and team members share in the management responsibilities of the team. Certain duties sometimes are delegated to certain team members, which, once again, depends on their skills. Some self-directed teams refer to their members as *team players* or give them even fancier names. Whatever works best.

Team leader

The team leader is first a team member who contributes to the work that all team members do but also serves as coordinator, facilitator, and the team's representative to management. As the point person with management, the team leader receives directions from management and facilitates their implementation by the team.

But the team leader doesn't exert supervisory authority and isn't the boss. The boss of a self-directed team is the manager to whom all team members report, including the team leader. In fact, whenever a team leader tries to order team members around, a revolt usually occurs.

Leaders among peers

I had the pleasure and privilege of working with a client for three years on the formation and development of self-directed teams. A key manager oversaw five self-managed teams and experimented initially with filling the role of team leader. At this company, serving as team leader meant facilitating team meetings and serving as the team's focal point and liaison for communicating with the manager. Team members who expressed interest in serving as leader, plus others appointed by the manager, rotated through quarterly assignments to the new job during the first year. All received training in facilitation skills to help them make the transition into this new role.

The shift to self-directed teams changed the traditional supervisor-to-subordinate organizational structure that had been in place at the company for many years. As a result, five teams now included five former supervisors who had become team members. Each of the ex-supervisors and other interested team members took turns serving as team leaders.

After a year of rotating everyone who was interested through roles as team leader, the manager decided to appoint one person from each team as its ongoing team leader. He told team members that he would receive their nominations for consideration but, in the end, would make the call himself. He wanted to appoint people who asserted the most positive influence on fellow team members and commanded their respect — in essence, people who were leaders among their peers.

In the end, only one of the five former supervisors was selected as a team leader. He was the one who really had strong and positive working relationships with his fellow team members. Managing by authority was never his style. In fact, the selection of the one former supervisor and four others as team leaders was met with near unanimous positive reception among the 40-plus team members, as these five were truly the leaders among their peers.

Playing the role of facilitator and coordinator is a tough one for many team leaders. You're asking that person to be a leader among peers — someone who's willing to be assertive; that is, action-oriented, positive, and firm, as needed, so that the team focuses on its responsibilities and the work that it must do. The team leader needs to be someone whom others respect.

Coach

The third role that impacts self-directed teams is sometimes referred to as *coach,* meaning the manager to whom the team reports. The coach's job is giving direction, setting parameters, obtaining resources, helping remove obstacles, and mentoring. Although coaches aren't part of the daily workings of the team, they're the ones who oversee what happens and, most important, they hold the team accountable for its results.

Now featuring: The features of self-directed teams

Self-directed teams generally have seven common features. Those features are

- ✓ **Horizontal structure — no hierarchy.** The organizational levels of most self-managed teams are flat. Almost everyone is a team member. Although skills and responsibilities may vary among team members, scales of titles and authorities are eliminated. The organizational structure is horizontal rather than vertical. Self-directed teams are egalitarian: All men and women are equal.

- ✓ **Discretion over daily work.** No supervisor or manager tells people what their assignments or schedules are. Team members handle all the day-to-day responsibilities. In fact, much of their time together is spent planning and deciding who's going to do what in getting the work done.

- ✓ **Frequent meetings.** All teams meet frequently, but self-directed teams often meet *more* frequently, for reasons noted in the previous point: They must plan and make decisions about getting the daily work done. Meetings may last only a few minutes but can occur almost daily. Longer meetings that go into greater depth on team-management and performance-related issues generally occur less frequently but, nevertheless, happen with some regularity.

- ✓ **Shared management responsibility.** Team members share responsibility for getting work done and managing the team. Specific management tasks include budgeting, scheduling, and other similar administrative issues. The team often works together on management matters.

- ✓ **Much cross-training and training.** Training is a continuous part of the life of a self-managed team. Training topics range from honing business administration skills to running meetings and solving problems. In addition, team members commonly teach one another their job functions to create more shared responsibilities (otherwise known as cross-training). Because of all their training, members of self-managed teams broaden and deepen their job skills, which contributes to their professional growth.

- ✓ **Shared concern about quality.** Self-managed teams with production-oriented functions have a quality-control function built in to the work process that often becomes a routine part of the job. That's different from the typical manufacturing or production work scene, where the quality-assurance or quality-control functions can be separate. Quality control is everyone's job on a self-managed team. It isn't the lone concern of a separate group of specialists in a different department.

> ✔ **Collective-based evaluation and pay systems.** This feature of self-directed teams occurs more often when teams have grown and matured over time, not with teams in earlier stages. Mature teams may spend considerable time collectively evaluating their overall performances and reporting the results upward to management. Team members employ peer review techniques for holding one another accountable.

Incentive pay also figures into the design of some self-directed teams. Traditionally in most business organizations, bonuses and commissions for hitting performance targets only apply to management and sales positions. In self-managed teams that have incentive systems set up, all team members share in a financial reward for the positive results of the team.

Moving Time: Making the Transition to Self-directed Teams

Getting started and moving forward with a self-directed team structure represents a major change in your organization. You're asking people to cast off roles and responsibilities that are as comfortable to them as an old pair of shoes, even though the old supervisor-led groups didn't move the way that you wanted them to as a manager. You can find tips in Chapter 4 that may help you lead regular teams through the changes as they move to a self-directed team structure.

This section provides you with tips about preparing to implement self-directed teams and handling the challenges that may arise once implementation takes place. Your role primarily is that of a manager/coach. (See also Chapter 3 for more about this role.)

Preparing for the move

Moving is a hassle regardless of how you handle it. Simply moving from one office space to another is bad enough, but what about moving your entire household? You don't just tell the movers to come get your stuff and haul it off. You have packing and preparation to do before the move can run as smoothly as possible.

Shifting into a self-directed team structure is much like making a personal move. Extensive preparation is required to make the move as smooth as possible. The following sections deal with some tips that will help.

Determining why you're implementing self-directed teams

People need to understand what's driving a change whenever you want them to support that change. So here are a few questions for you to answer first so that you're better prepared for communicating coherently to others when rolling out the teams:

- ✔ What are the business and organizational reasons for making the move to self-managed teams?
- ✔ What are we seeking to accomplish through this team structure?
- ✔ What will the future look like when the teams are running well?

Ultimately, your main reason for change must connect with better productivity and efficiency. Otherwise, why go this route? Maybe you run a large department and see a considerable amount of employee potential that's been left untapped. Maybe your department has a structure that promotes separation and turf issues and you want to break that down. Maybe you're a manager who's spread too thin and has a large number of people reporting to you. Maybe you've had a few supervisors leave your group and you see an opportunity to replace them with a team structure. Regardless of what is prompting your line of thinking, make sure that you can articulate it clearly and persuasively to other people who will be affected.

Laying the groundwork

Before going forward into self-directed teams, you may need to build support for a change among people outside of your department, including peer managers, management above you, the information technology group, human resources — likely all of them. You definitely want to have conversations with all the stakeholders, telling them where you're going with the self-directed team concept and what support you're going to need. A big part of this advance work is defining what investment is needed to make the teams work — investment in terms of money, resources, training and equipment, and in terms of the modifications that may be needed in personnel and information systems along the way. When the employees are union members, having early conversations with union representatives to build their awareness and understanding are crucial steps.

At the same time, laying the groundwork often means improving your grasp of the concept of self-directed teams — and doing the same for other key individuals who are involved in making the team structure work. Reading all the literature that you can lay your hands on and visiting other organizations that have adopted self-directed teams also are good steps.

Thinking long term

For self-directed teams to work, you, as the leader, need to think about the future. Where do you want to see the teams six months from now, a year for now, and a few years from now? Answering these questions helps you with defining your vision so that you can then communicate it to your team members, thus giving them a sense of direction and a positive outlook toward the team's future.

Making a hit-and-run change in management is a bad idea. By that I mean, don't announce any change in structure and then immediately remove yourself from active involvement. All that does is invite anxiety and chaos. Moving to self-directed teams takes time and never is a quick fix.

Thinking long term, you must understand how much time is needed for the teams to develop and perform effectively. You need to be able to plan *your* time, too. For this effort to change to work, plan on being actively involved for a good, long time before you're able to step back and provide mostly direction and oversight.

When you initially move into self-directed teams, you won't save time for yourself. New teams need much guidance. Making a good return on your investment must be your objective, especially with your investment of time, because you want the time you expend in the early stages to pay off down the road when your teams are more self-sufficient.

Creating a steering team to help

Depending on the scope of your transition into self-directed teams, forming a steering team can be one of the best things that you do. Your steering team can be made up of managers who will oversee the teams in a big-scale transition. The initial team leaders are probably involved in a medium-scale deal. And, when the transition is limited in scope, only a few key team members are involved.

A steering team plays two roles — planning and problem-solving. You want these people helping you plan the move into the teams and address issues and concerns that are likely to arise with that implementation. You may need to address a host of issues in a new self-managed team structure, such as evaluating customer or vendor relations, defining the size and shape of the teams, and redesigning the work processes.

Your steering team needs to remain in place for as long as you need it. Think months rather than weeks, so that you have help with leadership issues.

Deciding how you want to begin: Pilot team?

Starting with a pilot team or two quite often is a good way to go. Fewer people will be affected initially, which makes managing the change easier. If you elect to begin with a pilot team, be sure to take care in selecting team members who you think have a good chance of doing well. Succeeding with the first pilot improves your odds for success with later team transitions.

At some companies that wanted to turn only one or two conventional work groups into self-directed teams, I've suggested that managers first remake their work groups into teams — the entire emphasis of this book. After they're running well as teams, the transition for you or a supervisor, stepping out of the day-to-day management role and enabling the self-management aspect of the team, is going to be much easier than starting from scratch. You already have a group that knows how to work together as a team — the core concept of a self-directed team.

Drafting the implementation plan

With help from your steering team, outline the following factors (as they relate to your particular situation) that are essential for moving into self-directed teams:

- ✔ Key events and when they will occur
- ✔ Roles, responsibilities, and makeup of teams
- ✔ Short-term — three to six months — goals for the teams
- ✔ Training needs
- ✔ Any other issues to work on as you move forward
- ✔ Communication strategies for initial implementation and ongoing efforts

You don't have to figure out every last detail, but you need an implementation plan so that you're guiding your team members with care and focus into a self-directed mode. And, of course, you must plan how often you'll review progress on the total performance of the teams — usually at least quarterly for starters.

Tackling the challenges

Even the best-laid plans don't guarantee smooth transitions. When implementing self-directed teams, you can expect to encounter some challenges, and the first way to deal with them is to remain patient. Don't be upset or disappointed; think long term. (It's okay to be shocked when everything runs smoothly.) To make sure that you're fully prepared, this section discusses some of the significant challenges that often occur when you implement a self-directed team structure and some tips for tackling those challenges.

Deciding what to do with the supervisors

Dealing with supervisor issues often is the biggest challenge that you face when creating a self-directed team, and it's one that you want to plan for and address earlier in the process rather than later. The whole idea of *self*-direction is that you don't have supervisors monitoring and controlling day-to-day activities of the work group. But when you leave former supervisors floundering without defined roles, you add to their already high level of anxiety and may turn them into leaders of the resistance movement against self-directed teams. So what *do* you do?

You have two choices concerning what to do with a supervisor. One is integrating the supervisor within the team structure; the other is moving the supervisor out of the group. In neither case should the supervisor's pay be reduced.

- ✔ **Integration.** Former supervisors can play many important roles on self-managed teams. Some supervisors can be a big help on your steering team because they know the operations well. Following are some other possible roles:

  - Team leader — assuming that the former supervisor is able to lead through positive behavior rather than brute force

  - Trainer/mentor — based on the ex-supervisor's technical expertise and experience

  - Regular team member — a good fit for former supervisors who are happy not dealing with the headaches and responsibilities of their former role

  - Manager overseeing one or more teams — possible role for a select few ex-supervisor if they have good coaching skills

  Discuss these options with your supervisors and determine what roles best suit them and the team.

- ✔ **Reassignment.** When a supervisor shows little interest or aptitude for playing a role on the team, talk to human resources and other managers in the organization to see whether a transfer to another group can be worked out.

In the end, if you can find no good fit for an ex-supervisor within your teams or elsewhere in the organization, consider providing an exit package with a safety net, meaning a reasonable severance package, some kind of outplacement support, and a transitional period rather than immediate departure. A transitional period of a few weeks to a couple of months is reasonable. During this interval, the person can undertake special projects for you, such as documenting current work procedures. You can be flexible and allow them to take time off for job interviews. Your objective is fair treatment for the affected supervisor, thus alleviating concerns among other employees that someone is being pushed out the door abruptly and harshly.

Responding to concerns about job security

People worry when they see a reorganization in the works, because restructuring often means workforce reduction. So it's understandable that moving into self-directed teams can create worker anxiety over a fear of layoffs. When anxieties flare up for too long, you know the detrimental effect they can have on employee morale. What *do* you do?

Don't use a change into self-directed teams as a mechanism for eliminating jobs. Doing that nullifies the value that you can gain with teams and damages your credibility.

Whenever you hear that people are worried about job security, address their concerns directly through face-to-face communication, one-on-one and in groups. Certainly you need to mention that layoffs are not part of the plan, but don't spend a great deal of time dwelling on that point. Sometimes, the more you say that something *isn't* going to happen, the more people think that it *will*. Inviting people to talk about their concerns is a good strategy, but be sure to listen carefully and talk with them about the vision that you have for the teams and the plans that you have going forward to make your vision a reality. Emphasize that team members are actively involved in making these plans come to fruition. Listening with concern and focusing on the future helps your people work through their anxieties about the unknown.

When someone's role no longer is essential in the new team structure, do your best in helping that person find another job within the organization. If that option fails, spread the safety net as I explain in the previous section about "Deciding what to do with the supervisors."

Getting a team rolling and working

At the beginning of the transition, team members won't know what the self-directed thing is all about. They may speculate that it's just another one of management's flavors of the month that soon will pass. And when work remains undone from the previous structure, team members may be wondering how it ever will be handled under the new structure. If you neglect these concerns, your teams sputter rather than roll, and your team members grumble rather than perform. So what *do* you do?

You can get rolling early by implementing some of the strategies of the *focus cornerstone* outlined in Chapter 5. In particular, have your team develop a team-purpose statement and team guidelines, so that team members understand their overall roles and what specifically is expected of them.

As teams begin doing the work, make sure that team members understand the parameters of their decision making. Parameters define boundaries and members of self-managed teams need to know how far their authority extends and where they need to bring their team manager into the decision-making loop. When you delegate assignments, make sure that you spell out these parameters.

When team members experience significant changes from becoming self-directed, they often need some structure that helps them adapt to and make sense of the chaos. Figure 13-1 shows a simple daily planning sheet that self-managed teams can use for organizing their work and monitoring progress.

Daily Planning Sheet

Date _____

Assignment To Be Done	Team Member(s) Responsible

Training Schedule:

Progress Made From Yesterday:

Issues/Problems To Address:

Figure 13-1:
Daily planning sheet for a self-directing team.

Meeting for a few minutes every day to plan that day's work is a good practice in the early stages of a self-directed team. Some teams like using this routine so much that they continue daily meetings indefinitely, because doing so helps them build their own structure instead of living in constant chaos. At the same time, reviewing planning sheets every day reveals progress and issues the team must resolve.

Notice that a planning sheet like the one in Figure 13-1 contains a "Training Schedule" line, a topic that I address later at the heading "Establishing training as a regular business practice." Setting goals for the next three to six months also is a worthwhile exercise early in the implementation stage. Doing so gives team members a look at the big picture that their daily planning supports.

Dealing with behavior issues of team members

Self-directed teams are no different than any other kind of team structure — problems with personal working relationships often pop up. (See Chapter 2 for a list of the reasons that cause teams to struggle.) Problems can range from petty clashes over minor things to serious matters like withholding essential information from other team members. When such problems are left unattended, team chemistry easily becomes a bad mix, and you can say goodbye to your self-directed team. So what *do* you do?

In the early stages of a team's development, you can do yourself a big favor by being present and actively involved in the implementation process. On the coaching front, you provide constructive feedback to individual team members on behavior that positively contributes to and on behavior that detracts from good teamwork. Address individual issues early, clarifying your expectations and asking team members what steps they plan to take toward improving their respective behaviors. Check out Chapter 4 for details.

Two other chapters provide key references for you as training gets rolling: Chapter 8 discusses tools for interpersonal communication, and Chapter 10 talks about tools for constructive conflict resolution. You need to perfect these skills because they prepare you for coaching team members to address their own concerns with one another.

Coordinating the work of multiple teams

When you're operating with multiple self-managed teams, such as happens within an overall department, coordinating them all to keep them moving in the same direction often is a challenge. Each team may be developing and performing at a different level and thus may be unaware that what they do sometimes affects other teams. That means you don't want your teams operating in isolation with the left hand unaware of what the right hand is doing. So what *do* you do?

The key to coordinating the work of multiple teams is creating structures that pull together people from different teams. One way is creating a leadership team, composed of you and the team leaders, that meets regularly. Another approach is organizing an integration team, composed of a representative from each self-managed team, that meets periodically to plan and address cross-team issues. One more way is having all teams meet periodically for discussion of common issues.

Face-to-face communication is the core of cross-team coordination. Some of the face time directly involves you, but some also can also be accomplished by the team members. Your role in getting them started is clarifying expectations and checking on their progress.

Getting employees to let go of the past

Many employees view a changing to a self-directed team structure as a big change in their work lives. They no longer have a supervisor telling them what to do and letting them know what's right and wrong. As with any major change, some people react with glee and enthusiasm and others grow anxious and cling to the past. You may hear the latter group yearning for the good old days, even though they complained in those *good days* how bad it was. You may hear them dismissing the team thing as a fad that soon will go away. You may even see the skeptics dragging their feet on new work routines. So what *do* you do?

Keep three words in mind when you want employees to let go of the past: *celebrate, communicate,* and *educate.*

Start celebrating early in the implementation phase. One good party theme is saying goodbye to those good old days and welcoming the new. Neither trashing the past nor feeling bad about what lies ahead is necessary.

A party thrown by management, celebrating the past and welcoming the future often is well received, because such an activity shows that you recognize the changes employees are feeling. That knowledge helps them witness changes for themselves and adopt a positive outlook going forward, thus providing a boost in morale from the get-go. Remember that periodically celebrating the successes that teams are achieving, perhaps on a quarterly schedule, is good. Set goals with your teams, and when they meet or exceed them, have a little celebration. Bring in pizza or lunch and have a good time.

Tie celebrations to good team performances. Don't celebrate just for the sake of celebrating. Reward good performances so that teams see that successes are recognized and considered important.

Communication certainly is a big part of what helps team members let go of the past. Regular meetings at which team members are involved in shaping the work that they do — dispelling chaos with structure — can help move people forward. Periodic all-teams meetings help, too, and so do informal chats with individual team members.

Making yourself visible on a regular basis, showing that you care and support the teams and their members, also plays a major part in developing a positive outlook for the future.

Reiterate your vision and, most important, listen to individuals. Just acknowledging what people are saying and feeling can go a long way toward helping them adjust to new situations.

Education is important. In the early implementation stage, build in training as a routine part of team operations. Start educating team members about the concept of self-directed teams and the roles that they need to play in making teams work. This helps team members who need to find out how to think and do for themselves as opposed to waiting to be told what to do. Emphasize this point in both the training you have done and the expectations you spell out. From job skills to team skills, have your teams plan training as part of their work schedules.

Building Teams to Self-Manage and Grow

In this section, I offer guidance about where to direct your attention to help your self-directed team mature and flourish and about how to adjust your role as you progress from the early stages.

We have liftoff, now where do we go?

Getting started is one big challenge with a self-directed team, but keeping the team moving forward is another. You can do it by remembering to focus on the important elements of the early stages of implementation that are covered in the following sections.

Communicating

Don't abandon all those great communication programs that you put in place for liftoff. Teams meet frequently to plan and carry out their work, and you want to use those face-to-face occasions to provide leadership and direction and not have to rely so much on e-mail messages. Keep in closer contact by being present at occasions like these:

- ✔ Regular team meetings with your core group of team leaders who pass on information to the teams
- ✔ Periodic all-hands meetings at which you bring together all the team members
- ✔ Occasional drop-in visits with team meetings to stay in touch
- ✔ Regular *MBWA*, or management by walking around

MBWA is an effective form of informal communications. You walk around to people's work areas for a few minutes of social chatter. You have the rest of the day to handle business issues, so have a little fun. MBWA is a communication strategy that makes you a visible leader and enables you to gain a better knowledge of your team members as people and not just as employees.

Establishing training as a regular business practice

Stating your expectations about training and helping your team find the resources that it needs to meet those expectations is a vital part of your job. You can evaluate their success when you evaluate team performance.

Because your team members can't master everything at once, have them schedule their training. The basic areas of training are

- ✔ Team skills — skills that I cover in Part IV of this book
- ✔ Cross-training — mastering other job skills as required
- ✔ Computer application skills — for data management and processing
- ✔ Effective presentation skills — skills that prepare the team for periodically reporting results and recommendations
- ✔ Business administration skills — for budgeting, purchasing, scheduling, and handling other administrative functions of supervisors
- ✔ Coaching and facilitation skills — for your team leaders

As you can see, members of a self-directed team have much to discover. Pursuing these forms of ongoing professional development has at least two valuable results or consequences for your teams: It spurs individual motivation and builds skills that lead to higher levels of performance.

Expanding team responsibilities a step at a time

Ultimately, a truly self-managed team handles all responsibilities that a work group supervisor would. But a team can't assume all those responsibilities at once. Team members need time to discover and absorb various supervisory routines into their daily functions, especially administrative matters. When asking a self-directed team to take on new responsibilities, follow these steps to effectively delegate responsibilities:

- ✔ Spell out the results that you expect.
- ✔ Define the parameters that team members need to work within, especially limitations on time and authority.
- ✔ Provide the training and other forms of support that team members need to take on new duties.

> ✔ Set up checkpoints for reviewing progress.
>
> ✔ Evaluate the results.
>
> ✔ Set new goals.

Maintain ongoing accountability and focus with your self-directed teams by setting the frequency — quarterly, perhaps, but no less than once every six months — with which you plan to evaluate team results versus performance targets. Requiring the team to make presentations to you as part of this evaluation process really pushes the responsibility level for achieving results to everyone on the team. You may also want the team to produce an interim report of its performance, say, monthly, much as a supervisor is often required to do.

After a team evaluates its progress, with business direction provided by you, have team members reset their performance goals for the next time period and the plans on how they'll achieve those goals. That, after all, is why they're self-managed teams. Hold them accountable for achieving results.

I also recommend that members of self-managed teams provide each other with peer feedback once every six months. Chapter 7 describes in detail how executing this strategy promotes accountability and provides recognition of good teamwork and performance. Peer feedback is a great tool for team members to evaluate how they as individuals are staying on track as an effective part of the team.

Developing systems to fit the team structure

When venturing into self-directed teams, you often discover that the systems and policies of your organization don't always make a good match with the new team structure. For example, when company policy says that only someone in supervisory authority can sign off on vacations, employee timesheets, and purchase requisitions, you need to work within your company structure to modify these systems. Administrative areas that may require change include quality assurance practices, vendor relations, compensation, staff administration, work schedules, employee recognition, and performance reviews. You don't want your self-managed teams constantly colliding with internal obstacles when they are charged with managing those same functions. You need to serve as a barrier buster, helping your teams grow in managing their own performances. Chapter 15 provides you with some tips for designing team incentives and skill-based pay structures.

Continuously addressing issues and making improvements

When observing how your self-managed teams are progressing — from what's working well to what isn't — you have an opportunity to help them get better at developing solutions.

As much as you possibly can, delegate the development of solutions and periodic review of progress as a means of helping them maintain their accountability. Whenever people don't know what to do, show them and coach them, but seldom volunteer solutions yourself. Whenever you want a team to become self-managing, you want team members taking responsibility for addressing issues and making their solutions work.

Evolving in your role as team coach

During a team's evolution from early stages of implementation to a more experienced stage of development, your role as leader and coach also needs to evolve. You never want to become hands-off or uninvolved, nor do you want to perpetuate dependency by dictating how everything should be done. Here are a few tips for helping you develop and grow as leader of your self-directed teams:

- ✔ **Starting the function and then smoothly taking your hands off.** Your initial role is providing much guidance — helping facilitate team meetings, showing the team how an administrative duty is handled, and so on, but then you must turn the responsibility over to the team, checking in continually, giving lots of feedback, and reviewing progress until the team leader or team confidently handles the matter with good results.

- ✔ **Providing direction and vision.** In the beginning, much of your time is spent on day-to-day guidance and less of it is spent on the big picture. Those proportions reverse as the team develops and becomes competent in self-management. (You don't have time for the nitty-gritty, anyway.) Keep your teams looking toward the future and setting goals to get there.

- ✔ **Not biting off more than you can chew.** Take on only the extent of team responsibility that you can reasonably support; otherwise, you may leave your teams floundering and frustrated because you're not sufficiently involved in their development. Involving yourself in team development may mean that you must coach other managers to coach new teams.

- ✔ **Structuring your time and showing up when it counts.** Although you may have other projects going on or other issues to contend with that involve people upward and outward from your group, how you handle your time is key to managing your self-directed teams from their formation through ongoing development. Structuring your time so that you're available for the teams when they need it is important, because you must literally block off time on your calendar for each item on your to-do list. Don't leave the time that you spend with your teams open, because distractions and interruptions often eat away at the clock so much that you'll never get around to the issues or people you intend to deal with on a given day. As your teams evolve, your time commitments become more focused on events that are beyond the day-to-day — important meetings that you call or that your teams invite you to attend, business review sessions for planning and evaluation, celebrations of successes, and informal MBWA time. Monitor closely how you spend your time so that you function at the leadership level rather than down in the trenches, stuck dealing with day-to-day activities.

✔ **Continuously learning.** Never stop learning about your business, teams, leadership, and coaching. Use this book as your reference for teams and team leadership. For more about coaching, take a look at my book titled *Coaching and Mentoring For Dummies*, which also is published by Wiley. I know the author well!

Chapter 14

Managing Project Teams and Task Teams to Success

So you've been asked to lead a project team or a task team, or maybe you were the fool who thought up the idea of creating one of these teams and now you must deliver. Managing project teams and task teams can be quite challenging.

A *project team,* as the name suggests, is a group of interdependent people who come together to complete a project or a special assignment. A *task team* — sometimes known as a task force — is a group of interdependent people who commonly come together to study an issue and recommend solutions or courses of action. Project teams and task teams have several things in common:

✔ They work under deadlines, sometimes tight ones, and exist only long enough to do their work and then disband. So, they're not ongoing like regular work-unit teams.

✔ They often are cross-functional, meaning they are composed of people from different disciplines and departments whose expertise needs to be melded together for the project or the task.

✔ The members often have regular jobs that they do on a daily basis. Being assigned to the project or task team is an add-on to their regular duties. In some companies, people work solely in project teams, rotating from team to team as they are assigned.

✔ Management above sets the directions and objectives for the team, and everyone must live with those factors regardless of whether they agree with them.

Common factors between project teams and task teams also represent challenges to team managers. Whether you're called the project manager or task team leader, you're usually managing people who on an organizational chart don't actually report to you. You're not their direct supervisor. In addition, because they have other job demands on their time, this project or task team may not be as high a priority for them as it is for you. Add in occasional resentment for having to accomplish something that they didn't ask for, and no wonder managing such teams is quite a challenge.

Yet task and project teams have been growing in use throughout business organizations. The fact that they bring together a variety of specialties and talents often is the medicine that an organization needs for being able to tackle complex problems. These kinds of teams enable resources to be assembled for special assignments without incurring additional personnel costs. In short, project and task teams are a creative way of tapping into employees' abilities and generating good results.

This chapter provides you with the strategies and tools that you need to manage project teams and task teams for success — getting them started on the right track, moving productively to a conclusion, and asserting your leadership influence even though you lack supervisory authority over team members.

Beginning with the Essentials for Effective Project Management

The neat thing about projects is that they have a beginning and an end. The bad thing about projects is that when you don't get started on the right track, you may not end up where you want. Two keys that are particularly important as you begin are the team charter and the team project plan, which are the focus of this section.

Getting your charter set

Ships don't sail and planes don't fly without first determining in what direction they're headed and what destination they intend to reach. When you take on the leadership of a project team, you want to do the same thing. I call this *developing your project charter*.

You create the project charter with your sponsor, who usually is the person in senior management who endorses the work your project team is about to do. In many cases, the sponsor approaches and asks you to become the project manager (as in, "Boy, do I have a project for you!"). At times, you may initiate a project, but, in any case, you routinely seek out a sponsor so that you have upper management support for the initiative.

The following sections describe issues that you must work out and document for your project charter, including project objectives, staff resources, budgeting and material resources, working within specific time frames, and reporting your progress.

Project objectives

What do you need to accomplish with this project? What results are expected? Work with your sponsor to answer these questions. In most cases, you're looking at one or two main objectives for a project — any more than that may mean the scope of the project is too big for one team to handle.

In addition, ask your project sponsor why the project is important, so that you can pass along those same answers to team members when they ask.

Possessing knowledge of a project objective enables you to provide solid and clear direction when you launch your project team. Similarly, this knowledge prepares you to respond to team members who may have differing points of view about what the project team should do. The project charter helps you to steer them back along the same path as everyone else.

Staff resources

In some cases, you instantly know whom you want to serve on a project, based on what is needed for it, but in other cases, your resources already have been selected for you. You can often help determine who the right people are for the project by discussing staffing with your sponsor. When staffing a project, look for people with these three main qualities:

- ✔ The right technical skill sets for the project
- ✔ A record of good performance — plus enough time available to lend to your team's project
- ✔ The ability to coordinate and work well with others

You may want to recruit team members directly, which entails some negotiation, not only with your sponsor but also with other managers. I recommend recruiting and negotiating for the right staff, so that you can build a strong team from the beginning.

Ask your sponsor to pave your way for recruiting project personnel from other teams by speaking to the other managers on your behalf.

Budget and material resources

How much money can you spend on this project? What other limitations are in place? Asking these questions tells you upfront what constraints you face and enables you to remove any such obstacles, whenever possible. You also need to ask what material resources you need — equipment, technology, tools, and so on. And don't forget to discuss any support services that you may need from other groups. Work out all these issues with your sponsor.

Time frames

Most projects have deadlines. Knowing what those deadlines are and what to expect from them upfront is best, because you can tell members of your team what you're working with, timewise. By exploring the deadline issue with your sponsor before you start, you may be able to negotiate a more advantageous schedule for the project.

Your project management skills may come into question when you ask for a deadline extension after a project is underway. Even when a change is granted, your request makes it appear that you allowed an important deadline to slip. That's why explaining your concerns about meeting a deadline before you ever start a project is important. Even if your upfront request yields no change in the deadline, your sponsor at least knows that you had questions about meeting the deadline before the project began.

One other important point about deadlines: Even if your sponsor has no set deadline in mind for your project, set one anyway. Leaving your project timeline open makes pushing your team forward much harder, especially when you're working on a long-term project.

Progress reporting

The last item that you need to work out with your sponsor is how best to provide updates on the team's progress. You want to know when updates are expected, what's most important to report, and how it should be reported — written report or orally. Take the initiative by recommending how you want to handle these issues, and at the same time considering what your sponsor prefers. Keeping your sponsor in the loop and away from the need (or urge) to nag or micromanage is the idea here. Also, if any other key people or stakeholders have an interest in how your project progresses, find out who they are and how to keep them in the loop, too.

Document all the areas and issues that you discuss and resolve with your sponsor, and send him or her a copy. Voilá! — you have your project charter. You also have accurate directions for your new team.

Remembering to plan

The first piece of work that a project team needs to do isn't the actual project work but rather the plans it needs to make for the project. I'm amazed at how many project teams operate without a documented project plan. At best, they may have a schedule, but a good project plan contains more than that. The project plan is one of your essential tools for managing projects and the teams that work on them.

Various project management software packages exist for developing and updating project plans. You can keep it simple by using a form like the one in Figure 14-1.

Here are some tips for using the form in Figure 14-1:

- ✔ **Project name or subject.** When giving your project a name or subject, choose your words carefully so that they incorporate the outcome that you're expecting, such as "The Building Remodel Project." Doing so goes a long way toward avoiding the "Huh?" response from others outside the team who want to know what you're doing.

- ✔ **Project objective(s).** Listing your project objective (or objectives) fully defines the end results that you expect from the project. Project objectives connect the project charter to the project plan.

- ✔ **Deliverables.** Deliverables are products of work that the team creates to achieve its objectives. Describing what deliverables you're expecting explains to everyone on the team exactly what must be produced.

- ✔ **Schedule with milestones.** A schedule that highlights specific events is a major piece of the project plan, because it outlines key steps of the project and time frames for each step. Chapter 5 provides two main planning strategies that you can use when developing a project plan — the *going-forward* and *backward-planning* approaches. Both strategies help you outline your project schedule and milestones in a logical and sequential fashion.

- ✔ **Assignments.** This piece of the project plan explains what roles and responsibilities team members are going to play, like actors in a movie script. You can share responsibilities, but make sure that every team member plays a role in doing the project.

- ✔ **Checkpoints.** Checkpoints are times when the team meets to review its progress and to work, as needed, on other project-related issues. Don't leave these meetings to chance. Scheduling them upfront (often around project milestones or more frequently) tells everyone that your project is organized and that ongoing communication and accountability are expected.

Project Plan

SUBJECT/NAME: _____

DEADLINE: _____

OBJECTIVE(S): _____

DELIVERABLES:

Milestones   Project Completion Date

_____   _____

_____   _____

_____   _____

_____   _____

Assignments:

Checkpoints:

Figure 14-1:
A project
plan form.

Developing and using a project plan

The following tips describe the things that you can do to help you develop and implement a good project plan:

- ✔ **Involving team members in drafting a project plan.** A common theme throughout this book is developing the project plan *with* your team rather than doing it for them. Explain the objectives and the boundaries, but then have your team members help you map out the plan. Participating in that way helps them buy in to the plan. But a more important reason for having team members help you with planning is that they have much of the knowledge about the particular work that's needed to do the project.

- ✔ **Giving a copy of the plan to every team member.** A plan is fairly useless when you're the only person with a copy. Everyone involved in a project needs a copy of the plan so they too can live by it.

- ✔ **Coordinating task lists with the plan's milestones.** The project plan contains essentials for guiding the project, but it doesn't need to be refined down to the detailed task level. On the other hand, individual team members need to prepare their own detailed task lists that coincide with the milestones of the project plan, so they can provide copies for their team members. Their lists and descriptions of where the project is going compliment each another, helping the team and its members stay on track together.

✔ **Revising the plan as needed.** A project plan is a guide, but it isn't carved in stone. The longer that the term of a project runs, the more likely that changes will occur along the way. When changes occur, simply make sure that you update the master project plan and distribute new copies to your team members.

✔ **Managing by plan.** This last tip summarizes the previous four and serves as a reminder that the project plan is one of your most important project and team management tools. The plan helps in everything that you do in leading your team through the project. Details matter less and diversions are less of a distraction, because you have a strong focus on the direction in which you're headed and the results that your team needs to achieve.

Remember to set team guidelines with the members of your team. Guidelines serve as standards of excellence to the kinds of behaviors that members of your team can expect from one another when working together. Chapter 5 shows you how to facilitate the creation of your team's guidelines.

Starting a Task Team on the Same Page

Task teams offer challenges that sometimes are greater than even project teams. Generally the work that people do as part of a project team is part of their job, and they're performing many of the functions that are required of them in their regular jobs. However, where members of most task teams are concerned, you're asking them to work with you on something that is in addition to their regular jobs. Often task-team members are not even applying skills they use on their regular jobs but rather they're working on issues quite different from what they normally do.

With these challenges in mind, establishing the right focus with your task-team members is crucial from the beginning. In the sections that follow, I discuss preparing for and launching the work of your task team.

Before the team begins its work

Much of the preliminary work that you do with project teams also applies to task teams. Two main areas of emphasis are establishing focus and forming the team.

Establishing your task team's focus

In my experience, task teams tend to have fewer sponsors than project teams do and are treated more like extra credit projects that are nice to do than like the important work that project teams are charged with doing. Nonetheless, when you initiate an idea for a task team, establishing an overall focus is a good thing to do.

Building the support that you need when forming a task team means finding a sponsor — or turning to the manager who suggested the task to serve as your sponsor — so that you reach an understanding about the following topics before you start to work:

- ✔ Clarifying what issue is to be studied and why it's important

- ✔ Clarifying what outcomes are expected, such as a recommendations for a solution, a design of a program, the implementation of a new policy, and so on

- ✔ Clarifying what resources you need — from staff to finances

Forming the team

Finding the right team members often is your biggest task. People who show little interest can't be counted on to show up regularly for team meetings or tend not to follow through on assignments. They are not individuals that you want on your task team. (They'll do just fine, however, if *you* want to do all the work.)

When organizing your team, be sure to steer clear of these two problematic approaches:

- ✔ **Allowing management to select team members for you.** Whether the idea to select your team for you is coming from your sponsor or from others in management, push back and don't let anyone who isn't a direct part of your task team tell you who should be on the team. You can certainly listen to suggestions from anyone, but strongly reserve the right to select team members you think will work best.

- ✔ **Accepting anyone who volunteers.** Volunteers are good, because they usually already are interested in what your task team is going to do. On the other hand, volunteers may not have the kind of work ethic or team-work abilities that you need for your team to succeed. Whenever that's true of a particular volunteer, say, "No thanks," and then go after the people you think will work best.

You may not be aware of everyone who's talented and available for task-team service. So, define the main team-member criteria that you're seeking and ask managers from other groups whom they recommend.

When recruiting an individual you want for your team, cover these points in your conversation:

✔ What the purpose of the task team is all about

✔ Why you're so interested in having that person on the team — tie it to your criteria

✔ What the projected time and work commitments are

After discussing these points, you then can address any questions or concerns the potential team member may raise before closing the deal with the simple but direct question: "Will you join the team?"

Getting the task team rolling

Use initial task team meetings for making sure that everyone on the team is on the same page. Again reminding you to do as many things with (and not for) your team as possible, here's your checklist for those sessions:

✔ **Determining the length and frequency of team meetings.** Task teams need some kind of regular meeting schedule to do their work. Although you must, of course, factor in people's regular work schedules when considering the needs of the team with respect to its task, you also must keep this general rule in mind: The longer the interval between meetings, the slower the progress that the task team makes.

✔ **Developing a team-purpose statement.** Follow the process outlined in Chapter 5 for developing a team-purpose statement, which clarifies the overall role of the task team and sorts out differing points of view that people may have about the team's emphasis. Sorting out these differences upfront is better than running into obstacles they can occur later on.

✔ **Setting team guidelines.** What handful of expectations do team members have of one another when they're working together? Consider these team guidelines as a staple on your team's diet that builds a healthy coexistence.

✔ **Developing a work plan.** At the beginning of a task, nobody knows the exact outcomes or recommendations that you'll reach at the end, but you nevertheless want to make a plan for dealing with your issue. By outlining key steps or milestones that you believe will occur, and including target dates for reaching them, your team has a direction in which to go. The plan can (and undoubtedly will) be revised as you go.

✔ **Defining special roles.** Members of some task teams have special expertise or interests. Maybe one team member handles external relations well, another is best at handling policy research issues, and so on. Identify the expertise and special interests that exist among members of your team so that you can tap into it.

The task-team landmine

A Procedure Review Team was created for the overall purpose of reviewing, updating, and streamlining operating procedures at a company to better serve internal and external customers. The company's story relates that the idea for forming a task team came from a department head or two, although no specific designated sponsor had any regular connection or exercised any oversight. And although a certain amount of understanding about the team's role existed among some team members, no documented team-purpose statement was ever created.

The task team was composed of representatives from four main groups that had operating responsibilities within the company; however, just who from those main groups was supposed to serve as members of the task team never was determined. As a result, attendance at weekly meetings varied from six to sixteen people.

No one was designated as team leader, but two managers generally took turns facilitating the meetings. They came from the groups that had more operating procedures under review. The team had no plan or set goals.

Not surprisingly, without any foundation to provide a focus, the team sputtered during much of its first year of existence. And yet company management wanted the team to forge ahead on procedural issues, and so, the team, in its various forms, plugged along, occasionally getting something done, usually in response to a major customer complaint that had caught management's attention.

When an outside assessment was requested to explore why the team was struggling, determining the causes was easy. This task team became the lesson in how not to establish and operate a task team. Has your organization formed such a task team? Many still are running loose today.

Keeping a Team on the Productive Track

This section provides tips and strategies that you can use with project teams and task teams for managing their journeys successfully to their final destinations. It also give you tips for helping task teams with their fact-finding and recommendation-generating efforts.

Maintaining focus and pushing accountability

A laissez faire or hands-off approach ensures two outcomes that you don't want when you're leading a project team or a task team: The team never really coordinates its efforts and the results that you want never to see the light of day. But that won't be true in your case because you understand that after your team becomes organized, the hard work of keeping team members on track and producing really begins. How do you do that?

Here are a few key tips:

- ✔ **Meeting regularly and maintaining discipline.** Project teams and task teams need to meet on a regular basis — no less than once every two weeks and often much more frequently, depending on the work. You don't want to wait for a crisis to develop before pulling your team together. From planning to problem solving, from status review to creating work products, these kinds of teams have plenty of good reasons to meet.

  At the same time, insist on good meeting management habits at every meeting. In particular, make sure that you prepare well-defined agendas and have someone taking minutes that document all decisions, work done, and action items.

- ✔ **Addressing problems in a timely manner.** Encountering problems in team situations is inevitable, but whenever such a problem concerns the entire team, be sure to use the team meeting as a forum for addressing it. Problems with getting the work done well are the ones that you particularly want to put in front of the whole team. Problems with individuals, on the other hand, probably need to be addressed privately with the individual.

  Raising issues about problems and facilitating their resolution with the team are parts of your role as a leader. And *you* don't have to solve every problem. Getting the team involved is important if you ever want its members to assume responsibility. If an issue reaches beyond the team, you can help settle it by serving as an obstacle remover, but count on team members to help resolve inside-the-team issues.

- ✔ **Conducting regular status reviews with your team.** Reviewing team status is one of the key tactics that drives your team's accountability and results (Chapter 7 explains how). A status review is a follow-up progress check on how team members are doing with their assignments as well as a tool for planning the assignments for the next short-term period.

  Figure 14-2 provides you with a detailed status review form that's especially useful with project teams. It's based on one being used by a team that oversees municipal construction projects. The financial information is useful when budget management is an integral part of your project. Notice that the form also delves deeper into planning for the near term by looking one week ahead, then longer term, by looking four weeks ahead. Some projects require this kind of planning. Doing so helps team members break down a long-term project into more manageable bites and keep it on track toward meeting major milestones.

Project Management Status Review Tracking Report

Project _____ Date _____

Total Budget   Prior Week's Balance   Current Week's Balance

_____   _____   _____

Action Items For This Week	Team Member(s) Responsible	Current Status	1-Week Look-ahead	4-Week Look-ahead

Figure 14-2:
Status review form for a project team.

> ✔ **Recognizing achievements.** When you're reviewing progress and addressing issues that crop up with your teams, remember to stop long enough to offer recognition to successes as they occur. Hitting a milestone definitely is one such success and so is on-time delivery of good-quality work. Celebrate successes like these. From making announcements on the floor to taking the team out for lunch, *how* you recognize good performance matters less than actually recognizing it. Positive reinforcement goes a long way toward melding a team together and building a successful collective experience.

Managing task teams through a problem-solving process

Part of keeping a task team on track is employing the right kind of problem-solving system. The six-step problem-solving model described in Chapter 9 is one that I've used with success when leading task teams. Leading your team step by step as it works through the central issue is helpful, because you can move from defining the problem to analyzing it and from developing solutions to making recommendations. Such an approach helps team members understand how they've progressed throughout the process.

Whenever task teams deal with issues about their work, they often must gather information from outside of your business — research. But much of the information that they need, nevertheless, actually resides within your organization. In fact, periodically gathering information from internal resources is one of the more useful and important team functions for finding facts, gathering ideas, and testing plans that the team develops.

When task team members seek input and feedback from internal sources, here are some pointers that you can give them:

✔ **Decide each person's constituency.** Work with the team to decide who asks whom for input. Doing so helps on two fronts, ensuring that you speak to key people whose thoughts you want to include and avoiding the awkwardness of two team members talking to the same person.

✔ **Develop the questions.** You want to ask clear, specific, and in most cases, open-ended questions so that you get the information that you need.

✔ **Determine key messages that team members can convey in their introductions.** The people who team members interview need to know what you're doing and the context of your effort — a brief introduction does just that. For consistency and credibility, work with your team members so that they all use the same carefully crafted, but brief, introductory message.

✔ **Ask in person.** Soliciting thoughts from others works best when it's done in live conversation, over the phone or (even better) face-to-face. Most respond well to a short conversation in which they're asked a few questions — a painless experience. But many are much less willing to respond to e-mails and surveys. They don't need any more work.

✔ **Coach team members to listen and record.** When team members solicit facts and observations from their constituents within the company, their main role is gathering information — not filtering it, disagreeing with it, or attempting to rationalize what the team is doing. You don't want your team members engaging in debate with the people from whom they're gathering input. Doing so can bias the resource people you're interviewing and end up turning them off. Save the evaluation of comments until the team meets and after everyone shares what others had to say.

✔ **Set a deadline.** Setting a deadline for your team members to complete their interviews with constituents is important because all the information needs to be assembled before you can meet to evaluate it. Generally, sooner works better than later.

Managing with Influence Rather than Authority

One of the biggest challenges that you face when you manage project teams and task teams is that most, if not all, of the members of your team don't report directly to you. You're their team leader but not their boss. You don't write their reviews or direct what they do the rest of the time the way their own managers do. You don't have that authority.

This section explores how you can assert positive influence with your task team and project team members, driving their performance even though you don't have the title of boss and the authority that comes with it.

Explaining how leaders lead

Management positions in business organizations usually are viewed as leadership roles, but not all occupants of those positions are leaders. Why is that? Quite simply, they don't take charge much at all. They tend to sit back, let things run by themselves, and they're unable, for one reason or another, to steer a group of individuals toward achieving positive results.

Managers who take charge by asserting themselves are the ones who show leadership in their positions and tend to do so through one of two ways, *positional influence* and *personal influence*.

Positional influence

Positional influence is exhibited by someone in charge who asserts leadership through the authority of the management position that he or she holds. Authority comes with the title, and the person uses that authority to push others to perform and do what he wants them to do.

Personal influence

Personal influence is exhibited by someone in charge who asserts leadership through the quality of his or her character and the resulting behavior. Through everyday interaction and the development of working relationships with others, based on giving respect and asking for it, the person in charge asserts his or her personal influence with others, motivating them to perform.

You can achieve results using both kinds of influence. But each operates differently, and affects people differently, too, as you can see from the comparisons made in Figure 14-1.

Table 14-1	Comparison of Positional versus Personal Influence
Positional Influence	*Personal Influence*
Leading by title	Leading by example
Issuing directives	Seeking collaboration
When push comes to shove, pushing harder and relying on one-way communication	When push comes to shove, being firm as needed but opening up dialogue and solving problems together
Seeking control	Seeking involvement of others
Stimulating compliance	Stimulating commitment

Compliance means obedience — people do what they're told to do, but that doesn't necessarily mean that people give their best efforts and full support. That's the kind of behavior that you see when people have a sense of commitment to their jobs.

Asserting positional influence can be effective in running a regular work group, as long as group members are not the sort who tend to reject any kind of authority. In many cases, people don't like to be told what to do. But where any kind of team is concerned, one key for achieving success is including members of the team in the process rather than treating them as bystanders waiting for orders. That's why heavy doses of positional influence tend to negate team development — although they're often good for inciting dissension, especially among bright, creative people.

More than any title, your behavior is what helps you to gain employee commitment. People are more likely to follow you and work with you when you show them that you care about and respect them. Demanding good performance while building caring and respectful working relationships is a mutually *inclusive* effort.

Asserting your personal influence

Because most of the people serving on your project or task team are not your subordinates, you are, in essence, a team leader. You're a facilitator, a coordinator, and a point person, but you're not the boss. You don't have boss-type authority, and whenever you try to push that type of authority anyway, you'll probably be rejected so fast that you may end up as the sole member of the team.

Leading others requires neither a title nor a granting of authority. What it requires is your assertion of personal influence. When you're passive in your behavior — wishy-washy, hesitant, the sit-back type — you have no personal influence. Of course, when you come on too strong and attempt to dictate and brow beat, say hello to a revolt.

Asserting your personal influence, especially in leading task teams and project teams, requires that you consistently:

- ✔ **Exhibit a positive and confident manner**
- ✔ **Collaborate and engage in two-way conversation**
- ✔ **Follow through on your commitments**

Some additional ways of asserting leadership are

- ✔ **Sharpening your facilitation skills.** Asserting positive leadership with your project or task team begins with your being able to run meetings effectively. Prepare those agendas and have *working* meetings, not merely information-passing meetings. As facilitator, use tools that stimulate participation and, at the same time, positively and firmly push the group to stay focused when working through its agenda. Chapter 12 provides more detail about the skills of effective meeting facilitation.

- ✔ **Giving constructive feedback frequently.** Part of leading any team as a coach — a key theme of this book — is acknowledging performance of team members as they perform in real time. Cover all important aspects of their performance, including their behavior. Make your feedback specific, direct, sincere, and based on observations, not interpretations. Acknowledge what people do well and what they don't do so well, providing positive and negative feedback, and not just one or the other.

Team members appreciate this honesty and become more open to hearing your feedback the more they recognize that doing so is just a regular practice in the way that you operate as a team leader.

Acknowledging performance by individual team members is best done one-on-one. Giving individual feedback in a public setting can make for a strained interaction, because some people are embarrassed even when positive feedback is given in front of their peers. Know your people. Acknowledge collective performance in front of the team. In fact, when the team as a whole performs well, lead the charge in orally recognizing the quality results to which everyone contributed.

- ✔ **Setting the team guidelines early.** Focusing people on achieving good performance is so much easier when expectations are clear and people are involved in setting those expectations with you. Use the team guidelines as criteria for giving constructive feedback.

✔ **Addressing issues of concern in a timely manner and with a focus on solutions.** As coach of the team, you work on two levels: the collective, whole team level, and the individual level. When issues of concern come up with team-member performance, don't avoid the situation and let the problem fester and grow. Go talk to that person — don't use e-mail. Firmly and constructively state what you have observed, listen to what the other person has to say, and then discuss a solution that addresses yours and the other person's ideas. Use the team's guidelines as a framework for improvement efforts. Remember to assess progress at follow-up meetings.

You don't have to be someone's boss to address an issue. Stepping up and tackling an issue privately and timely earns you credibility, especially with fellow team members who see that you demand good performance and firmly yet positively deal with problems that may get in the way.

Ultimately, when someone is not responding to your intervention efforts, discuss the consequences and let him know that you'll talk to his manager. If good faith efforts to work out solution fail, removal of the person from the project or task team is a reasonable conclusion.

✔ **Sending feedback to your team members' managers.** Because people are being asked to spend time and perform on a team that may be outside their day-to-day jobs, the least you can do is ensure they get credit for it. Let your team members know in the beginning that you plan to periodically pass along feedback about their performance to their managers and to offer your input when the time comes for their respective performance reviews. Doing so promotes accountability, avoids surprises, and most important, recognizes good performance.

Manage your task team and project team members as if they reported directly to you. Thinking of them that way helps you to become deeply involved in what they're doing — the way a *coach* is.

Chapter 15

Show Us the Money: Incentives and Other Rewards for Teams

*B*ehavior that's rewarded is repeated. I use that old line as an important theme when working with managers. The idea is that when you positively acknowledge good performance that you see occurring, you're likely to see it happening again. That's the principle of *positive reinforcement.*

Conversely I've seen many times and places in which wrong behaviors are rewarded, and it keeps coming back in that case, too. For example, every time a staff member who habitually does sloppy work makes another error, you step in and fix it. I'll say it again: *Behavior that's rewarded is repeated.*

Whether you're managing individuals or teams, recognizing and rewarding the right behaviors is the point. Taking good performance for granted never has been much of a motivator.

You can recognize good performance in many ways; that's the topic of this chapter. Historically, in business organizations, *incentive pay* — that is, pay beyond a person's regular base salary, usually in the form of bonuses or commissions — was limited to people in management and sales positions. In recent years, however, incentive pay has been extended to many levels of employees.

This chapter explores how you can create incentive plans for teams, especially the kinds of plans that create a link between performance and financial reward. The chapter also explores a reward system known as *skill-based pay* — rewarding individual team members for the new skills that they develop and apply in helping the team do its work.

But money alone is not enough. To complement pay-based rewards for good performance, this chapter also shows you how to recognize good work in ways that cost little or nothing but richly express your appreciation.

Getting the Incentive for Team Incentive Pay

Traditionally employees earn a living based on the pay scale for their position, modified by changeable factors such as labor market conditions, where a position fits within the hierarchy of an organization, and how long a person has been in a job. Your base salary is what you see in your paycheck every pay period, no matter how many good days or bad days of performance you've experienced. Unless you're being terminated, your base pay remains constant until your manager and organization give you a raise, such as once a year.

Incentive pay is a form of variable compensation. Sometimes called a bonus, it's a component of wages that varies by performance and is proffered in addition to your base salary. Incentive pay is a way of rewarding good performance with money rather than with promotion and without adding costs to base salary structures.

Incentive pay for teams can be a strong management tool that drives teamwork and performance. It's also a tool that can be helpful when you're working with work-unit teams and project teams (which are defined in Chapter 1). The sections that follow explore some of the reasons for using incentive pay systems with teams and how to design an incentive pay structure that works with your teams.

Hey pal, here's the rationale

When you consider developing a team incentive plan, first ask yourself: Why do I want such a plan? What do I hope to accomplish with it? You want to be able to communicate answers to these questions to your team members so they understand where you're headed with an incentive plan.

Some objectives to aim for with a team incentive plan are

- ✔ **Stimulating increases in productivity.** Increased productivity is the number-one reason for establishing an incentive plan. You're pushing performance so that you gain good results — even better results than before. You want to create a link between performance and reward. When you do, you have a mechanism in place that helps you achieve the productivity that you're after.

✔ **Rewarding key behaviors that you need for good productivity.** Remember, behavior that's rewarded is repeated. A team incentive plan is a tool that helps you reward the right behaviors for stimulating strong performance. In most cases, these behaviors deal with teamwork, output of work, and quality of work and service. These positive behaviors are what you need team members to exhibit so that they produce the work results that are in demand. A team incentive plan serves as a tangible reward for such behaviors.

✔ **Increasing an understanding of business needs and the kind of performance required for meeting those needs.** A good incentive plan paints pictures for team members of the business targets that need to be achieved and the progress they must make in meeting those targets. Information gives people the power to make decisions and act. A good incentive plan helps your team achieve that objective.

✔ **Aiding in the retention of good performers.** Labor markets often are quite competitive, especially for good employees. The dilemma you face: Although you can't afford to give people more money just to stick around, you can be creative with your salary systems so that you remain competitive in the job market, giving employees reasons to stay with the organization because you reward them for helping deliver the results that the business needs, a win-win situation. That's one objective of team incentive plans.

Money alone is not the be-all and end-all for team member motivation and retention. Many factors other than pay come into play — the challenge of the work, the chance to grow, and the quality of your management are but a few. So, think of a team incentive plan as just one tool among many.

An incentive pay plan can turn some people off. Some team members take great pride in their work and don't view money as a motivator for this pride. They approach their work with passion and treat what they do as a special craft. For some of these people, extra pay in the form of incentives is an insult. They're already getting paid, and that's fine. The way they see it, they don't need some sort of bribe to produce good results.

Before you design and implement a team incentive plan, talk with your team members about your main objectives and ask for their feedback. When your team thinks incentives are unappealing, you don't need to bother with designing such a pay plan. More often than not, introducing the idea creates excitement, but check it out first.

Recipe for success: Designing the incentive plan

A good team incentive plan rewards team members equally for the collective results of their work. When designing an incentive plan so that you reap the benefits that you seek, make certain that it meets the criteria discussed in the following sections.

Offering rewards that attract attention

Incentive pay has to be big enough to be interesting. Otherwise you'll hear comments like, "When you give us peanuts, or $50 a year, to do everything you're asking of us, why even bother?" What the right amount is is impossible to determine. But one thing is certain: Thousands work better than hundreds or tens.

Budgeting for the rewards

A team incentive plan is more than a reward system. When used wisely, it also serves as a financial planning tool. By determining the monetary level that team members find worthwhile, you can budget for that amount. Thus, you have the incentive pool in place and don't need to figure it out after the fact. One caveat: Cover yourself in case a major downturn occurs by making sure that everyone understands that incentive payouts are based on economic and business conditions.

Defining performance criteria

Team members must understand the goals or targets that form the basis for the incentive plan. Quite often, you want to involve team members in defining what those targets are. Including them in the design of the incentives builds their willingness to buy in to the process, of course, but it also recognizes that they're the ones who are doing the work and ought to know what the unit needs to accomplish.

How many goals or targets do you need? I'd say three to five, at most, because you don't want a cumbersome plan. On the other hand, you do want to include the areas that are most relevant to the collective performance of your team. Here are some areas to consider:

- Output or production targets
- Quality standards
- Profit or revenue targets
- Cost-control levels
- Customer satisfaction
- Completion of special projects
- Implementation of new initiatives

Measuring the results

Every goal that you set for the incentive plan needs to be measured in a reasonable way; otherwise, it isn't a goal that will work. You may need to create new mechanisms for measuring results — from survey forms to software applications. Provide performance information that is generated to the team so the team members can see what's happening.

Connecting performance and payout

In compensation lingo, the connection between performance and payout is called *line of sight*. In other words, the plan offers team members a clear understanding of the relationship between what they need to achieve in their performance and the financial reward they receive for it. If team members do *x* in their performance, then they each will earn *y* in dollars for their efforts. Connecting performance and payout gives team members a sense of control over their destinies.

Including a beginning payout level and a top end

Does payout of incentive begin when the team reaches 50 percent of the target, 80 percent, or when 100 percent of the targets is reached? No right or wrong answer exists. Generally, I favor teams receiving some incentive for going a good part of the way toward the intended target — definitely more than halfway before receiving any cash reward. When the team hits the 100 percent level, it should receive 100 percent of the incentive pool. When a team *exceeds* its target, the incentive payout also should be proportionally higher up to a predefined level. The idea is to define payout levels so team members know where rewards begin and realize that they can be rewarded for going above and beyond the 100 percent target.

Paying out frequently

Longer intervals between payouts mean a lesser impact by incentives on performance. For instance, incentives paid only once a year occur too seldom to have much of a driving effect on performance. Six months may be the maximum interval for incentives to have at least some effect. Designing your incentive program to pay every three to four months can have a much greater impact on team performance.

Producing positive outcomes

Incentive plans focus on improvements in productivity, such as increases in output per person. But when the agenda includes the elimination of jobs, an incentive plan is seen as a punitive rather than a positive tool. A good incentive plan achieves outcomes that benefit the business and team members.

Keeping your plan simple to understand and administer

A good team incentive plan sticks to the keep-it-simple approach. Although numbers and formulas usually are involved, nobody needs a PhD in calculus to figure out the plan. Whenever people can't understand how a plan works, it has little effect on performance. Furthermore, whenever tracking results and administering the plan is cumbersome, it won't last long. Those things said, you're nevertheless likely to experience a few kinks and more work when first implementing your new incentive pay plan. That's normal.

Sampling a few incentive plans

Incentive plans can take on many shapes and forms. This section shows you a few samples that incorporate key ingredients that this chapter covers. Although a plan can have more detail, these samples aim for the keep-it-simple approach and preserve a clear connection, or *line of sight,* between performance and reward.

THE MEDIA-RELATIONS TEAM

This work-unit team is part of a public-relations agency. Its main job is providing media-relations services for the firm's clients and helping to grow the firm's business. Here are the key elements of the incentive plan:

The goal areas. The team has three goals for which it sets targets:

- ✔ **Client retention** — how many clients it starts with and ends with in each incentive period
- ✔ **Client satisfaction** — what clients think about the services rendered by the team and how well the team is meeting their needs
- ✔ **Revenue** — how much money the team earns for the firm and whether earnings come from new business or current clients

The incentive cycle. The incentive plan works on a quarterly cycle. Each quarter, results are tabulated, appropriate incentives are paid out, and new goals are set for the next period. Adjustments made each quarter make it possible to set goals that are challenging and realistic.

The payout formula. In evaluating the results at the end of each quarter, multipliers are used for determining how much incentive is rewarded to team members. The multipliers are:

> *0.0 = Target not met*
>
> *0.75 = At least 75 percent of target achieved*
>
> *1.0 = 100 percent of target achieved*
>
> *1.5 = Exceeded 100 percent of target*

The three goals are weighted evenly. Each goal equals one-third of the total regular incentive of $900. The multipliers are applied to each goal and then added together to determine the full amount of the incentive payout.

Example

The Media Relations Team set these targets for the quarter:

- ✓ **Client retention:** Keep 8 of 10 current clients.

- ✓ **Client satisfaction:** Achieve a 90 percent average approval rating from all clients served during the quarter. The team surveys its clients at the end of each quarter to obtain this feedback.

- ✓ **Revenue:** Achieve a target of $200,000 in business income.

At the end of the quarter, here are the results and how the multipliers work:

- ✓ **Client retention (Goal 1):** Seven of the 10 clients still are being served at quarter's end — 0.75 payout level.

- ✓ **Client satisfaction (Goal 2):** Overall rating average is 90 percent — 1.0 payout level.

- ✓ **Revenue (Goal 3):** Thanks to adding two new clients, the target is exceeded by $25,000 — 1.5 payout level.

Given that the 100 percent payout level for each of three goals is $300 per team member, the math works like this:

- ✓ **Goal 1:** .75 × $300 = $225 payout

- ✓ **Goal 2:** 1.0 × $300 = $300 payout

- ✓ **Goal 3:** 1.5 × $300 = $450 payout

Total incentive payout per team member for the quarter = $975

THE ORDER FULFILLMENT TEAM

This work-unit team is responsible for receiving orders from the sales department and shipping products to customers. Orders usually consist of many parts and pieces. The work involves packaging orders accurately and shipping them to meet time commitments. The team also services existing orders by providing part replacements and upgrades when needed.

The goal areas. This team set targets in four areas:

- ✓ **Meeting deadline commitments for current orders**

- ✓ **Meeting accuracy rates for current orders**

- ✓ **Meeting deadline commitments for replacement and upgrade needs**

- ✓ **Meeting accuracy rates for replacement and upgrade orders —** Accuracy for this team goes right to the heart of quality because it means that not only the right products are shipped but they must be in working order.

The incentive cycle. The Order Fulfillment Team operates on a quarterly basis so that it can stay up to date with the flow of business.

The payout formula. Because all goal areas are critical for results, each is weighted equally — in this case, one-fourth of the total regular incentive of $800. The multipliers work as follows:

> *0.0 = Target not met*
>
> *0.9 = At least 90 percent of target achieved*
>
> *1.0 = 100 percent of target achieved*
>
> *1.25 = Exceeded 100 percent of target*

Example

The Order Fulfillment Team set these targets for the quarter:

- **Deadline commitments for current orders:** 90 percent

- **Accuracy rate for current orders:** 95 percent

- **Deadline commitments for replacement/upgrade orders:** 90 percent

- **Accuracy rate for replacement/upgrade orders:** 95 percent

The team follows up each order with the customer to determine whether fulfillment is accurate, products are in good working order, and delivery is on time. This information is recorded in a database that serves as the measuring instrument for the team's incentive pay system. Here are the results at the end of the quarter:

- **Deadline commitments for current orders (Goal 1):** 75 percent of the time, less than 90 percent of the intended target — 0.0 payout.

- **Accuracy rate (Goal 2):** 95 percent on all current orders shipped — 1.0 payout level.

- **Deadline commitments for replacement/upgrade orders (Goal 3):** 85 percent of the time — 0.9 payout level.

- **Accuracy rate for replacement /upgrade orders (Goal 4):** 100 percent — 1.25 payout level.

The incentive pool allotted $200 per goal area for achieving 100 percent of target level. For the quarter, here are the incentive calculations:

- **Goal 1:** $0.0 \times \$200 = 0$
- **Goal 2:** $1.0 \times \$200 = \$200$

✔ **Goal 3:** 0.9 × $200 = $180

✔ **Goal 4:** 1.25 × $200 = $250

Total incentive payout per team member = $630

The example of the Order Fulfillment Team illustrates a benefit of an incentive plan that sometimes is overlooked. By measuring results, the plan can place greater emphasis on areas where a team may be having difficulty — such as hitting delivery deadlines on certain orders. With performance data in hand, you can begin solving a problem like that.

THE PRODUCT DEVELOPMENT TEAMS

These cross-functional, technical project teams create new products and upgrade current products. Their projects last four to six months.

The goal areas. The incentive plan has two main goals:

✔ Hitting target dates for *deliverables* (work products defined by a team)

✔ Making deliverables that work — no malfunctions

The incentive cycle. Based on project timelines.

The payout formula. It works like this:

✔ If a project team meets both goals, all team members receive 100 percent.

✔ If a project is delayed but still is completed within one month of the intended deadline and has the right quality, 75 percent of the eligible incentive pool is rewarded. A project is not considered to have met deadline, however, if quality problems exist. No payout occurs for a project that's more than a month late and still has quality problems

✔ If a team hits its quality target and gets its project done at least two weeks ahead of schedule, it receives 120 percent of its eligible incentive.

Example

The Product Development Team has four months to complete a project. If they hit their time and quality targets, each team member receives $750. This is how the incentives are scaled:

✔ **Hits time and right quality targets:** 100 percent × $750 = $750.

✔ **Hits quality target but comes in one month late:** 75 percent × $750 = $562.50.

✔ **Beats the deadline and achieves quality standard:** 120 percent × 750 = $900.

A well-conceived incentive plan is easy to understand and administer and, above all, clearly links performance outcomes and rewards.

Rolling out the incentive plan

Design is fine, but you'll pout without a good rollout. So, as you put together a team incentive plan, pay attention to the tips for success that I describe in the following sections.

Involving others in the design

You need to include team members who are covered by the plan in helping you define and set the targets to serve as the performance criteria. Emphasize to them that you want goals that are challenging yet attainable, that define results, and that can be measured. Team members can help with finding ways to measure results when those mechanisms are not yet in place.

Consult with your manager, human resources, and finance people as you design the plan, because their support often is needed, especially for budget and policy reasons. Involving the managers of these departments is beneficial during the planning stage, because when you seek their *advice and counsel* rather than their *permission,* you can assertively lead the campaign for an incentive plan.

Communicating the plan to educate team members

Make sure that your team members understand why you're pushing the incentive plan. Educate them on how the plan works and how they can earn cash payouts. Run through some examples for them so they can see the plan in action. When your team members understand the plan, they're much more likely to make it work and drive forward with the performance that you want.

Don't forget to articulate clearly the timeline of events that needs to occur, including deadlines for setting team goals and evaluating results, and the exact length of the performance period.

Addressing problems as they arise

Monitor progress when the incentive plan is rolling. Snags sometimes occur in setting goals, measuring results, and working with the payroll department to receive timely incentive payments, just to name a few problems that are possible. Whatever difficulty arises, get involved quickly to preserve the plan's momentum.

Gain sharing

Gain sharing is another form of incentive reward that can be applied to some teams. Traditional gain-sharing programs are aimed at improving performance and often target cost reductions. The idea behind gain sharing is that if costs are reduced, everyone responsible shares some portion (commonly half) of the savings. Because team members are sharing in a financial gain that they have produced, such incentive programs are self-funding to a large extent.

Gain sharing generally is applied to a large business unit or an entire worksite. However, the concept can be even more effective when applied to a smaller unit in which people feel more directly able to control certain financial outcomes. Administration can be a snap — as easy as splitting the pot 50/50.

Here are some areas where a gain-sharing plan can be applied:

- Waste reduction
- Operating expenses
- Sales margin increases
- Cost per production unit
- Cycle time for product development, claims processing, or fulfilling customer orders
- Equipment and machinery downtime
- Attendance
- Loss time from on-the-job accidents

Reviewing how the plan is working

Periodically, say once every couple of cycles, take a look to see whether the plan is doing what you want or expect in terms of meeting certain performance objectives or improving motivation. Make sure that the administrative side of the plan remains simple and direct. Talk to team members as part of your assessment, and make adjustments accordingly.

Rewarding Individual Team Members: Skill-Based Pay

This section explores a pay structure that can be used with some work-unit teams, but it works best where team members have the opportunity to gain and apply a multiple level of skills in helping their team achieve top performance. This structure, known as *skill-based* or *competency-based* pay, rewards individual team members rather than the entire team.

Counting the pluses of skill-based pay

The main idea of a skill-based pay structure within a team is rewarding individual team members for the skills that they possess, acquire, and apply toward helping the team achieve its goals. Thus, when team members develop new skills and put them to work, they earn increases in their base salaries. A skill-based pay plan is worth exploring with teams that have operations that feature many different functions that people can discover how to perform over time. The benefits of skill-based pay are that it:

- ✓ **Focuses acquisition of skills on supporting business needs.** A good skill-based pay program identifies the skill areas that you want team members to develop — skills that are known to help the business run more effectively. That's the idea — reward the skills that are needed for the work of the team and for the business overall. As business needs change and new technologies develop, you identify and reward the new skills that team members need. This link usually translates into productivity gains.

- ✓ **Increases workforce flexibility.** Because a skill-based pay structure encourages team members to broaden their skills, you gain more team members who can do more kinds of work, making it easier to shift team members around to meet work demands. Say hello to greater flexibility and productivity.

- ✓ **Allows for pay increases without creating a hierarchy.** For their accomplishments, team members are rewarded with pay rather than new titles. No one rises to a higher level than anyone else. You avoid building a hierarchy, and the equality concept of a team remains intact.

- ✓ **Recognizes individuals without reducing the team structure.** The idea that "we're all in this together" is important for team success. That's why team *incentive* plans (which I discuss in "Recipe for success: Designing the incentive plan" earlier in this chapter) reward all team members equally. Skill-based pay is a way of rewarding individuals for their contributions without affecting the collective sense of a team. As individual team members receive certification for their skill acquisition, they are rewarded financially and their skills go directly toward supporting the team. But, at the same time, skill-based pay recognizes the desires and interests of the individual — not all team members want to acquire all possible skills, which results in a diversity of skills and interests.

- ✓ **Provides for job enrichment.** The entire concept of skill-based pay focuses on building competencies — greater knowledge, skills, and abilities. Training and cross-training are key elements in the execution of this kind of pay program. When people are encouraged to acquire and apply new skills, their jobs become fuller and more challenging — factors that stimulate employee motivation, teamwork, and performance.

Designing a skill-based pay plan

This section explores the elements to consider when designing an effective skill-based pay plan for your team. Such a plan can be used successfully in many job functions where duties and tasks can be shared — in production, technical, administrative, service, maintenance, and professional functions.

Don't fall into a skill-based pay plan that means your team members constantly are in training but getting little work accomplished. The demands of work and training must be balanced.

Another pitfall is rewarding employees who receive training in skills that are not applied on the job, for whatever reason. Similarly, budgeting for only the amount of skills training that you can afford is important. Theoretically, every team member in a skill-based pay structure can rise to the top by acquiring and applying all possible skills. Although not all team members want to do that, you still have to figure out what you can afford to spend for critical skills that you most want to reward.

Work with the help of your manager and human resources department when you design a plan that replaces the traditional salary system with a system that pays for personal growth and teamwork — skills-based pay. Such a plan usually means introducing broader salary ranges so that growth from skill acquisition can be rewarded. Prepare to introduce a skills-based pay structure for your teams by spending some time on five main elements of the framework, which are described in the following sections:

Identifying the skill set areas

What sets or blocks of skills are needed to perform the tasks and duties on the team? You can identify skill blocks from two angles — depth and breadth. *Depth of skill* means the extent of specialization in an area of work. *Breadth of skill* describes the variety and number of skill functions. Depending on what your team does, you may have skill blocks for both depth and breadth.

Skill blocks can encompass such areas as:

- **Job-duty skills (the core work of the team)**
- **Computer applications**
- **Team skills**
- **Customer service**
- **Administrative duties**
- **Project management**
- **Team leadership**

Defining the levels of skill or competency within each set

Subdividing a skill block helps you determine where a person needs development. For example, in the block called computer applications, you have data entry, word processing, spreadsheets, database development and administration, graphics, and programming, to name a few.

When you're defining a block of skills — again, with team member input — also determine your *base level*, which means the skills needed by a team member new to the job. The base level can be, for example, a handful of functions that cut across a few blocks. Thereafter, your skill-based pay program builds upon the base level.

When you're defining skills in the pay plan, stick to skills that team members can discover through formal training classes and cross-training. Keep in mind that you're not looking at functions that require a college degree in a professional field. That's why this pay structure doesn't work for teams that are multidisciplinary. You're not going to have accountants doing engineering work and vice versa.

Determining the pay value

Determining the pay for acquiring new skills may mean grouping skills within a block instead of considering only a single skill. Although budget considerations need to come into play, you want to make mastering and applying a valued skill financially worth something to team members. Pay value doesn't have to be the same amount for each new skill developed. You can vary dollar amounts based respectively on the complexity of skills and the amount of performance value they add to the team. For instance, project management skills, because they're more difficult to acquire and master, may carry a higher price tag with your team than regular job-duty skills in performing the projects.

Developing an evaluation mechanism

How do you determine whether a team member has mastered a skill? Do you use a performance or demonstration test? A written test? Do you gather feedback from team members who provided the training? Or do you use a combination of evaluation methods? The *how* is less important than the fact that some sort of mechanism is in place to assess and certify that a team member has acquired a new skill.

Setting the application time period

The monetary reward kicks in when the new skill has been demonstrated on the job in a good skill-based pay plan, and setting a time period for that to occur is important. Don't make the time period long between when a skill is gained and when it's used on the job — three months can work. You may want to set longer or shorter time frames based on the complexity of the newly acquired skill.

Document your plan as a permanent record. The plan becomes your tool for educating your team members and for administering the pay program going forward.

Keeping the system running

Designing a good skill-based pay plan takes a great deal of work, but developing a team with members discovering how they can perform multiple functions can enhance overall team performance, making the plan well worth the effort. Here are a few tips to follow for keeping the system running well:

- ✔ **Supporting cross-training.** Work with your team members on identifying their interests in skill development and developing a schedule that balances workload needs with cross-training time. Remember that not every team member masters and applies every possible skill that's identified for a reward all at once. At best, team members who are ambitious may add a few skill sets to their repertoire during the course of a year. But cross-training and even outside training are part off regular business practice if a skill-based pay system is going to work.

- ✔ **Assessing the program periodically.** Do team members believe the program is rewarding their development? How easy or difficult is the pay plan to administer? What confusions have surfaced since implementation? Overall, how is the plan working? Ask questions like these quarterly to start and at least every six months thereafter. Get feedback from team members as part of this assessment. Modify the pay program wherever needed and communicate the changes to your team.

- ✔ **Adjusting to incorporate new skills.** As business needs change, and sometimes as technology developments occur, your team needs to acquire new skills. When the work that you do begins to require those new skills, be sure to adjust your plan so that it acknowledges and rewards them.

Showing You Love Them in Other Ways

Money doesn't motivate everyone and generally isn't the sole motivator for anyone. So you need to think about other forms of rewarding team performance. Sometimes nonmonetary rewards may be of necessity. Perhaps despite your good plans, you don't have the financial means or management support for implementing variations on traditional pay practices. This section provides you with ideas for showing your appreciation without cash-in-the-pocket rewards.

Performance contest: Competing against yourself

Tammy led a team at a temporary technical staffing company. The performance contest that she organized had a clear objective: clean up the company's database of two thousand job applicants by determining who was active, what their skill sets were, updating contact details, and other things of that sort. If everyone pitched in, the team could do the job in two months, Tammy said. She challenged the team to meet the deadline and promised they'd celebrate hitting the target by having a night on the town.

Tammy ran reports each week, checking the team's progress and sharing the results with everyone. Sure enough, within two months the team had hit its target. The celebration featured tickets to a popular musical on a Saturday night, with spouses and significant others included. Even Tammy's boss came along to thank the team for its fine performance. As Tammy pointed out, the contest wasn't a competition among team members. It was, instead, the team competing against a target — in essence, competing against itself. Team members rallied together to do the job. That's the way to run a performance contest.

Gratitude at a cost

Often you can budget for the cost of suggestions like the ones that follow. But even when you sometimes have to cover the expense yourself, the cost is well worth it for celebrating success with your team.

- ✔ **Entertainment outings.** Examples include going to a ballgame, a movie, the theater, or having a night on the town. The whole team comes together — sometimes even with their families — for fun and entertainment at no expense to team members.

- ✔ **Social play outings.** A boat ride, a golf outing, bowling, an afternoon at the amusement park or video game arcade — choose something that your team members like to do.

- ✔ **Eating events and parties.** You never go wrong when food is involved. Whether it means taking the team out for lunch or a fancy dinner, or throwing a party, the idea is celebrating your success through the dependable eat-drink-and-be-merry approach. One set of teams hauls out the old barbecue and grills steaks whenever the quarterly results come in and all teams have met their goals. A good time is had by all — at the company's expense.

- ✔ **Gift certificates.** Adding a little something to your words of thanks for a job well done never hurts. Gift certificates can be for shopping or dining or just cash, and the amounts don't need to be high.

✔ **Time off.** Leisure time is a valuable commodity. The idea: For the good results that you've recently delivered, take a little time off at company expense. This time off doesn't count against vacation time or sick leave. You handle it discreetly and probably don't have every team member take the time off all at once.

Appreciation at little or no expense

The following ideas for showing appreciation for team performance generally cost little or nothing in terms of dollars and require only a bit of time and attention; however, they sometimes are the best investment you can make in motivating team members.

✔ **Educational field trips.** Team outings on company time that have some job-related value are great ideas. You can try attending a speech at a public gathering, visiting another company to witness its workings, or touring some place of interest that the team can gain knowledge from — probably with company-paid lunch as part of the deal. The idea: "We as a team go explore and discover together, and we don't have to use our own personal time to do so. Neat!"

✔ **Letters giving credit.** You show your appreciation for the team's good performance by writing letters to the team and to individual members for the record. The letters can go in each team member's official personnel file. For team members who don't report directly to you, a copy goes to their manager. Sometimes you can even ghostwrite letters for management above you to sign and send to your team members. Recognition from above can mean a great boost for team morale.

✔ **Little gifts.** Sometimes called *chachkes,* little tokens of appreciation costing no more than a few dollars take advantage of the adage that "it's the thought that counts." Inscribed trophies and plaques fall into this category, and so do medals and ribbons — like the ones they hand out at 10K runs and marathons. You can even make your little gifts in the form of edible treats — always welcome.

✔ **Recognition meetings.** A team gathering to express appreciation for a job well done also is an opportunity to recognize individual team members in front of their peers in a positive way. Recognizing something good about each person is a good idea, so that nobody is left out. Be specific: Identify and acknowledge particular contributions instead of just saying thanks for good work. Recognizing specifics shows that you have noticed and that you care, which goes a long way toward boosting motivation. Sometimes, you can invite management from above to attend and show its appreciation, too. Make sure that you prepare management guests well so that they can comment briefly but knowledgeably about what the team has been doing and why recognition is in order. A few words of appreciation from above often provide a big boost for team morale.

✔ **Articles in the newsletter.** A little publicity outlining your team's accomplishments is another idea that often triggers a positive spark of recognition and appreciation. Spreading the word publicly about what your team has done usually leads to informal expressions of appreciation by others in the organization — a sort of two-for-one burst of gratitude.

✔ **Positive feedback.** I push this idea throughout this book: A few words of positive feedback through informal conversation is the cheapest and yet one of the most powerful ways of showing your appreciation for good performance. Positive feedback is far more than general praise. You state specifically what you've seen in performance that was good. This tactic works well for a team as a whole, in the form of public recognition, and for individual team members as they perform good deeds.

Use positive feedback early and often so that team members know that good performance counts. Remember: *Behavior that's rewarded is repeated.*

Recognizing accomplishments the same way every time gets pretty stale; everyone likes variety. So, periodically ask team members, "Money aside, when the team performs well, what should we do so that people know that they *are* appreciated?" Keep a few notes on what team members tell you, and remember: What motivates one person may not be the same for everyone else.

We're celebrating *what?*

The key point about showing appreciation is to reward good performance. That means *results*, not merely activity. You may think that your team is working hard, but if they haven't produced any results, it isn't party time, yet.

That simple idea was lost on a group of 50 people working in a start-up operation at a large corporation. They had been working in teams to launch a new product and were well funded. The company expected them to deliver a new product — not exactly a radical concept.

One day, senior management of the unit decided to shut down operations for the afternoon and take everyone to the movies at company expense. They rented a nearby theater and bused everyone over to watch the latest release of a *Star Trek* film. (My timing was good

because I'd been doing some work that morning with a few people in another department and ended up getting invited to go to the movies. Hey, what the heck!)

When I inquired about the reason for the celebration, I found out that no major milestones had been passed nor had any other contributions been made. In fact, senior management of the unit had already convinced their funding source to move the target date back for delivery of the product. So, in essence, the team was out celebrating its hard work, without any real accomplishments to show for it. Everyone enjoyed the afternoon at the movies, however.

About four months later, after another couple of deadlines were missed, the funding company removed the senior management of this team.

Part VI
The Part of Tens

The 5th Wave   By Rich Tennant

"Right here ..., 'Crimegroup.com'. It says the well-run small criminal team should have no more than nine goons, six henchmen, and four stooges. Right now, I think we're goon heavy."

In this part . . .

The short chapters in The Part of Tens provide you with quick tips for managing management teams; for getting a team back on track when it's slipped off; and for identifying the qualities of effective team players — the kind of people you want on *your* team.

Chapter 16

Ten Tips for Management Groups to Work as Teams

In This Chapter
▶ Overcoming managers' natural tendencies
▶ Tactics for reshaping a management group into a team

Management teams are one of the five most common types of teams, but they're also the rarest — in true team form, anyway. Just pulling management staff together and declaring they're a team doesn't necessarily make a real management team.

A team has a common purpose and focuses on the greater good. Team members share accountability for results of their whole unit. But many management groups don't work that way. Each manager/member tends to focus most on his own territory and doesn't become involved much with the *sum of all these parts,* so to speak.

Yet management groups have the potential for functioning as real teams when the management leader wants to see it happen. This chapter contains tips for making a management team really work.

Spell Out the Need and Expectations

When your job is leading the management team, Job One is explaining to your colleagues why you want your management group to function as a team and what doing so means to you. For instance, you may see that your organizational entity can function more effectively if your management staff is involved with you in shaping and contributing to its success — which can be accomplished better when you work as a team rather than as a collection of individuals.

You want your managers to put aside their individual interests and take on the interests of the entire unit. Mention, too, that you need them to speak up and offer their ideas and opinions. Although you're still the leader and the buck still stops on your desk as the final decision maker, you need and want your managers to be actively involved in helping to operate the overall unit.

Get Everyone in Line: Draft a Purpose Statement and Guidelines

Chapter 5 provides you with a strategy for involving your team in the development of a purpose statement and team guidelines. The purpose statement defines why you exist and what your team's overall role is. Here's an example of a team purpose statement developed by an executive team with my facilitation:

> ***The purpose of our executive team is to work together in support of one another and to provide leadership and direction that promotes excellence in our organization.***

A management team's purpose statement doesn't need to be revolutionary or really catchy — you're not creating an advertising slogan. All you need is one clear sentence that defines why you exist as a team and what your overall role is as a team.

Team guidelines spell out how all the team members, you included, expect to work with one another inside and outside of team meetings. The guidelines are a handful of key behaviors that define expectations and focus every team member on mutual support and productivity.

By starting early in the process on the purpose statement and guidelines and working with your team (not *for* them), you're creating what I call *alignment*. You're laying the foundation that points everyone on the team moving in the same direction and starts them thinking and functioning as a team — an essential ingredient for having a real management team and not merely a management group.

Work on Organizational-level Issues

For the management group to function as a management team, you must work together on issues that affect the whole organizational entity that you run. So, work on planning, problem-solving, and making decisions critical to the success of the entire operation. Having your managers report periodically on matters affecting their own groups is okay, but spending most of your time on individual operational issues means that you won't develop a team — and probably don't need one.

Meet regularly, meaning once every one or two weeks. Make your meetings working sessions concerning common issues. In addition, assign subgroups of two or more team members to work outside of meetings on various organizational-level issues that especially need to be studied. Delegating responsibility helps connect team members and takes some of the burden off your shoulders as the only one concerned about big-picture issues.

Conclude each management team meeting by discussing for a few minutes how to communicate information coming out of the meeting back to each manager's groups. The troops want to know and need to know about issues the management team addresses and new directions they take. Otherwise, they wonder what members of the management team do when they hang out together.

Set Organizational Priorities and Tie In Group Plans

What are the goals or priorities that the overall organizational unit needs to achieve during the next six months to a year? Establish these goals together as a team, deciding to address a handful that involve everyone on the management team.

Then have each manager/member on the team develop plans and priorities for his or her group that support organizational-level priorities, and have that manager/member share the plans with everyone else on the team. Sharing this information is good to do because managers need to be aware of one another's priorities. Furthermore, doing so can spotlight opportunities for cross-group cooperation and promote teamwork outside of the management team meetings.

The organizational level/group level goal-setting process creates alignment throughout business operations. All managers are planning and executing in the same direction. That cohesiveness reinforces the focus cornerstone (Chapter 5) and makes each team member much more aware of the entire operation and not just his own piece of it — adding the kind of perspective that a real management team has.

Conduct Periodic Business Review

When you're setting goals and plans at the organizational- and manager-group level, reviewing progress periodically at both levels is important. This strategy promotes the accountability cornerstone (see Chapter 7) and demonstrates that your management team is serious about driving good performance.

Periodically means some kind of regular basis. Consider quarterly (but no less than twice a year) reviews for ensuring that all of you really *do* see the progress that your business unit and constituent groups are making. Remember that adjusting your plans to keep up with the needs of your business also is important to do.

Play "Switch" with Team Members

In the game of "Switch," as I call it, one person takes on another person's perspective, and vice versa. The parties to a discussion can't talk from their own perspective; otherwise, others in the group can call them for not switching effectively.

Why play Switch? One of the challenges of leading a management group that functions as a real team is getting members to think beyond their own group needs and interests. For instance, on every issue, the operations manager talks mostly about his interests; the sales manager does the same. Each has difficulty seeing what's important to the other person and what's important for the greater good of the entire organization — sales, operations, and all the other functions together.

Periodically, in your management team meetings, call for a switch. Assign one team member to represent the needs and interests of another team member's area of responsibility. Other team members won't hesitate in blowing the whistle when their perspective is not accurately represented. On a simpler level, without calling for a switch, you can ask team members to paraphrase one another's points of view, an exercise that ensures that everyone is listening and understanding.

Another way to stimulate different perspectives on issues is encouraging team members to raise questions like:

- How will this idea or point of view help the team and unit as a whole?
- How will this point of view help another team member?
- (Spoken to the sales manager, for instance): How will this suggested approach work for operations? What are the pros and cons?

Outcomes that are good for all of us are far better than outcomes that are good for only one of us.

Set Direction and Define Parameters

Your role as leader of a management team is communicating a vision of the future that you're aiming for and what's important to you within this so-called big picture. Then you facilitate your team's involvement in helping you define the course of action necessary to realize your vision.

At the same time, define your parameters. Explain to your manager/members the boundaries within which they need to work when they help you with an issue. Parameters include the type of decision-making mode that you want to use when a decision is needed. Train them in the modes, especially the consultative and consensus modes (see Chapter 11), so that they understand how to use them. Also, be clear about the distinction between an agenda item that is intended only for discussion or review and one that ends with a decision.

Avoid relying primarily on consensus as the way to settle issues. Not every issue lends itself to consensus. What's more, as Chapter 11 points out, overuse of consensus can lead to *analysis paralysis* — no decisions made, no action taken.

In all likelihood, your managers want to see decisions made and feel just fine when sometimes you take them upon yourself with some kind of input from the team. Stick to involving your team members on the organizational-level issues and they'll feel secure about being included and truly part of a management team.

Evaluate the Team's Progress

Take time out on occasion to evaluate together how the team is doing — say once or twice a year. Ask each team member to respond to questions such as these:

- ✔ What are we doing well as a management team?
- ✔ What are we not doing as well as needed as a management team?
- ✔ What have been the pluses and minuses of our team leadership?
- ✔ How effective has our communication with one another been?
- ✔ How productive have we been as a team in leading our organizational unit?

Add your feedback to that of each team member, but let them go first so that you don't bias their observations. Likewise, listen openly and receptively to their feedback — a good test for you. The issues that are identified from this feedback discussion become items for team problem-solving sessions.

You can even solicit peer feedback periodically (a strategy that is covered in Chapter 7): Each team member comments on the support and effort of all the other members — an assessment, of sorts, on how team members individually are helping the team. Use your team guidelines as criteria in the process.

Evaluating the team's progress promotes the shared accountability that you so greatly need, if you're going to have a true management team. Evaluating progress also challenges you and your team members to have open and honest dialogue with one another. You can lead by example as a team member giving honest feedback and listening openly to what others have to say.

Reinforce Good Team Playership

As boss of the entire organizational entity, you write performance evaluations for each of your managers. When you do, remember to include an evaluation of how well they work with and contribute as a member of the management team and to provide continuous performance feedback on an informal basis, acknowledging their contributions and shortcomings as part of the management team. From the formal, written evaluation to the informal, day-to-day feedback, your efforts reinforce the message that being an effective team player is an important part of their jobs.

Retreat Periodically

Sometimes getting away together is a good thing. (That's what I mean by *retreat,* as opposed to running, hiding, and giving up.) A management team benefits greatly by taking time away from the office — say, once a quarter to twice a year.

A retreat of a day or so is an opportunity for concentrated work on major issues and plans. Retreats also are good for doing some of that *team-building* stuff — activities that strengthen working relationships (see Chapter 6 for details). You can have some fun but also set direction, so that when you return to the office, you're better able to move forward on that direction and accompanying action items determined during the retreat.

Chapter 17

Ten Tips for Getting a Team Back on Track

In This Chapter

▶ Sorting out your toolkit

▶ Looking at your leadership role

Most teams don't reach a high-performing and self-sufficient level overnight. After all, achieving perfection takes a bit of time. Along the way, teams sometimes hit bumps and veer off the track.

Even more frustrating is watching a team start to come together and do well and then seeing it decline in performance and teamwork. You can see the slippage in deadlines missed, internal clashes and conflicts, communication breakdowns, and quality problems, to name just a few factors.

Besides pulling out your hair or wishing for a miracle (Where's that genie when you need her?), you can take steps toward moving your team back on track and urging team members to perform and work well together again by jotting down the ten tips in this chapter on your to-do list.

Assess — Figure Out Where You Are

You can assess the situation by talking individually with team members, asking them what's working and not working within the team. When more formality is required, you can have a neutral party from outside the team interview each team member for the assessment. Either way, explain to your team members what you're doing: You're finding out how the team is functioning and what issues are affecting it.

The best kind of assessment asks everyone the same questions so that you get specifics and greater depth to the data you're collecting. Ask people for *observations* — what they see happening with the team. You want to ask questions that get at people's observations (and not their opinions) about how the team is functioning. Observations make for more objective and substantive results than opinion surveys do. Better data enables you to clearly identify problems. When I conduct assessments for teams, I ask how a team is functioning in key areas like these:

- Interpersonal communications
- Cooperation
- Addressing problems
- Performance outputs
- Performance quality
- Dealing with conflicts
- Sharing information
- Reliability and meeting commitments
- Team leadership

You can build questions around any of these key areas, for example:

> *In terms of team members doing their fair share of the work and following through on their commitments, what have you noticed?*

To wrap up the assessment you can pose a broad question like one of the following:

> *Overall, what's working well within the team?*

> *What key issues need to be addressed for enhancing the team's functions and performance?*

When the assessment is finished, summarize your findings in a report for all team members to read and discuss. This assessment begins the problem-solving process, helping the team determine the issues on which it needs to focus so that it gets back on track.

Solve Problems

If your plan for getting the team back on track begins with an assessment, you've probably identified a number of problems to solve. Go to it! Chapter 9 is your reference for the problem-solving process. You may want to make problem-solving the emphasis of an entire meeting, the way some managers do.

Tough love at Toni's team

Toni called a special team meeting, because she was upset about the decline in performance and work ethic that her contract staffing team had experienced during the last month or two. She worked hard building the group into a well-functioning team. Now, it seemed, they were resting on their laurels. Team members had become lax and inconsistent in their performance — coordination of communications, follow-through, careful documentation, and timely responses to customers all were lacking.

As she began the meeting, Toni told team members that she wasn't pleased about their performance and that the focus of the meeting was on how to improve. Speaking firmly, she outlined problems as she saw them. Team members could tell that Toni was serious, because you could hear a pin drop in the meeting room.

Toni invited team members to comment but indicated that she didn't want to spend a great deal of time rehashing the problems; she wanted them solved. A few people spoke up, agreeing with the manager's points. Then Toni facilitated a brainstorming session (see Chapter 9). The energy level in the room picked up and ideas for solving the problems began to flow. The discussion was lively and an action plan was set.

After the meeting, many team members told Toni that this meeting was the best the team had ever had. At a follow-up meeting a month later, it was clear that team's performance had picked up. Reflecting on her recent experience, Toni realized that some of the discipline that she had built into the team at its inception had drifted away. Team meetings had become superficial discussions of assignments with little attention to identifying and addressing problems at an early point. Her tough love meeting had pulled the team back on track.

Address Conflicts

Internal conflict can derail a team. When two or more team members are at odds with each other, and you neglect the situation, the tension they create festers and grows like a cancer. Factions sometimes even form when employees start taking sides with and against one another. The point: Make sure that you act sooner rather than later, if you ever want your team to refocus and get back on track. Chapter 10 offers the tools you need for addressing conflicts.

You may need only to coach team members individually and let them go forward to settle their differences. Telling them that you're going to follow up to see how everything is going puts them on notice that you think the situation is important. When team members would rather not address their concerns with one another, explain your expectations to them regarding professional conduct and teamwork and that you intend to conduct a progress review.

In most cases, team members resolving their own conflicts is best. When they do, you can coach from the sidelines, but don't insert yourself when you're not wanted or really needed; just clarify your expectations and hold team members responsible. If your help as a facilitator is essential, prepare the parties individually before bringing them together and then work with them to develop a solution that they can hammer into an agreement. Always set a follow-up date to monitor progress.

Only when a conflict involves most of the team do you want to address it in front of the entire team. Team members may be uncomfortable doing this, which is okay, but you can prepare them with a detailed agenda. Maintain your focus on working out a resolution and setting a time to follow up and review progress.

Develop Teamwork

A big part of what derails teams relates to teamwork. Team members aren't communicating, problem-solving, or dealing with conflicts effectively, and that isn't unusual. Just because you organize people to work together doesn't mean that they have the skills to do so smoothly. Building the skills that team members need to work effectively in teams is a worthier endeavor. Part IV of this book outlines six skill areas, including interpersonal communication and problem-solving, that team members vitally need to perform well together. Quite simply, when a team is off-track, invest time in training them, and *retraining* them, in essential team skills.

Clarify and Reset Team Goals

With everyone running double time to keep up with the work plan and coping with what seems like constant change, a team sometimes can feel like it has lost direction and faded out of focus. When that happens, the time is right for setting or resetting a team's goals and making sure that everything is up to date. Working with the team, define what outcomes need to be accomplished and clarify your plans and assignments.

With the team is the operative phrase when you talk about goals. Don't make these plans *for* your team. The full involvement of team members in identifying issues or obstacles and clarifying their goals and overall direction is critical to encouraging a strong performance. People support most that which they help create.

Regularly Review Status

Status review is one of the biggies for team managers. It's a critical mechanism for promoting accountability within your team. Chapter 7 describes the strategy for the accountability cornerstone in detail.

Status review means following up in your team meetings on the action items that the team has set for itself, with team members reporting the results of what they've done. Regular status reviews keep a team on track, or nudge it back on when it happens to slip off. Status reviews establish that assignments aren't forgotten and that follow through is expected.

Lead the Battle against Outside Obstacles

Teams sometimes get into trouble because of outside problems, such as failing to receive the cooperation they need from other groups. That can mean resources or support the team needs from elsewhere within the organization didn't arrive or came in at a less than adequate level. In these cases, your team needs you to step in and play an active role in removing obstacles. Don't leave your team members fending for themselves. Instead, speak directly to managers of the outside groups that need to offer support and cooperation. Be persistent, but instead of just raising the problems, explore options that help settle the problems. That's how you fight for your team without becoming a bloody attacker on the prowl that no one wants to deal with. Whenever support problems persist, don't hesitate to speak with your boss.

Dealing with obstacles that occur outside the team does take time. So, inform your team members about what you're doing so that they know you're acting on their issues and so you can ask for their patience.

Evaluate the Full Team, Quarterly

Teams that aren't performing consistently and positively need more accountability. Instituting the practice of a full team evaluation on a quarterly basis helps out.

Evaluate with your team the results it achieved versus goals that it set. Problem-solve whatever issues and shortcomings come to light. Revisit the situation in the next quarter and have team members again report their progress.

In addition, ask your team to evaluate how well it's functioning as a team. Team members can evaluate such issues as teamwork, communication, and meeting deadlines as a team and then problem-solve the issues that they raise, including the solution steps they create as part of the team's next set of goals.

As you enhance the discipline of your team's performance, add peer-feedback sessions into the process, say once every six months. Doing so builds in team member accountability. I explain the peer-feedback process in Chapter 7.

Deal with Individual Performance Issues

All that it takes for team morale and performance to sink to the bottom of the tank is one or two individuals not pulling their weight, clashing with other team members, and doing other disruptive things. So, dealing with performance issues sooner rather than later is extremely important.

Take the individual aside for a private conference. Gather the facts and then report your concerns in observation-based terms, not as opinions or interpretations. Coach the team member by defining your expectations and mapping out a plan with that person to meet your expectations. Follow up with a review of the team member's progress a few times during the next few months. You can take this coaching-to-improve approach even when you're not the person's supervising manager — just make sure that you keep the other manager in the loop.

Chapter 10 covers other details, including what to do when you don't see any improvement.

Manage by Plan

Planning is the sum of all the other tips in this chapter. When you lead as a coach, you manage by plan. You run your teams from work plans, and you measure their progress by comparing results achieved against the goals that you set in your plans. When problems come up, the solutions become part of the plan.

But managing by plan as a coach doesn't mean you must micromanage — just the opposite. You can lead your team members toward figuring out their own ways of accomplishing their goals and plans. You're in the bullpen only to provide support and review progress and results (what a relief!).

As you lead your teams, using a little bit of discipline goes a long way toward fulfilling the plan — at a high level of performance.

Chapter 18

Ten Qualities of an Effective Team Player

In This Chapter

▶ Looking for people who have the right stuff

▶ Recognizing quality when you see it

*I*f you had the opportunity to start a new team and select anyone from your organization to be on it, who would you pick? Assuming that people have the right technical skills for the work to be done, what other factors would you use to select your team members?

Teams need strong team players to perform well. If you're like most people, you want the best players on your team. But what defines such people? No dictionary definition exists, and every so-called expert has his own opinion. Through the years in my team workshops I've asked participants to define what they see as qualities that make for an effective team player. Here's the list of the ten qualities that come up most often.

Demonstrates Reliability

You can count on a reliable team member who gets work done and does his fair share to work hard and meet commitments. He or she follows through on assignments. Consistency is key. You can count on him or her to deliver good performance all the time, not just some of the time.

Communicates Constructively

Teams need people who speak up and express their thoughts and ideas clearly, directly, honestly, and with respect for others and for the work of the team. That's what it means to communicate constructively. Such a team member does not shy away from making a point but makes it in the best way possible — in a positive, confident, and respectful manner.

Listens Actively

Good listeners are essential for teams to function effectively. Teams need team players who can absorb, understand, and consider ideas and points of view from other people without debating and arguing every point. Such a team member also can receive criticism without reacting defensively. Most important, for effective communication and problem-solving, team members need the discipline to listen first and speak second so that meaningful dialogue results.

Functions as an Active Participant

Good team players are active participants. They come prepared for team meetings and listen and speak up in discussions. They're fully engaged in the work of the team and do not sit passively on the sidelines.

Team members who function as active participants take the initiative to help make things happen, and they volunteer for assignments. Their whole approach is can-do: "What contribution can *I* make to help the team achieve success?"

Shares Openly and Willingly

Good team players share. Unlike some little children, they have no problem sharing. They're willing to share information, knowledge, and experience. They take the initiative to keep other team members informed.

Much of the communication within teams takes place informally. Beyond discussion at organized meetings, team members need to feel comfortable talking with one another and passing along important news and information day-to-day. Good team players are active in this informal sharing. They keep other team members in the loop with information and expertise that helps get the job done and prevents surprises.

Cooperates and Pitches In to Help

Cooperation is the act of working *with* others and acting together to accomplish a job. Effective team players work this way by second nature. Good team players, despite differences they may have with other team members concerning style and perspective, figure out ways to work together to solve problems and get work done. They respond to requests for assistance and take the initiative to offer help.

Exhibits Flexibility

Teams often deal with changing conditions — and often create changes themselves. Good team players roll with the punches; they adapt to ever-changing situations. They don't complain or get stressed out because something new is being tried or some new direction is being set.

In addition, a flexible team member can consider different points of views and compromise when needed. He or she doesn't hold rigidly to a point of view and argue it to death, especially when the team needs to move forward to make a decision or get something done. Strong team players are firm in their thoughts yet open to what others have to offer — flexibility at its best.

Works as a Problem-solver

Teams, of course, deal with problems. Sometimes, it appears, that's the whole reason why a team is created — to address problems. Good team players are willing to deal with all kinds of problems in a solutions-oriented manner. They're problem-solvers, not problem-dwellers, problem-blamers, or problem-avoiders. They don't simply rehash a problem the way problem-dwellers do. They don't look for others to fault, as the blamers do. And they don't put off dealing with issues, the way avoiders do.

Team players get problems out in the open for discussion and then collaborate with others to find solutions and form action plans.

Treats Others in a Respectful and Supportive Manner

Team players treat fellow team members with courtesy and consideration — not just some of the time but consistently. In addition, they show understanding and the appropriate support of other team members to help get the job done. They don't place conditions on when they'll provide assistance, when they'll choose to listen, and when they'll share information. Good team players also have a sense of humor and know how to have fun (and all teams can use a bit of both), but they don't have fun at someone else's expense. Quite simply, effective team players deal with other people in a professional manner.

Shows Commitment to the Team

Strong team players care about their work, the team, and the team's work. They show up every day with this care and commitment up front. They want to give a good effort, and they want other team members to do the same.

Team players who show commitment don't come in any particular style or personality. They don't need to be rah-rah, cheerleader types. In fact, they may even be soft-spoken, but they aren't passive. They care about what the team is doing and they contribute to its success — without needing a push.

Team players with commitment look beyond their own piece of the work and care about the team's overall work. In the end, their commitment is about winning — not in the sports sense of beating your opponent but about seeing the team succeed and knowing they have contributed to this success. Winning as a team is one of the great motivators of employee performance. Good team players have and show this motivation.

Index

• G •

• H •

• S •

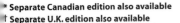

SPORTS, FITNESS, PARENTING, RELIGION & SPIRITUALITY

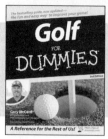

0-471-76871-5

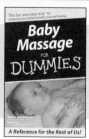

0-7645-7841-3

Also available:

- Catholicism For Dummies
  0-7645-5391-7
- Exercise Balls For Dummies
  0-7645-5623-1
- Fitness For Dummies
  0-7645-7851-0
- Football For Dummies
  0-7645-3936-1
- Judaism For Dummies
  0-7645-5299-6
- Potty Training For Dummies
  0-7645-5417-4
- Buddhism For Dummies
  0-7645-5359-3

- Pregnancy For Dummies
  0-7645-4483-7 †
- Ten Minute Tone-Ups For Dummies
  0-7645-7207-5
- NASCAR For Dummies
  0-7645-7681-X
- Religion For Dummies
  0-7645-5264-3
- Soccer For Dummies
  0-7645-5229-5
- Women in the Bible For Dummies
  0-7645-8475-8

TRAVEL

0-7645-7749-2

0-7645-6945-7

Also available:

- Alaska For Dummies
  0-7645-7746-8
- Cruise Vacations For Dummies
  0-7645-6941-4
- England For Dummies
  0-7645-4276-1
- Europe For Dummies
  0-7645-7529-5
- Germany For Dummies
  0-7645-7823-5
- Hawaii For Dummies
  0-7645-7402-7

- Italy For Dummies
  0-7645-7386-1
- Las Vegas For Dummies
  0-7645-7382-9
- London For Dummies
  0-7645-4277-X
- Paris For Dummies
  0-7645-7630-5
- RV Vacations For Dummies
  0-7645-4442-X
- Walt Disney World & Orlando
  For Dummies
  0-7645-9660-8

GRAPHICS, DESIGN & WEB DEVELOPMENT

0-7645-8815-X

0-7645-9571-7

Also available:

- 3D Game Animation For Dummies
  0-7645-8789-7
- AutoCAD 2006 For Dummies
  0-7645-8925-3
- Building a Web Site For Dummies
  0-7645-7144-3
- Creating Web Pages For Dummies
  0-470-08030-2
- Creating Web Pages All-in-One Desk
  Reference For Dummies
  0-7645-4345-8
- Dreamweaver 8 For Dummies
  0-7645-9649-7

- InDesign CS2 For Dummies
  0-7645-9572-5
- Macromedia Flash 8 For Dummies
  0-7645-9691-8
- Photoshop CS2 and Digital
  Photography For Dummies
  0-7645-9580-6
- Photoshop Elements 4 For Dummies
  0-471-77483-9
- Syndicating Web Sites with RSS Feeds
  For Dummies
  0-7645-8848-6
- Yahoo! SiteBuilder For Dummies
  0-7645-9800-7

NETWORKING, SECURITY, PROGRAMMING & DATABASES

0-7645-7728-X

0-471-74940-0

Also available:

- Access 2007 For Dummies
  0-470-04612-0
- ASP.NET 2 For Dummies
  0-7645-7907-X
- C# 2005 For Dummies
  0-7645-9704-3
- Hacking For Dummies
  0-470-05235-X
- Hacking Wireless Networks
  For Dummies
  0-7645-9730-2
- Java For Dummies
  0-470-08716-1

- Microsoft SQL Server 2005 For Dummies
  0-7645-7755-7
- Networking All-in-One Desk Reference
  For Dummies
  0-7645-9939-9
- Preventing Identity Theft For Dummies
  0-7645-7336-5
- Telecom For Dummies
  0-471-77085-X
- Visual Studio 2005 All-in-One Desk
  Reference For Dummies
  0-7645-9775-2
- XML For Dummies
  0-7645-8845-1

HEALTH & SELF-HELP

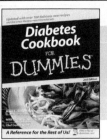

0-7645-8450-2

0-7645-4149-8

Also available:

- Bipolar Disorder For Dummies
  0-7645-8451-0
- Chemotherapy and Radiation
  For Dummies
  0-7645-7832-4
- Controlling Cholesterol For Dummies
  0-7645-5440-9
- Diabetes For Dummies
  0-7645-6820-5* †
- Divorce For Dummies
  0-7645-8417-0 †

- Fibromyalgia For Dummies
  0-7645-5441-7
- Low-Calorie Dieting For Dummies
  0-7645-9905-4
- Meditation For Dummies
  0-471-77774-9
- Osteoporosis For Dummies
  0-7645-7621-6
- Overcoming Anxiety For Dummies
  0-7645-5447-6
- Reiki For Dummies
  0-7645-9907-0
- Stress Management For Dummies
  0-7645-5144-2

EDUCATION, HISTORY, REFERENCE & TEST PREPARATION

0-7645-8381-6

0-7645-9554-7

Also available:

- The ACT For Dummies
  0-7645-9652-7
- Algebra For Dummies
  0-7645-5325-9
- Algebra Workbook For Dummies
  0-7645-8467-7
- Astronomy For Dummies
  0-7645-8465-0
- Calculus For Dummies
  0-7645-2498-4
- Chemistry For Dummies
  0-7645-5430-1
- Forensics For Dummies
  0-7645-5580-4

- Freemasons For Dummies
  0-7645-9796-5
- French For Dummies
  0-7645-5193-0
- Geometry For Dummies
  0-7645-5324-0
- Organic Chemistry I For Dummies
  0-7645-6902-3
- The SAT I For Dummies
  0-7645-7193-1
- Spanish For Dummies
  0-7645-5194-9
- Statistics For Dummies
  0-7645-5423-9

Get smart @ dummies.com®

- **Find a full list of Dummies titles**
- **Look into loads of FREE on-site articles**
- **Sign up for FREE eTips e-mailed to you weekly**
- **See what other products carry the Dummies name**
- **Shop directly from the Dummies bookstore**
- **Enter to win new prizes every month!**

Separate Canadian edition also available
Separate U.K. edition also available

Available wherever books are sold. For more information or to order direct: U.S. customers visit www.dummies.com or call 1-877-762-2974.
U.K. customers visit www.wileyeurope.com or call 0800 243407. Canadian customers visit www.wiley.ca or call 1-800-567-4797.